AMERICA

CAN WIN
The Case for Military Reform

GARY HART
WITH
WILLIAM S. LIND

ADLER&ADLER

Published by Adler & Adler,
Publishers, Inc.
4550 Montgomery Avenue
Bethesda, Maryland 20814

Library of Congress
Cataloging-in-Publication Data

Hart, Gary, 1936–
   America can win.

   Includes index.
   1. United States—Military
policy.   2. United
States—Armed Forces.   I.
Lind, William S.   II. Title.
UA23.H365   1986   355'.0335'73
85-15047
ISBN 0-917561-10-4

First Edition

Printed in the United States
of America

To the men and women who serve our country

Contents

Preface

I MMEDIATELY AFTER MY ELECTION to the United States Senate, I sought membership on the Armed Services Committee. While I had no special expertise in defense matters, I felt that, in the aftermath of our involvement in the Vietnam War, we needed to rethink our defense policies in some fundamental ways.

I spent a good deal of time on the committee listening and learning. But most of what I heard was disappointing. It had little to do with what seemed to me to be the central issue: insuring that the country had an effective defense. Instead, most of the debate was about money. Conservatives wanted to give the Pentagon more money. Liberals wanted to give it less. Neither seemed to think about much else. I came to conclude that fighting over how much we spend had little to do with whether or not our military forces could win in combat.

I began to try to develop a new approach to consider defense issues, one that focused more on effectiveness. In 1978, I joined with former senator Robert Taft, Jr., to issue a white paper on defense, *A Modern Military Strategy for the United States,* which was an update of an original white paper produced by Senator Taft in 1976. This began one of the military reform movement's most important traditions: Republicans and Democrats, liberals and conservatives working together for reform. I was considered a moderately liberal Democrat; Senator Taft was regarded as a moderately conservative Republican. None of that mattered. Both of us believed our military forces should be effective, and each was willing to think seriously about what was needed to restore effectiveness.

The white paper also marked the entry of two other individuals into the battle for military reform: Norman Polmar and William S. Lind. Polmar was already a noted naval writer and editor of the American sections of the famous naval annual, *Jane's Fighting Ships*. He was Senator Taft's principal outside adviser on the white paper's proposed shipbuilding plan.[1]

William S. Lind, coauthor of this book, was hired by Senator Taft in 1973 as his legislative assistant for foreign affairs, economics and transportation, and ultimately became his adviser on defense policy and drafter of the original defense white paper.

Lind's activities with Senator Taft ranged from questioning the direction of the navy's shipbuilding program to stimulating a debate about land warfare. In 1976, he received a briefing on the army's new tactical doctrine called the "active defense." He wrote a lengthy critique, a central point of which was that the "active defense" reflected attrition warfare, warfare based on a mutual casualty-inflicting contest like the First World War battle of Verdun. Instead, Bill argued, our tactics should reflect maneuver warfare, warfare like the German blitzkrieg or most Israeli campaigns, where surprise and rapid movement shattered the enemy's ability to fight effectively. Bill's critique was published in the army's principal journal, *Military Review*. It stimulated a wide-ranging debate on the theme of attrition versus maneuver warfare, which became a major theme of the reform movement.

In 1977, Bill Lind joined my staff, and together we began to develop ideas about the navy and express them in a series of amendments to the annual defense authorization bills. Those amendments promoted such concepts as smaller aircraft carriers, affordable in large numbers; vertical takeoff fighters to fly from the small carriers; diesel-electric submarines to complement our expensive nuclear submarines; and modular naval weapons and sensors. Ultimately, the navy was able to block most of these innovations, but the debates over them brought the issue of military effectiveness before a growing number of senators, the press, and some serving military officers who became allies.

Gradually, these individuals began to see interrelationships among what each was doing. Common themes, such as maneuver warfare, the need for weapons affordable in adequate numbers, and the importance of innovative ideas in war, began to be recognized. It was increasingly clear that, if we were to restore military effectiveness, we needed a large number of far-reaching, fundamental changes in our defense policies. We needed something similar to what, in other countries and in earlier times, had been called military reform.

The term "military reform" was introduced publicly in January of 1981, when I wrote a column for the *Wall Street Journal:* "The Case for Military Reform." Among the people who read it was a conservative Republican congressman from Virginia, G. William Whitehurst. Congressman Whitehurst, a senior member of the House Armed Services Committee, agreed with the basic premises of the article. He contacted me and said, "I wonder what a Republican congressman and a Democratic senator could do to move this forward if they worked together?" The answer was the Congressional Military Reform Caucus, a bicameral, bipartisan group of members of Congress founded in the summer of 1981.

The reform movement has grown slowly but steadily since. The defense debate is increasingly a three-way debate among the old "cut the budget" group, the "give the generals what they ask for" group, and the reformers. In 1982, the army sponsored a major conference on military reform at West Point, inviting the most prominent reformers to present their views and subsequently publishing the proceedings as a book. That year the army also adopted maneuver warfare as its doctrine. The Military Reform Caucus had its first major success in Congress in 1983, passing an amendment to the defense bill that established a strong, independent office for testing weapons under realistic combat conditions.

Where is the military reform movement going today? That is the subject of this book. Thucydides wrote:

> War of all things proceeds least upon definite rules, but draws principally upon itself for contrivances to meet an emergency; and in such cases the party who faces the struggle and keeps his temper best meets with most security, and he who loses his temper about it with corresponding disaster.

Preface

This is not a book about war. But it is a book about what
Thucydides called "contrivances"—the training and readiness; the
insight and inventiveness; the ideas in designing equipment; most
of all, the genius in conceiving and executing strategy, tactics, and
doctrine in combat that represents true national security. It is a
book about the difference between success and failure—perhaps
between the survival or defeat of our nation.

War is an anomaly. It is, on the one hand, such an awful
breakdown of order and civility that some resist even the thought
of armament and defense. On the other hand, war is so often the
expression of the noblest form of patriotism and sacrifice that it
causes others to form an unhealthy preoccupation with the instruments of death and destruction.

To be prepared for war, George Washington said, is one of the
most effectual means of preserving peace. He didn't say the only
means or even the best means—simply one of the most effectual
means.

Americans of good will and genuine patriotism, regardless of
party or ideology, must learn to think about and discuss the issues
of modern defense, of being "prepared for war," without the outdated political rhetoric that has come to charge and corrupt this
vital subject. Concerned and informed citizens must replace the
extremists in the marketplace of defense ideas.

Unquestionably, the new terror of nuclear annihilation has
fundamentally altered thinking about defense and the military in
our time. All policymakers must take this fact into account. The
potential of nuclear war has severely restricted the notion of war
as a carrying out of political intercourse by other means.

Nuclear war cannot be prevented by vastly expanded nuclear
arsenals. But the danger of nuclear war, indeed of most wars, can
be limited by an effective conventional defense that deters aggres-
sion against us, our allies, and our legitimate interests. It is this
defense that calls forth this book.

It takes more than money to achieve strength. It takes judgment as well. That is why the current and popular political debate
about spending more or spending less is largely irrelevant. Defense
dollars must be wisely spent and they must be spent in pursuit of

defense objectives that make sense in the modern age. Right now, we are not doing that. We have spent one trillion dollars for defense over the past five years. But we are less well prepared to meet a military challenge than if we had spent less more wisely.

Harry Truman, echoing Jefferson, used to say the American people wanted to hear common sense. This book is designed to promote common sense. It is not about abstract theory, weapons technology, or sophisticated jargon. It is a book for Americans genuinely concerned about their security and the avoidance of unnecessary conflict and loss of lives. It is meant for all those citizens frustrated by a defense roller coaster driven by politicians and military "experts" who have kept the defense debate closed to most Americans.

Peace will not come through unilateral disarmament, a reckless nuclear arms race expanding into space, new miracle weapons, or force-feeding defense contractors. It will only come from those who wish us ill knowing full well that we are prepared to meet any threat to our security—whether an isolated terrorist or a modern superpower—with an effective response. But even the often-discussed "threat" is not a simple one. It must be judged on at least two scales—its size and its likelihood. The biggest threat may not be the most likely. And the most likely may not be the largest.

Some individuals, mesmerized by ideology, see the Kremlin's hand in every threat to American interests anywhere. Others, fearful of the responsibilities of power, refuse to count Soviet tank divisions in Eastern Europe and helicopter gunships in Afghanistan. As usual, reality rests somewhere in between. Total preoccupation with the Soviet Union helps make us muscle-bound to the terrorist car bomber or radical hostage taker. Avoidance of superpower responsibility makes our friends and allies suspicious of our commitment to the defense of democracy.

Our interests cannot be defended until they are defined. Our security cannot be guaranteed until we understand what genuinely threatens it. We do not have a clear definition of American interests as we close the twentieth century. And we are not sure what forces within the Kremlin walls or shadows along the darkened alleyways of the Middle East might emerge to challenge our security.

Preface

Times change. Circumstances change. Interests and threats change. To make America truly secure in a period of great change, two things are necessary: an appreciation of some basic truths about the nature of conflict, truths as old as the human race, and a willingness to think and act anew. Most current political and military leaders plunge ahead as if nothing ever changes. If change occurs in our defense thinking, it is almost entirely the result of some new technological gadget, not because of new perceptions.

No one should seek to lead this nation who is not totally committed to its security. In the years remaining in the twentieth century, our security must include limitations on the nuclear arsenals of the superpowers and the spread of nuclear weapons to other nations, a clear understanding of our legitimate interests and commitments, an appreciation for a variety of threats to those interests, and an effective conventional defense.

This book seeks to establish that, despite great expense, we do not today possess that effective conventional defense. It is a warning that we are headed for disaster if a different approach is not undertaken immediately. Disaster can mean either a humiliating military defeat on the conventional battlefield or a nuclear war brought on by the failure of the conventional deterrent. More importantly, this book seeks to outline the steps necessary to reform our military and political institutions, to change the kinds of weapons we buy and the way we buy them, and to change the way we think about our defense in this revolutionary era.

History teaches more than one lesson. We know well the stories of weaker nations defeated by stronger adversaries. We know less well the many instances of numerically superior forces successfully overcome by theoretically inferior—but more clever—challengers. Joshua was one of the first military commanders to defeat a vastly superior enemy with numerically inferior forces—and a divinely inspired strategy. The strategy was based, as you will recall, not upon a new-technology weapon but upon a trumpet. He surprised the Philistines, frightened them, and caused them to run. But the trumpet was crucial, and it had to be sounded properly. The Bible asks: If the trumpet gives an uncertain sound, who will follow?

Today our defense trumpet does not give a certain sound. And

xiv

until it does, we will not be safe or secure. Military reform is meant to give the trumpet a certain sound—a sound of effectiveness and a sound of true national security. If we undertake the historic task of military reform, we can all be sure that America can win.

Gary Hart
Washington, D.C.
January 1986

Acknowledgments

ANY OF THE PEOPLE who have helped with this book cannot be named. They are serving military officers, noncommissioned officers, or civilians working where they would be vulnerable to retribution from the Defense Department. While they must remain anonymous, they have given generously to this book, especially to the tiresome task of reviewing and commenting on portions of the draft. They are due deep and sincere thanks.

Among the individuals who have contributed vitally important help are the central figures in the military reform movement: John Boyd, Steve Canby, Norman Polmar, Chuck Spinney and Pierre Sprey. Without them, there would be no military reform movement. They are owed thanks for ideas, for facts, and for substantial amounts of their time spent reviewing the manuscript.

Other individuals who have given their generous assistance include: Dr. Richard A. Gabriel and Dr. Paul L. Savage of St. Anselm College, Dr. Earl H. Tilford, Jr., Jeffrey Ethell, Winslow T. Wheeler, Patrick J. Garvey, Michael Burns, Kenneth S. Brower, John L. Petersen, Dr. Thomas S. Amlie, Fred Reed, Major Charles A. Leader USMCR, Robert W. Bartels, Dr. Donald D. Chipman, Lieutenant Colonel David Evans USMC, and Peter T. Tarpgaard.

The Congressional Research Service of the Library of Congress provided its usual timely and excellent help. The minority staff of the Senate Armed Services Committee was also extremely helpful, despite the chronic heavy demands on its time. The armed services themselves responded thoroughly and, generally, quickly to our

Acknowledgments

requests for data, even though they knew the information would be used for a book that would be critical of them.

We take full and sole responsibility for any errors of fact reflected in this book. Whatever proves useful in the book, however, is very much a collective product of the hundreds of military officers and noncommissioned officers, serving and retired, who have freely offered their candid advice about defense issues. They, far more than any civilians, are the heart, soul, and future of military reform. Their ideas, concerns, and frustrations with business as usual in defense have shaped not just this book but the whole reform movement. They are its inspiration, its ever-flowing source of ideas and new information, and, in large part, the book's reason for being. They are owed an incalcuable debt.

Introduction

The Military Reform Movement

THE PURPOSE OF MILITARY FORCES, if they have to fight, is to win. Are our military forces today able to win in combat? The question is seldom seriously asked. That is perhaps because the answer is so discomfiting. Our military record over the past thirty-five years has, to say the least, not been one of consistent success. Our last brilliant victory was in 1950: General Douglas MacArthur's audacious Inchon landing. Unfortunately, it was followed by a bitter retreat through North Korea in the face of Chinese intervention and a stalemate along the 38th parallel.

Since Korea, we have unsuccessfully fought a ten-year war in Southeast Asia. Understandably, we have tried to forget about that war. It was an intensely painful experience for everyone it touched —for those who went to fight and for those who stayed home, for those who supported the war and for those who opposed it. It remains a bitter memory for us all.

But more than fifty thousand Americans died in that war, and we owe it to them to learn all we can from it. It holds many lessons. Army colonel Harry G. Summers, Jr., points out a number of them in his excellent book, *On Strategy: The Vietnam War in Context.* He discusses how our strategy in Vietnam violated most, if not all, of the principles of war. Today our strategy is one of doing everything, everywhere. That again violates the principles of war.

Colonel Summers argues that we confused preparing for war — organizing, training, and equipping military forces—with the conduct of war, which centers on tactics, operational art, and strategy. He states that "there was a general feeling that strategy

I

was budget-driven and was primarily a function of resource alloca-tion."[1] Budgeting and resource allocation still consume the vast bulk of the time and attention of the Pentagon and the congressio-nal committees that oversee defense. And, more than ever, the strategy is shaped to justify the budget.

We do not seem to have done better in learning the Vietnam War's lessons about military organization, tactics, or overly com-plex, high-tech equipment. Out of a peak strength of approximately five-hundred-fifty thousand soldiers, only about eighty thousand were combat troops. The rest were part of a huge, sprawling, vul-nerable "tail" of headquarters, supply services, and maintenance depots that got in our way more than in the enemy's. Ten years after Saigon fell, our "tail" is still enormous. Our army in Europe has more soldiers working as "communicators" than it has infantry-men.

We poured billions of dollars into technologically complex systems, such as the "McNamara line," a network of fancy tech-nology sensors designed to spot infiltrating North Vietnamese. The line and the rest of our complex weaponry were beaten by an enemy who relied on strategy and tactics, not technology, and simplicity, not complexity.

Since Vietnam, the failures have continued. We rescued a ship, the *Mayaguez,* and its crew from Cambodian hijackers. However, we handled the operation so badly that forty-one marines were killed rescuing forty seamen—who were in the process of being released, with their ship, by the Cambodians.

The attempt to rescue the hostages from Iran was an ignomini-ous failure. Commando operations, like all combat, are character-ized by uncertainty, surprises, and things that go wrong—what von Clausewitz called "friction." Plans and commanders must be agile and adaptable to deal with friction. Our planning for the Iran raid was so rigid that when just one thing went wrong—we found ourselves short one helicopter at the Desert I site—we called off the whole operation. We were too rigid even to do that well. The attempt to withdraw broke down into confusion, panic, and finally tragedy. Eight U.S. servicemen died, intact equipment and clas-sified documents were abandoned to the enemy, and the nation was badly embarrassed. In contrast, Israel, West Germany, Britain, and the Netherlands, among others, have carried out daring commando operations successfully. It can be done. But it has not been done, so far, by the United States.

In 1983, 241 American marines died when a lone terrorist drove a truck bomb into the Beirut building where they were living. Why were so many marines in one building, in a city where car bombs were common weapons? Why were barriers inadequate and sentries armed with unloaded weapons? Why was no one held responsible?

Even Grenada, where we "won," raises more questions than hope. The marines and the army's rangers performed well there. But the once-elite Eighty-second Airborne Division did poorly in the face of a few hundred Cuban construction workers. It advanced only about five kilometers in three days, so slowly that at one point the chairman of the Joint Chiefs of Staff telephoned the Eighty-second Airborne commander and said, "We have two companies of marines running all over the island and thousands of army troops doing nothing. What the hell is going on?" Discipline broke down in some of the Eighty-second's units. One combat-experienced officer who monitored the division's radio communications later said it sounded as if the whole division were on the verge of panic. The army subsequently awarded 9,800 medals for Grenada, even though only about 7,000 soldiers were ever on the island.[2]

This long string of military failures is the most important reason we need new defense policies. A military system that consistently fails in combat endangers our existence as a nation. It is also unfair to our men and women in uniform. The large majority of them work sixty hours a week or more, shoulder heavy responsibilities, and often take great personal risks because they believe our country needs a strong and effective defense. But our current military system ensures that much of that effort goes for naught. The "input" is great, but there is little "output" of real military strength. We owe our servicemen and servicewomen something better.

Another reason we need fundamental change is that even large increases in defense spending fail to yield any real improvement in our military strength. Since 1980, we have spent more than one trillion dollars on defense. The defense budget has increased by 33 percent, with inflation discounted, in the past six years. Are we a third stronger than we were then? Hardly.

What has happened? A quick look at aircraft procurement provides the answer. In the Fiscal Years (FY) 1978 through 1981, we obligated $69.9 billion (in FY 1985 dollars) for air force and navy aircraft. Those dollars bought 2,040 aircraft, at an average price of $34.3 million each. In FY 1982 through 1985, we obligated $122 billion (also in FY 1985 dollars), a 75 percent increase. But we bought only 1,799 aircraft, an 11 percent decrease. Why? The average cost per aircraft rose by 98 percent, to $67.9 million.[3]

Not a single unfavorable element of the U.S.-Soviet military balance has been reversed by all the spending. In 1980, NATO was inferior on the ground in Europe. It still is. We were similarly inferior in Korea. We still are. The balances in Southwest Asia, at sea in submarines, and in fighter aircraft are still unfavorable. One trillion dollars has not turned inferiority into superiority anywhere.

These twin problems— our record of military failure, and our inability to spend ourselves strong again—make fundamental changes in defense policy vitally important, not just to our men and women in uniform and to policymakers in Washington, but also to every citizen. The safety of each and every one of us depends on effective defense forces. Today we do not have them. It is time we did.

Military effectiveness is what the military reform movement is all about. But what is the military reform movement? Who is in it?

The Core Group
The military reform movement is an attempt to discover the root causes of our military failures, develop the ideas necessary for restoring military effectiveness, and turn those ideas into policy. It has two wings, one composed of civilians, the other of serving military officers. At the core of the civilian wing lies a group of

4

five people: John Boyd, Steven Canby, Bill Lind, Norman Polmar, and Pierre Sprey. These individuals do not in any sense control the movement—it is too loosely organized for anyone to control. Rather, these five people provide much of the grist for the reform mill, in the form of catalyzing ideas.

John Boyd, a retired air force colonel, is in many ways the intellectual leader of the group. As a captain, he developed the tactics that are still the basis of our approach to air-to-air combat.[4]

Colonel Boyd's briefing, "Patterns of Conflict," is, in the words of Congressman Newt Gingrich of Georgia, "a substantial portion of the original military theory developed in this century." Its origins lie in Boyd's noting some unexpected results from mock air-to-air combat conducted at Edwards and Nellis Air Force bases in 1974. His observations of those tests led him to undertake an examination of air-to-air combat during the Korean War. American aviators were very successful in that conflict. They achieved a ten-to-one kill ratio over their North Korean and Chinese opponents. Colonel Boyd began his study with the question: "How and why did we do so well?"

He noted that in several traditional measures of aircraft performance, the principal communist fighter, the MiG-15, was superior to the American F-86. The MiG could often climb and accelerate faster, and it had a better sustained turn rate. But in two less obvious measures of aircraft performance, the F-86 was much superior to the MiG. First, the pilot could see out much better. Second, the F-86 had quick, high-powered hydraulic controls, and the MiG did not. This meant that, although the MiG could perform many individual actions—including turn, climb, and accelerate—better than the F-86, the F-86 could *transition* from one action to another much more quickly than the MiG.

Using these two superiorities, the American pilots developed tactics that forced the MiG into a series of actions. Each time the action changed, the F-86 gained a time advantage, because the F-86 pilot could see more quickly how the situation had changed, and he could make his aircraft shift more quickly to a new maneuver. With each shift, the MiG's reactions became more inappropriate, until they were so inappropriate that the MiG gave the F-86 a good

5

firing opportunity. Often it appeared the MiG pilot realized what was happening to him and panicked, which made the American pilot's job all the easier.

Colonel Boyd began studying ground combat to see if there were situations similar to what he found in the air war over Korea. He discovered that in numerous battles, campaigns, and wars a similar pattern emerged. One side had presented the other with a sudden, unexpected change or a series of such changes to which the other side could not adjust in a timely manner. As a result, it was defeated, and it was often defeated at small cost to the victor. The losing side had frequently been physically stronger than the winner. And, in many cases, the same sort of panic and paralysis the North Korean and Chinese pilots had shown seemed to occur.

Colonel Boyd asked himself: what did all these cases have in common? His answer was what is now called the Boyd Theory, which is explained in "Patterns of Conflict." It is the theory of conflict that underlies much of the military reformers' work.

The "Patterns of Conflict" briefing takes about five hours, but it can be summarized as follows:

Conflict can be seen as time-competitive Observation-Orientation-Decision-Action (OODA) cycles. Each party to a conflict begins by *observing.* He observes himself, his physical surroundings, and his enemy. Then, on the basis of his observation, he *orients;* that is to say, he makes a mental image of his situation. That, in turn, leads him to *decide* to do something. He puts the decision into effect, that is, he *acts.* Finally, because he assumes his action has changed the situation, he observes again and starts the process anew. His actions continually follow this cycle, sometimes called the Boyd Cycle or OODA Loop.

If one side in a conflict can consistently go through the Boyd Cycle faster than the other, it gains a tremendous advantage. By the time the slower side acts, the faster side is doing something different from what it had observed, and the action of the slower side is inappropriate. With each cycle, the slower party's action is inappropriate by a larger time margin. Even though it desperately strives to do something that will work, each action is less useful

6

than its predecessor; the slower side falls farther and farther behind. Ultimately—and often suddenly—it ceases to function effectively. Frequently, it panics.

This is what happened in many of history's most decisive battles and wars. Hannibal followed this pattern against the Romans at the battle of Cannae, where he won one of history's greatest tactical victories. It is also what the Germans did to the French in 1940. Sometimes a single action was enough. At other times, a series of Boyd Cycles was required. But in every case, the critical competition was in *time.*

Dr. Steven Canby is the West Pointer among the reformers. As a young captain, Canby was tasked to write a manual on small-unit infantry tactics. The Infantry School's many departments each sent him their views to be incorporated in his work. Canby threw them all out. Instead, he wrote the new manual to reflect actual combat experiences. It was then circulated to all the Infantry School departments. Each without exception was complimentary and approved of the many changes as long overdue—except in its own area, where it was clear the author "did not understand."

After leaving the army, Canby got his doctorate from Harvard and went to work for the Rand Corporation as a defense analyst. In the 1970s, he moved to Washington and established himself as an independent defense consultant. While he is not well known in the United States, Canby has a widespread reputation in Europe, where he frequently works with both NATO and neutral militaries.

Norman Polmar, author, analyst, and defense consultant, was editor of the American section of *Jane's Fighting Ships* from 1967 to 1977. He was fully responsible for almost one-third of that volume, called "the bible of the world's navies." He left that position, in part to edit two reference books published at three-year intervals by the U.S. Naval Institute, *The Ships and Aircraft of the U.S. Fleet* and *Guide to the Soviet Navy.*

Polmar has consulted for several U.S. and foreign aerospace and shipbuilding firms, as well as the navy, army, Defense Nuclear Agency, and Office of the Secretary of Defense. He is currently a member of the secretary of the navy's Research Advisory Committee as well as of a Defense Department panel examining long-term Caribbean issues.

Pierre Sprey, the reformer most interested in hardware effectiveness, started as an engineer and statistician working on fighters and radar aircraft in the aerospace industry. During a five-year stint in the late 1960s in the Office of the Secretary of Defense, he led the concept design team for the A-10 close-support aircraft and, with John Boyd, started the F-16 program. Both aircraft were remarkable in that they were more effective and much less expensive than their predecessors. Despite these initial aircraft successes, Sprey saw an even more pressing need for fundamental improvements in ground equipment. As a consultant, he worked intensively in the 1970s to improve the effectiveness of tanks, antitank and antiaircraft weapons, and armored personnel carriers. To provide the basis for their improvement, he pioneered the use of combat history to derive crucial effectiveness characteristics. Sprey has also contributed heavily to military reform thinking on the need for changes in weapons acquisition, especially in the areas of competitive procurement, operational testing, and competitive prototyping. He is currently president of his own consulting company.

These four people, with Bill Lind, remain the core of the civilians among the reformers. But a number of other individuals have played prominent parts in the reform movement. Most must remain anonymous because of where they work; the Defense Department is quick to isolate and suppress any reformer it can identify.

But two reformers inside the Defense Department have already been identified and thus can be named here. The first is Franklin C. "Chuck" Spinney. In March 1983, he appeared on the cover of *Time* magazine in recognition of his innovative and critical work on the defense budget. Over strong objections from the secretary of defense, Spinney testified to Congress that the major increases in defense spending sought by the administration would not bring the anticipated increases in military strength. Spinney's continuing work on what he calls "the plans/reality mismatch" provides the basis for the military reformers' approach to defense budgeting.

The second reformer is A. Ernest Fitzgerald, who gained considerable fame when, in 1968, in response to a direct question from Senator William Proxmire of Wisconsin whether there was a $2-billion cost overrun on the C-5 aircraft, waffled, mumbled, and finally said, "Maybe." He was hounded out of his air force civilian job for his answer and spent many years in litigation to get his job back. He finally was reinstated, by court order, in 1982. Today he continues to be active in crusading for improved management and cost control in the Defense Department.

Other reformers outside the Defense Department include Dr. Jeffrey Record, a prominent author on national security affairs and a former aide to Senator Sam Nunn; Dina Rasor, Paul Hoven, a former helicopter pilot in Vietnam, and Joe Burniece, who work for the reform-oriented Project on Military Procurement; and Drs. Richard Gabriel and Paul Savage of St. Anselm College.

The reform group, like the movement as a whole, has no set organization. It does not meet regularly. It is almost an overstatement to call it a group. Members often disagree among themselves —which they see as no bad thing, since disagreement is often the wellspring of new ideas. They are perhaps best characterized as a loose band of intellectual and political guerrilla fighters, ambushing the defense establishment with unexpected questions, unwelcome facts, and innovative alternatives to current policy. They are thoroughly unpopular with most of the Pentagon brass. But members of Congress, the press, and many younger military officers find their ideas refreshing contrasts to the standard policy of insufficient military strength at increasing cost.

The Caucus

The second major component of the civilian wing of the military reform movement is the Congressional Military Reform Caucus. From its founding in 1981, it has grown to include more than 130 members of Congress. It is the only group in Congress that includes both liberals and conservatives, other than a few caucuses that represent geographic areas.

The caucus' first major legislative success came in 1983, when it passed an amendment to strengthen the weapons testing process by establishing a new, strong, independent Office of Operational

Introduction

Testing and Evaluation. Operational testing is the field tests given
to a weapon after it is developed, to determine whether or not it is
suitable for use by troops in combat. Unfortunately, until the caucus amendment was passed, operational testing was controlled by
the same Pentagon official who controlled weapons development.
In effect, the developers being tested wrote, administered, and
graded their own tests. The result, not surprisingly, was that the
tests were seldom very thorough. For example, a new armored
personnel carrier for the infantry was never filled with fuel and
ammunition, then shot at with Soviet weapons. Instead, "simulations" were done, often with computers. They usually failed to
replicate real vulnerabilities or battlefield conditions.

The caucus' initiative was strongly opposed by the Pentagon,
but it passed the Senate ninety-five to three and sailed through the
House unopposed. So do we now have honest, effective testing for
weapons? Unfortunately, the answer is still generally no. The administration, which is opposed to military reform, hired as the new
operational test director someone it knew would not make too
many waves—a senior test pilot from one of the large aerospace
firms, McDonnell Douglas. The reformers were not strong enough
to block his confirmation by the Senate, and under his control, the
office has not been hard-hitting. Congress can only do so much to
force reform on an unwilling administration, even when it passes
appropriate laws. The problem has nothing to do with political
parties; the Carter administration was as hostile to military reform
as its Republican successor.

Since its success with the testing amendment, the caucus has
had a number of smaller legislative victories. They include providing some better equipment for the Air and Army National Guard,
mandating warranties on some types of military equipment, providing estimates of what a weapon should cost early in a program
so that future price increases are easily detected, requiring some
tough new tests of the army's Bradley Infantry Fighting Vehicle,
and protecting whistle-blowers in the Defense Department. In
1985, the House caucus passed a number of important reforms, only
to see them substantially weakened by the House-Senate conference on the defense authorization bill, a conference controlled

by the two Armed Services committees—both of which tend to protect rather than critically examine "business as usual" in the Pentagon.

Perhaps more important than these pieces of legislation has been the defense education the caucus continues to provide to many members of Congress. Through its ties to the reform group, the caucus has heard presentations on many defense issues that reflect the reformers' concern with winning in combat. Since the Armed Services committees primarily hear witnesses who are spokesmen for the Defense Department, this has brought some needed balance into Congress' study of defense issues. The caucus, in turn, has given the reform philosophy valuable exposure among the press and the public.

But the caucus must do better. It suffers from many weaknesses inherent in the Congress, including the inability of any member of Congress to spend much time or effort on any single area, a general reluctance to challenge the committees officially entrusted to supervise the Defense Department, and the push and pull of political and parochial interests. Most caucus members are members in name only. They have not done anything more to push military reform forward than put their names on the caucus membership list.

If the caucus succeeds in convincing most of its members to become active, overcomes inevitable parochial pressures on weapons systems, and systematically challenges the usual congressional rubber-stamping of Pentagon "expertise" on military matters, it will have a dramatic effect. It could change the terms of the congressional defense debate from "spend more or spend less" to "what do we need to do differently to restore the combat effectiveness of our armed forces?" Ultimately, even a hostile administration would be affected by such a change. And because it recognizes this potential, the military must pay more attention to reform ideas than if there were no caucus.

The Uniformed Reformers

The second wing of the movement is, in the long run, the more important. It is composed of the military reformers within the armed services. They are present in all the services, and they can be found at all ranks. A few are generals and admirals. Most are younger officers—lieutenants, captains, majors, and lieutenant colonels in the army, air force, and marines; ensigns through commanders in the navy. Their motivation is simple: if they are sent into combat, they want to win. They recognize that many of our present practices and policies undermine what is necessary to win in combat, and they want them changed.

The reformers inside the armed services and those outside are linked by common motivations and goals, and through some interchange of ideas. But the uniformed wing of the reform movement is by no means dependent on, or an offshoot of, the civilians. The uniformed reformers do their own thinking, and they include some intellectuals of the first rank. They remain anonymous, because the leaders of their respective services, with the exception of the army, are hostile to reform. They are not rebels or subversives; they try to work loyally within the system. But they do seek change.

Why are they the most important element of the reform movement? The movement's goal is to create an ongoing, self-renewing process of reform within the armed services. Military effectiveness demands constant adaptation to new ideas, weapons, and strategies. To be effective, a military must always be open to change, always seeking new ideas, new perspectives, new ways to outsmart the opponent. The civilian reform movement sprang up because today's peacetime armed services have lost sight of the art of war and its unceasing demand for innovation. The civilians' principal goal is to make our armed services self-reforming and, thereby, to put themselves out of business.

What Military Reform Is Not
What is military reform's content? The rest of this book attempts to answer that question. But at the outset it is necessary to make clear what reform is *not*, because it is often misrepresented and misportrayed.

Military reform is not an effort either to reduce or increase the defense budget. Some reformers favor increasing defense spending; some favor reducing it. The movement has not attempted to develop a consensus on this issue. Its goal, instead, is to reduce the amount of attention devoted in the Pentagon, the Congress, and the press to the size of the defense budget and to give more attention to whether we are buying and doing the right *kinds* of things —right for what is needed for success in combat.

The size of the defense budget now dominates the defense debate. How much to spend in total, or for this or that program, is what gets talked about. But total resources are only one factor in determining the outcome of a conflict, and they are generally not the most important factor, unless there is great disparity between the two sides. France spent billions of francs on the Maginot line in the 1920s and 1930s. But all the spending was to little avail because the nature of warfare had changed, and the Maginot line was ineffective against the blitzkrieg. Great Britain spent millions of pounds on the defenses of Singapore in the same period, but the defenses were built against an attack from the sea. When the Japanese attacked overland from the Malay Peninsula, Singapore's defenses were useless. Just spending money does not guarantee an effective defense.

Military reform is not an effort to buy large numbers of individually inferior weapons instead of smaller numbers of superior weapons. Opponents of reform have made the charge that the reformers want "quantity instead of quality." That is not true. The weapons that reformers advocate are selected first and foremost to be more effective in combat than the establishment's weapons. Because of the dictates of combat, they generally turn out to be smaller, simpler, and less expensive than those sought by the Pentagon. Reformers believe that characteristics such as small size and simplicity help give a weapon true quality— quality in combat.

The Pentagon generally defines quality in weapons in terms of technology: the more complex and expensive the technology, the higher the quality. Reformers also believe technology is very important, but they insist it be used in militarily appropriate and useful ways. Reformers argue that quality must be defined as *tactical* quality: the characteristics that make a weapon effective in combat. What are they? In each case—for tanks, fighter planes, or warships—they must be carefully analyzed on the basis of combat

13

experience. For example, in every war since the beginning of air combat in World War I, 60 to 85 percent of all aircraft shot down were destroyed by a plane they never saw. What does this mean? It means that small size is very important in fighter aircraft, because the smaller the fighter, the harder it is for an enemy to see it. The two fighters most preferred by the Pentagon, the navy's F-14 and the air force's F-15, are among the largest, easiest-to-see fighters in the world. Both have proved inferior in mock combat to the smaller and less expensive F-16—the design of which was strongly influenced by reformers John Boyd and Pierre Sprey.

Although specific desirable characteristics differ from weapon type to weapon type, effective weapons are generally small and hard to see, easy to operate and maintain under combat conditions, reliable, quick to achieve kills, and affordable in large numbers. Numbers are important in war. Quantity is itself a quality. In World War II, huge numbers of Russian T-34 tanks overwhelmed the tactically superior Germans on the Eastern Front. But the crudely built T-34 was also individually superior to the finely machined, more expensive, and more complex German Panzer III and Panzer IV tanks.

Most of the Pentagon's preferred weapons offer neither quality nor quantity. The reformers want both. They believe that with fundamental changes in the way we design our weapons, we can have both.

Military reform is not a call for more centralized management in the Pentagon in a quest for "efficiency," like that pushed twenty years ago by Secretary of Defense Robert S. McNamara. Military reform has effectiveness, not efficiency, as its goal. Effectiveness means the ability to win in combat. Efficiency is the ability to reach that goal at minimal cost. Both are important, but effectiveness is the more important of the two.

Another way to understand this is to view effectiveness as the "output," the desired end product of the whole defense process. Efficiency is one "input" into that process—an important one—but still just one among many. It makes no sense to adopt policies that sacrifice the "output" in order to improve an "input." The actions we take to improve efficiency cannot contradict what we need to do to be effective.

Efficiency is important. In fact, in combat, it is one of the principles of war, called "economy of force." The army defines economy of force by saying, "Skillful and prudent use of combat power will enable the commander to accomplish the mission with minimum expenditure of resources." The army is not being stingy here. If a general uses more divisions than he really needs to win a battle, another general somewhere else may lose a battle for want of those divisions.

In peacetime, efficiency means getting the most combat power for each dollar we spend for defense. This is necessary because resources are limited for defense and for the government, just as for every citizen running a household. If defense resources are wasted through inefficiency, they are not available to buy the weapons, ships, aircraft, and ammunition our forces need to be effective.

It is important to make clear the distinction between effectiveness and efficiency because too many politicians have confused them in the past. They are not the same. For example, we could have a very efficient horse cavalry division, one that buys its remounts cheaply, has a good retention rate for its troopers, feeds no horse more grain than it needs, and saves money by contracting out to local farriers. Its effectiveness on the modern battlefield would still be zero.

Further, if efficiency rather than effectiveness is defined as the goal, our ability to win in combat can be hurt severely. Too often, past actions designed to improve efficiency in the military have caused more centralization, generated more paperwork, and diverted more of the combat unit commander's time from training, tactics, and caring for his men to writing up reports and collecting data. This hurts combat effectiveness. Effectiveness in combat demands decentralization. To have a fast Boyd Cycle, decisions must be made on the lowest possible level. What happens to the Boyd Cycle if the observations must be passed way up the chain of command, the decision taken there, and the orders transmitted back down the chain? Obviously, it is dramatically slowed. Our current approach to management in the armed services—one created in part by Congress — drives decisions to ever higher levels as we strive to oversee everything to make sure no one is wasting money. If this habit carries over into combat, and habits tend to carry over, it will hurt us seriously.

Military reform is not political partisanship. Reformers do not seek to use the issue of military reform to attack or advance either political party. The reform movement has been happy to include anyone of either party and any ideology who will work for improved military effectiveness and who will criticize whatever works against it. The Carter administration and the Reagan administration have been equally deficient in seeing the need for military reform. Reform is not a threat to either party, and it can be of value to both. It is a matter of national policy, not partisan or ideological politics. It is too important for the future of the country to let politics hinder it in any way.

Military reform does not seek to define a new national or military strategy. Rather, its concern is to make the military instruments of strategy, the armed forces, effective. Why do we draw this distinction? In our fast-changing world, strategy may change quickly. Just over a decade ago, the People's Republic of China was a strategic opponent; today it is a strategic friend. In this century, Russia has twice been an ally; now it is an opponent. Germany, now an ally, was twice an enemy.

In contrast, changes in military doctrine and tactics, in style of warfare, in the institutional culture of the armed services, and even in military equipment are slower. The navy's big aircraft carriers may be in service for half a century. The British army has been remarkably consistent in having excellent small units and mediocre generalship for at least two centuries. A leading Western specialist on the Soviet military, John Erickson, once said to a visitor, "Do you want to understand today's Soviet army? Ask yourself what the Russian army was like under Czar Nicholas I."

Many a freshman congressman has tried to sound knowledgeable on defense by saying, "You must tell us what the strategy is before we can decide anything else." That is not a useful way to approach the problem. Of course we need a sound, clear strategy. Choices such as whether to put the majority of our resources into naval power or land power must reflect our strategy. And our armed forces must be employed within a correct strategy in wartime if they are to win. We need an effective system for thinking about and deciding on a strategy—and that system *is* a concern of the reformers. But most of the issues that affect whether or not our forces can win in combat on the tactical and operational levels must be independent of strategy, because strategy is likely to change more rapidly than we can change our policies and practices in these other areas.

A Definition

What, then, is military reform? It is an effort to make all our defense policies and practices—from the infantry squad through the Office of the Secretary of Defense and the Congress—serve the purpose of winning in combat.

In an age when even the simplest subject seems to demand vast numbers of acronyms, bar graphs, and flow charts, this definition seems very simple indeed. That is because the choice we face is clear-cut. In view of our more than thirty-year record of military failures, we have just two rational choices. We can do whatever is necessary to make our military forces effective again. Or we can take the advice one Danish candidate for parliament gave his countrymen: get rid of the armed services and install in their place a recorded phone message that says "we surrender" in Russian.

Armed forces that are not militarily competent endanger the nation. They also waste the lives of the dedicated men and women who serve in them. They waste lives in peacetime by throwing obstacle after obstacle in front of those who pursue military excellence. They waste them in war with unnecessary casualties and defeats caused by bad tactics, strategic failures, incompetent commanders, inadequately trained troops, and poorly designed weapons. One need only to recall the scene in Beirut in October 1983, as we dug the bodies of more than two hundred marines out of the rubble, to see how high the price of military incompetence can be for those who serve.

Introduction

Nuclear War

There is one major area to which military reform does not directly apply: nuclear war. There are two obvious reasons. First, it makes no sense to speak of winning a nuclear war. A nuclear conflict would be a cataclysm for all those it touched. There would be nothing to distinguish victors from vanquished among the corpses. Second, and obvious after a moment's reflection, is the fact that there is no such thing as nuclear war except as a hypothesized form of combat. We know the power of nuclear weapons, so we know their use would be a catastrophe. But beyond that, we know nothing. There is no combat experience in nuclear war, so all thinking is pure speculation. The basis for military reform-type analysis does not exist. It is impossible to reform speculation.

For the most part, so-called tactical nuclear weapons also lie outside the boundaries of military reform. What is tactical to us is Düsseldorf to our allies. At least in Europe, tactical nuclear weapons are "linkage" to the strategic nuclear arsenal, not practical battlefield weapons.

To say that the realm of nuclear weapons lies outside the boundaries of military reform does not mean the two are entirely separate. There are three relationships. First, because both superpowers and several middle-rank powers possess nuclear weapons, conventional wars in which the superpowers are directly or indirectly involved are likely to be limited wars.

Limited war is not new. Between the end of the Thirty Years War in 1648 and the French Revolution in 1789, most European wars were limited. They were limited in their goals; nations seldom sought to destroy one another. The Thirty Years War had shown both the futility and the price of attempts to destroy other nations or beliefs. By some accounts, Germany's population was cut from 16 million to 6 million in that war. European wars were also limited in means. Armies were very expensive and took a long time to train in the elaborate, formal tactics of the time. No one wanted to lose his army. Frederick the Great's father was in this respect typical of European kings of the later seventeenth and eighteenth centuries. He built the finest army in central Europe but resolutely refused to use it. "War ruins armies" was his watchword. Frederick put that fine army to use, and the ensuing wars did largely ruin it. But even he sought only a province or two, not the destruction of his neighbors.

Today, as then, limited war means the goal will seldom be an enemy's complete destruction. The threatened destruction of even a client of a nuclear power could move the world uneasily close to the brink of total devastation. In the 1973 Middle East War, the superpowers both acted to prevent a complete defeat of Egypt by Israel after the Israelis crossed the Suez Canal and encircled the Egyptian Third Army, for fear that such a defeat might lead to a U.S.-Soviet confrontation. Superpowers' armies are likely to find similar constraints put on their actions. It may often be necessary to build a "golden bridge" across which a defeated enemy may retreat with some remnants of both his army and his prestige intact.

That does not mean there will be no such thing as winning. Had we maintained a free and independent South Vietnam, we would have won the Vietnam War. As it was, we clearly lost. Israel has won her wars, even if she did not end up occupying Damascus, Amman, or Cairo. Great Britain won the Falklands War. For conventional forces, winning remains the bottom line. If victory usually will not mean World War II-style unconditional surrender, it will still mean the victor ends up controlling the situation and achieving his limited goals. The winner will emerge with his power and position enhanced, the loser with his diminished, and the world will take note.

Military reform relates to the nuclear threat in a second way. Some commentators portray the world situation as similar to that of the late 1930s. The Soviet Union is seen as the successor to Hitler's Germany, planning aggressive war and just waiting for a good opportunity to strike. There is no doubt some truth to this portrayal. The Soviet leadership traditionally has been eager to fish in troubled waters, to take advantage of the West's weakness, and to stir up trouble. It has supported many so-called wars of national liberation aimed at Western allies and interests.

But on the whole, today's situation seems more like that before 1914 than before 1939. All-out war between the superpowers, including strategic nuclear war, seems more likely to come as the unintended result of a series of escalating crises than from a coldly calculated Soviet attack on the West. Here, the position of the United States may pose the greater danger. Because our conventional forces are relatively ineffective, we have adopted a doctrine of first use of nuclear weapons. In Europe and possibly elsewhere —including the Persian Gulf, where our Central Command has been spoken of in this context—we have stated that if our conventional forces suffer defeat, we hold open the option of using nuclear weapons.

A scenario is not too difficult to envision. A crisis erupts and turns into war between U.S. and Soviet clients. Our client is being worsted, and we introduce substantial American combat forces in its support. Those American forces are defeated, either by the Soviet client or by Soviet forces introduced in response to our own. The Eighty-second Airborne Division is decimated. The First Marine Division is driven into the sea, and thousands of marines are killed. An American aircraft carrier is reduced to a flaming hulk. The decision makers in Washington face an enormous national humiliation. Nuclear weapons appear to offer a way out. It looks as if a few well-placed "tactical" nuclear weapons will destroy the opponent's armies and save what is left of ours. Desperate, we use them. The Soviets feel they must respond the same way or be shown up as a "paper tiger." They use tactical nuclear weapons at sea, annihilating what is left of our navy in the area and sealing our armies off from both reinforcement and withdrawal. In Washington, it seems the only answer is to drop a few more nuclear weapons, this time aimed at Soviet naval bases. American nuclear weapons land on Soviet soil. Again they retaliate, and World War III has begun.

Because of the danger inherent in any escalating crisis, we must be able to control events on the conventional level. That means we must have conventional forces that can deter or, if deterrence fails, prevail. Again, winning may not mean annihilating the enemy; doing so may push the Soviets into being the first to use nuclear weapons. But we cannot hope to control a situation with forces that are losing. When our forces are being defeated, events are beyond our control.

Military reform aims at giving us conventional forces effective enough to keep us off the nuclear hook. Military reformers seek to establish an effective conventional deterrent in Europe and elsewhere. With such conventional capability, a doctrine of nuclear first use would be unnecessary. Although a policy of "no first use" would have to be discussed and coordinated with our allies, it would be highly desirable. Increasing numbers of Europeans, who realize that nuclear war will occur first on their territory under current doctrine, seem to feel the same way. The movement for stronger, more effective conventional forces, at a cost all can afford, is gaining strength in Europe as it is here.

Military reform relates to nuclear weapons in a third way. The purpose of our nuclear arsenal is to deter wars, not to fight them. The same is true for the reformed, effective conventional forces the reformers envision. No reformer wants conventional forces that can win because he wants to fight wars. The price of modern conventional war is far too high for that. No one wants to see more monuments on the Mall in Washington covered with the names of dead Americans. Reformers want forces that can win because they are more likely to deter war than forces a potential enemy thinks he can beat.

Military Reform: The Diagnosis

How do military reformers diagnose our military weaknesses? There are problems on three levels.

The first level is the "superstructure." It is called that because, although it includes most of the issues the public reads about in the newspapers, problems on this level derive from deeper, more fundamental deficiencies in our military system and structure. Superstructure problems include such things as:

• Weapons so poorly designed they won't work in combat. An example is the army's new Bradley Infantry Fighting Vehicle. Although troops are supposed to stay in the Bradley much of the time on the battlefield and fight from it, it has very thin armor—

so thin even the smallest antitank weapon will easily go through it. Worse, the armor is aluminum, which when hit by a "shaped charge" antitank weapon, vaporizes and burns at the point where it is hit, adding to the effect of the warhead. Because of the Bradley's turret, troops can no longer ride on top to keep themselves alive if the vehicle hits a mine. They must ride inside, where a mine will throw them against the roof and kill them. The Bradley is supposed to be an improvement over the M-113 personnel carrier because it has a light cannon and an antitank missile. But the highly explosive ammunition for these weapons, stored behind the Bradley's flimsy armor, makes the vehicle a powder keg, lethal to the troops inside. The Bradley's deficient design concept may cost thousands of American infantrymen their lives if a major war breaks out.

• Training time. The average American fighter pilot only gets about half as many flight sorties each month as an Israeli fighter pilot has traditionally received. On a visit several years ago to the First Marine Division at Camp Pendleton, California, a visitor asked how many days the battalions had spent in the field as full battalions during the previous year. The average was about thirty days for the infantry battalions—not very much. The tank battalion had not gone to the field at all as a complete battalion in the previous twelve months.

• Inadequate ammunition, spare parts, and war reserve equipment (equipment to replace combat losses in wartime). We have so few torpedoes for our submarines that after each sub shoots just one full load, there will not be enough to give it a complete reload. Then we will be out of torpedoes. The subs will have to tie up at the docks for the rest of the war.

• Unit cohesion. In combat, troops do not fight so much for "king and country" as for their buddies—the people in their fire team, squad, and platoon. Today most of those people will be strangers. We rotate people so rapidly that we often have a personnel turnover rate of 25 percent per quarter in an infantry company, one of the highest rates in the world. Strangers do not fight well together; sometimes they won't fight at all.

• Outdated force structure. Today our navy depends on just thirteen huge aircraft carriers. Each one is highly flammable, filled as it must be with explosive aviation fuel and ordnance. Soviet antiship missiles have very large warheads—several times the size of those on the French-built Exocet missiles the Argentines used in the Falklands War— designed to penetrate deep and explode in a carrier's magazines. The Soviets also have about three hundred attack submarines, each of which can sink a carrier. We have only about one hundred attack subs, in part because the carriers, their planes, and their escorting cruisers and destroyers soak up most of the money.

These problems are all serious. But to deal with them effectively, the question must be asked, how did they come about? Why have we made so many mistakes? This leads us to the second level of the military reformers' analysis of our defense weakness: problems in officer education and promotion, the way we structure our military decision-making bodies like the Joint Chiefs of Staff, the way our weapons development and procurement process works, and the role Congress plays in the defense debate. This book examines each of these areas in detail.

The third level of analysis looks at the "corporate culture" of the military services. How do they behave as institutions? They behave like the bureaucracies they are. All bureaucracies—military and civilian, government and private—tend to do what is comfortable internally, not what is effective externally. In the services, most of the senior leaders, the generals and admirals, are not warriors but "milicrats"—bureaucrats in uniform, who behave no differently from their counterparts in other government departments. And the result is the same as in other departments: the more money we put in, the fewer useful results we get out. Solving defense problems by throwing money at the Pentagon works no better than solving social problems by throwing more money into the welfare bureaucracy. If military reform is to be effective, it must change the way our armed services think and behave as institutions. It must change their corporate cultures.

Many knowledgeable people reply, "This all sounds great, but is it realistic? Is it practicable? Can these huge, powerful and entrenched institutions be made to change their most basic habits, the way they think and behave?"

The answer is yes, for three reasons.

First, it *must* be done. The most basic responsibility of any government is to protect its citizens. Today, with armed forces ill prepared for combat, we are insecure, and no matter how much we spend we will remain insecure. Only military reform can give us genuine national security.

Second, military reform has strong support from many people in the armed services. Once they understand what military reform really is and what it seeks to do, it will have active support from the large majority.

Third, there are historical precedents. They include the "Root reforms," changes driven by Secretary of War Elihu Root in the period after the Spanish American War; the reform of the Royal Navy by Admiral Sir John Fisher in the early 1900s, a reform that saw, among other things, the introduction of the famous "dreadnought" type of battleship; and the reforms enacted in Prussia after its disastrous defeat by Napoleon in 1806, reforms that created the justly famous Prussian General Staff.

Perhaps the strongest historical evidence that military reform is possible comes from our own wartime experiences. Three times in our history—in the Civil War, in World War I, and again in World War II—the United States fielded large and reasonably effective armies and navies in a remarkably short time, starting with very little. Although we do not usually think of these great expansions of our military power as reforms, in many ways they were. If we look at the transformation of the U.S. Navy in the Civil War from a third-rate fleet of wooden ships, little changed from Nelson's day, to what may well have been the world's most powerful navy, built largely around steam-driven, armored warships with their guns in revolving turrets—the famous monitors—we see a tremendous amount of reform in just five years. Similarly, if we compare the U.S. Army that carried out the Louisiana maneuvers in 1940 to the fast-moving, hard-hitting Third Army of General George Patton in 1944 and 1945, we see tremendous qualitative improvement, not just an expansion in size.

Some will say, "Yes, but that was under the pressure of war." Is the pressure on our country really any less today? We remain a primary guardian of the values and freedoms of Western civilization. Those values and freedoms are threatened by myriad hostile forces, from the might of the armed forces of the Soviet Union through the fanaticism of various religious movements in the Middle East to the assassinations and bombings carried out by European radicals of both the left and the right. The threat of nuclear war looms over us all, a threat made all the more serious by our dependence on nuclear weapons to make up for the weakness of our conventional forces.

It is time to rip down the cobwebs of daily routine and political and bureaucratic complacency and confront our central military problem: our conventional forces are not effective enough to defend us. Unless we make them effective, in every crisis we will risk a choice between national humiliation and nuclear war.

Military reform is a threat to some Pentagon and defense industry bureaucrats who do not wish to see their comfortable and profitable routines disrupted. However, it is a promise to everyone else, most of all to the vast majority of those serving in our armed forces. They want the opportunity to give the nation the military excellence it needs. They are deeply frustrated by "business as usual" and by the current practices that put financial management, career politics, "dog-and-pony-show" inspections and demonstrations, endless reports to higher headquarters, and even base beautification and the Combined Federal Campaign above preparing for combat. They did not join to be losers, and they know they can be winners, if we will only change the system so they can do their jobs.

PART

ONE

Superstructure

T he term "superstructure" will be familiar to any readers on the other side of the Iron Curtain. It is used here in the same way Karl Marx used it: to describe phenomena which, however dramatic, compelling or momentous, are nonetheless not things complete in themselves, but rather manifestations of other, often hidden systemic problems. The concept is useful in understanding what is really happening within our military, and why we have the problems we do.

The military superstructure includes such issues as style of warfare, guiding military concepts, weapons and other equipment, personnel issues, training, and force structure. They are all important. But to understand why and how problems in the defense superstructure have come about, it is necessary to dig deeper.

What are the problems in the superstructure? What policies and practices should replace those we can see are deficient?

1

Ground Forces

THE UNITED STATES today has two armies: the United States Army and the United States Marine Corps. The army has about 785,000 personnel, making it the fifth largest army in the world in manpower. It fields 17 divisions, has 11,053 tanks, 3,491 artillery pieces, 9,785 personnel carriers for its infantry, and 5,343 helicopters. To put this in some perspective, the Soviet army has 193 divisions, about 51,000 tanks, 34,000 artillery pieces, 70,000 personnel carriers, and 4,100 helicopters. The People's Republic of China has 158 divisions, 11,450 tanks, 12,800 pieces of artillery, and 2,800 personnel carriers.[1] These comparisons show that we are a substantial land power, but not exactly in the top league numerically.

Then we have our second army, the Marine Corps. It has 198,000 personnel, from which it produces only 3 divisions, although it also mans its own air force. The Marine Corps likes to pretend it is not another army, so as to avoid competition. Marines argue their only mission is to conduct amphibious attacks. But the idea that we could have 3 divisions out of a total of only 20 that just took a beach and then went home is nonsense. We have used the marines as an army in past wars, and we will undoubtedly continue to do so. Furthermore, the potential competition is really the best reason for having two armies; if one gets stuck in a rut, clinging to outdated concepts or tactics, the other can still move forward.

Concepts

One of the most important questions about an army is, what is its style of warfare? Reformers think this is one of the most important factors in determining whether an army is likely to win or lose. An army's style of warfare is, simply, the way it fights. There are two basic elements to an army's style: what ideas it tries to follow —its doctrine—and what ideas it is actually capable of following in combat. The two are not always identical.

There are two basic styles of warfare: firepower/attrition and maneuver. In firepower/attrition warfare, the object is simply to pour firepower on the enemy—artillery shells, bombs from aircraft, bullets, etc.—to kill his troops and destroy his equipment. To win, you need to kill enough of his troops and blow up so much of his equipment that he can no longer fight. That was how we fought in Vietnam; you may remember the daily reports of the "body count" during that war.

Perhaps history's grimmest and therefore best example of firepower/attrition warfare is the Battle of Verdun in World War I. The chief of staff of the German army, General von Falkenhayn, wanted to bleed France to death. He believed that if he attacked the strategically insignificant fort of Verdun, the French would defend it, as the Allies defended each foot of ground in that war. If more French soldiers were killed than German soldiers, Germany would be brought closer to victory— or so he thought.

The general got his wish. The French did defend Verdun, considering it a symbol of French pride and French courage. In the end, at least 700,000 men, German and French, were killed or wounded. Slightly more Frenchmen were killed than Germans. The greater attrition of the French proved to be strategically meaningless.[2]

In contrast to Verdun, when Germany attacked France in 1940 it defeated her quickly and with relatively few casualties. Why such a difference? It is because in 1940 the Germans used a different style of warfare: maneuver warfare. The object in maneuver warfare is not to kill enemy soldiers, but to shatter the ability of whole enemy units—divisions, corps, even whole armies—to fight in an organized, effective way, and to panic and paralyze enemy commanders. The main means is not firepower, but maneuver. In the term "maneuver warfare," the word maneuver means Boyd Cycling the enemy: presenting him with surprising and dangerous situations faster than he can react to them, until he comes apart.

Maneuver warfare is not new. The first clear example of it is the battle of Leuctra in 371 B.C., between Sparta and Thebes. The Thebans outmaneuvered the Spartans by launching a surprise attack into the Spartan's right flank. One of the greatest tactical victories of all time, Hannibal's defeat of the Romans at Cannae in 216 B.C., was also an example of maneuver warfare. The Carthaginians tricked the Romans into attacking in the center, then swept around both flanks and encircled them. The Romans were annihilated. The Roman response, Scipio's invasion of North Africa, was equally an example of maneuver and was strategically decisive.

In modern times, the Germans have been the greatest practitioners of maneuver warfare. Their best maneuver warfare campaign was that against France in 1940. Contrary to popular wisdom, the numbers were about equal, 135 Allied divisions to 136 German divisions. The number of tanks was almost equal, 2,541 Allied to 2,574 German. And the Allied tanks were on the whole better than those of the Germans.

But the Germans had a new idea: blitzkrieg. The Germans outmaneuvered the Allies by attacking where they were not expected, through the forests of the Ardennes mountains. They followed up their breakthrough there with stunning speed, with one tank corps covering 230 miles in just fourteen days. The French high command could not react in time to the fast-moving Panzer divisions. Each time they tried to build a new defensive line, the Germans were through it before it was completed. The realization that they simply could not move fast enough brought the French to panic and despair, and France collapsed.

Germany conquered France, Belgium, and Holland in only forty-three days, with the loss of just 27,000 killed—small casualties by World War I standards. Blitzkrieg had managed to substitute speed for weight of metal and ideas for blood.

Israel has been another successful practitioner of maneuver

warfare. In the 1967 war, the Israelis shattered the Egyptians with a surprise attack and a blindingly fast advance. In just six days, the Israelis had reached the Suez Canal, and the war was over. In 1973, Israel recovered from her initial surprise and defeat along the Suez Canal with a bold maneuver. Israeli forces suddenly crossed the canal, drove south, and encircled the whole Egyptian Third Army. In both wars, Israeli casualties were relatively few, and her victories were quick.

Historically, the United States generally has adhered to a firepower/attrition style of warfare. We usually had the great superiority in numbers of men and equipment to fight this way and win. The Union rolled over the Confederacy with firepower and attrition, and we defeated both the Central Powers and the Axis in like manner.

The cost was often high. In 1864, General Ulysses S. Grant was locked in a series of battles with General Robert E. Lee around Richmond, Virginia. Grant had superiority in numbers. The Union army in Virginia had more than 110,000 men, Lee about 65,000. Grant could and did use firepower/attrition warfare. At the battle of Cold Harbor, Grant ordered his troops to charge directly into Lee's entrenched riflemen. In half an hour, 7,000 Union troops were killed or wounded. The wounded were left lying between the lines for three days. Only two survived.

The troops understood what this kind of warfare meant for them. Before the battle of Cold Harbor began, many had pinned notes on their backs with their home addresses so that their families could be told of their deaths. One young Union soldier had written in his diary, "Cold Harbor. I was killed." He was.

Firepower/attrition warfare is no longer viable for an American army, even if the nation were willing to accept its high casualties. It can only work where one side either has a great technological advantage—for example, British machine guns against spear-armed tribesmen in nineteenth-century Africa—or where one side greatly outnumbers the other. Today the United States has neither advantage over the Soviet Union. Nor does NATO have such an advantage over the Warsaw Pact.

We cannot afford to fight long, drawn-out wars. Firepower/attrition warfare is usually slow. Although the Germans conquered France in 1940 in just forty-three days, the Allies, using firepower/attrition warfare, took almost ten months to cover the same distance going the other way in 1944 and 1945, even though they had great numerical and material superiority.

Both our armies need to follow a maneuver style of warfare. Maneuver warfare means such major changes as:

• Imaginative tactics. In attrition warfare, tactics generally follow rigid formulas and recipes. Officers are taught that for each situation there is one correct response, the "school solution." That does not work in maneuver warfare. If formulas are followed, the enemy will quickly figure them out, and our forces will not be able to surprise him, to present him with dangerous situations faster than he can deal with them.

• Decentralization. Today we have a very centralized military. Partly because of the quest for "better management," we have pushed decisions to ever-high levels. Maneuver warfare demands the opposite: decentralization. Only a decentralized military can have a fast Boyd Cycle, which is the basis of successful maneuver warfare.

• Mission-type orders. Currently, most military orders tell the subordinate exactly what to do, and he is kept closely under the control of his superior. That is not true in maneuver warfare, which can only be fought with mission-type orders. A mission-type order tells the subordinate what *result* his commander wants but leaves him a great deal of latitude in determining how to achieve it. Why is this important? The dominant characteristics of combat are uncertainty and rapid change. The commander immediately on the scene must be able to adjust his actions to unexpected and sudden changes. Mission-type orders let him do so. Without them, he must report the new situation up the chain of command and wait for new instructions. Often, by the time he gets them, the situation has changed again, and they are useless. Back he goes for more orders. His Boyd Cycle is slow.

Some junior officers have begun calling tactics based on mission-type orders "trust tactics." That is a good name for them. The commander trusts his subordinate to make sure his actions serve the commander's intent. The subordinate trusts his commander to make his intent clear and to back him up when he shows initiative —even when that initiative results in a mistake. There is no room for the typical managerial "zero defects" atmosphere with mission-type orders. Better to have initiative with some mistakes than no mistakes and no initiative.

• The "operational art." Traditionally, Americans have thought of two levels of war: tactics and strategy. Tactics is the art of winning battles. Strategy is the art of winning wars. The Germans in the past had, and today the Soviets have, an intermediate level between tactics and strategy—the operational art. This linkage between tactics and strategy is the art of *using* tactical events—battles or refusals to give battle—to strike *directly* at the enemy's strategic center of gravity. For the commander, it is the art of deciding where and when to fight on the basis of the strategic plan.

A good example of the operational art is the North Vietnamese and Viet Cong's Tet offensive in 1968. Tet was a tactical defeat for the communist forces; the Viet Cong in particular suffered very heavy casualties, and the communists were not able to take and hold any important cities. But they won a great operational victory. The American strategic center of gravity was the growing popular discontent with the Vietnam War. The American government was trying to maintain popular support by assuring the American people that the war was going well and would soon be won—the infamous "light at the end of the tunnel." By showing they could carry out a large offensive, including an attack on the U.S. embassy in Saigon, the communists shattered that claim and struck a devastating blow at the American people's support for the war. The people felt, rightly, that their government had been misleading them. They were never to trust that government's claims about the war again.

Why is the operational art so important? Because it is more through the operational art than through maneuver in tactical battles that a smaller force can defeat a larger one and that maneuver warfare can bring a quick victory without high casualties. Traditionally, American armies have tried to win strategic victories by accumulating tactical victories. This is attrition warfare, even if each battle is won through maneuver. Only by using battle sparingly, by trying to fight only where and when a tactical victory will have an important strategic effect, can maneuver warfare really be effective, especially for a force that is outnumbered.

This is just a sketch of the different perspectives maneuver warfare demands.[3] Where do our two armies stand in terms of adopting a maneuver style of warfare?

In 1982, in a change of historic proportions, the army adopted maneuver warfare as doctrine. It published a new version of its basic doctrinal manual, field manual *FM 100-5,* based on maneuver concepts.

The new manual includes many statements that reflect maneuver warfare concepts, such as:

> Airland Battle [the army's term for its new doctrine] emphasizes flexibility, speed, surprise and initiative as well as mission orders. ... Even in conventional combat, operations will rarely maintain a linear character. ... Subordinate leaders will be expected to act on their own initiative within the framework of the commander's intent. ...
>
> Commanders must also take time to train subordinate leaders and staff members, building their confidence and requiring them to exercise initiative. This is best done by training them to react to changes which require fast, independent decisions based on broad guidance. ... Operational art thus involves fundamental decisions about when and where to fight and whether to accept or decline battle. Its essence is the identification of the enemy's strategic center-of-gravity and the concentration of superior combat power against that point to achieve a decisive success. ...
>
> Among the intangible factors [of combat power] are state of training, troop motivation, and leaders' skill, firmness of purpose, and boldness—their ability to perceive opportunities, decide rapidly, and act decisively. ... Maneuver is the dynamic element of combat—the means of concentrating forces at the critical point to achieve the surprise, psychological shock, physical momentum, and moral dominance which enable smaller forces to defeat larger ones. ... Effective maneuver protects the force and keeps the enemy off balance. It continually poses new problems for him, renders his reactions ineffective, and eventually leads to his defeat. ...
>
> Applied to individual soldiers and leaders, [initiative] connotes a willingness and ability to act independently within the context of the higher commander's intent. In both senses, initiative requires risk-taking and an atmosphere that supports it. ... Overcentralization slows action and precludes seizing fleeting opportunities. At the same time, decentralization risks the loss

of some precision in execution. The commander must constantly balance these competing risks, recognizing that loss of precision is usually preferable to inaction.

All of these precepts, and many more included in the field manual, express basic maneuver warfare concepts.

But adopting maneuver warfare as doctrine is just the first step. It takes more than correct doctrine to win in combat. It takes an army that can put those ideas into effect in the chaos of war. What changes are necessary to enable the army to do that?

One is truly *having* a doctrine, a shared way of thinking. Just publishing a manual does not guarantee that everyone understands it and thinks in the way it prescribes. Today most commanders practice in training whatever they understand best: maneuver warfare, frontal assaults, the "active defense," linear warfare, cavalry-style charges, or a series of "trap play" ambushes. The army does not yet have a shared way of thinking, although it is working to build one.

Other changes should include developing excellence in tactical techniques, the "how-to-do-it" aspects of war; educating officers in the art of war, in how to think, not just in terminology, formats, and procedures; promoting officers with the strength of character, the imagination, and the boldness combat demands (qualities that often do not fit very well into a peacetime army routine); creating a force structure that provides a sufficient number of combat soldiers; fostering cohesion, good morale, and esprit de corps in the combat units (which means sending the best quality soldiers to the combat arms not to the technical branches); and purchasing equipment that is reliable, simple to operate, and fixable with field expedients—hammers, wrenches, bailing wire, and tape—rather than computers.

Almost everything an army does reflects its choice of either a firepower/attrition or a maneuver style of warfare.[4] Is the U.S. Army moving to make the necessary changes?

It is beginning to do so. In fact, the army, alone among the armed services, is today making a serious and sincere effort to reform itself. The effort has not yet touched everything—weapons design and procurement, for example, so far remain immune—but genuine progress is being made. It is being made largely because of efforts from inside the army, not in response to the civilian reformers.

One of the most important changes under way in the army is in the people who lead it. A new generation of officers is beginning to reach the ranks of colonel and brigadier general. These are individuals who were platoon and company commanders in Vietnam. Many have bitter memories of that war. They saw how a technologically inferior enemy was often able to outsmart and outmaneuver us. They were deeply frustrated by overcentralization, by the layers of helicopters circling overhead carrying colonels and generals trying to run the platoon and company battles on the ground, and usually doing it badly. Most of them are strong supporters of maneuver warfare. They believe the army must devote greater attention to the art of war and less to management and career politics. As their influence grows, it will fuel the army's own reform movement.

The army's effort to reform itself is something every American should praise and support. But it should not be taken to mean that no aspects of army policy should be criticized. The army is still not working to correct its own problems in all areas. The poor performance of the supposedly elite Eighty-second Airborne Division on Grenada is a good example. No steps have been taken to root out that division's deep and serious problems.

On the whole, however, the army is making headway. If its current efforts to reform spread, deepen, are sustained, and succeed, the world will see a much different and far more effective United States Army from the one to which it has become accustomed in recent years.

What about our second army, the Marine Corps? The Marine Corps provides an instructive, if disheartening, example of how an attempt at self-reform can go astray. In the mid-1970s, when the debate about maneuver warfare began, the army was hostile. But the Marine Corps was open. Marine officers generally had resisted the pressures of "managerialism" better than their colleagues in the other services. They remained interested in the art of war and in finding better ways to fight and win. Maneuver warfare was recognized by many marines, especially junior officers, as a way to improve the corps' chances of winning.

The movement for maneuver warfare blossomed rapidly in the corps. The principal Marine Corps journal, the *Marine Corps Gazette,* opened its pages to a lively and intense discussion of the subject. Individual units began experimenting with maneuver tactics, mission-type orders, and decentralization of authority. Both in the schools and in combat units, military reading, discussion, and war-gaming seminars were formed. In 1981, the commander of the Second Marine Division, Major General A.M. Gray, Jr., proclaimed maneuver warfare as doctrine in his division. He established a Maneuver Warfare Board, made up largely of junior officers, to promulgate the concept in the division, and he began a series of maneuver warfare, free-play field exercises at Fort Pickett, Virginia. In 1982, the head of the Tactics Department at the Amphibious Warfare School, the Marine Corps' school for captains, began teaching maneuver warfare as doctrine. The commandant of the Marine Corps at this time, General Robert H. Barrow, allowed this grass-roots movement for reform to flourish and even gave it some encouragement.

A mark of the marines' progress occurred in the 1983 invasion of Grenada. The marine battalion on the island, Second Battalion, Eighth Marines, came from the Second Marine Division. The battalion commander was himself a strong proponent of maneuver warfare, and he had trained his battalion in it. The decentralization and use of mission-type orders had gone so far that the junior officers had a hand-and-arm signal for it: putting your hand under your arm and waving the elbow up and down transmitted the order, "Wing it."

Second Battalion, Eighth Marines, did extremely well on Grenada. It moved so fast it threw the Grenadian forces completely off guard. A senior Grenadian officer captured by the marines said that marine units had appeared so swiftly where they were not expected that his army's high command was convinced resistance was hopeless. That is the best possible outcome in maneuver warfare, since it results in quick victories with few or no casualties.

Unfortunately, since General Barrow retired as commandant, the senior leadership of the Marine Corps has turned against maneuver warfare and military reform generally. Not only has the new leadership not undertaken the changes maneuver warfare requires—such as adopting a new doctrine that reflects it, reforming the Marine Corps schools so they teach it, and making the bulk of field training the free-play exercises that foster it—that leadership has moved to suppress maneuver warfare where it had been flourishing.

Progress in maneuver warfare continues in the Second Marine Division. But most Marine Corps field training is still rigid and mechanical, and tactics are generally taught as recipes and formulas. Education and doctrinal development are at a standstill, except at the Amphibious Warfare School, where some progress is still being made. No equivalent to the army's excellent new second-year course at Fort Leavenworth is in the offing, much less a Marine Corps counterpart to the army's field manual *FM 100-5*. Senior marine leaders have denounced the small groups of marines who meet to study maneuver warfare. "Stability," a code word for resistance to reform, has been proclaimed as the Marine Corps' policy.

This is not to say that maneuver warfare and military reform are dead in the Marine Corps. On the contrary, they are very much alive, especially among the younger officers, the lieutenants and captains, and with a slowly growing number of their superiors as well. Many junior officers continue to believe maneuver warfare is vitally important if the corps is to succeed on future battlefields. This means more to them than the negative attitudes of the corps' senior leadership. They continue to study maneuver warfare, avidly preparing themselves for the day when the corps adopts it as doctrine, as surely it someday will. To the degree they can, they practice it in their platoons and companies. Because of their commitment to reform, the long-term future of the Marine Corps is bright, even though it appears that in the short run, rigidity and orthodoxy are prevailing.

Equipment

Ideas and people are more important for winning in combat than equipment; however, weaponry is still a vital concern. Weapons that don't work in combat or cannot be bought in sufficient quantities will bring down even the best people and ideas.

Anyone who reads the newspapers knows our armed forces have some serious problems with their equipment. Many of our weapons are badly conceived and designed. They will let our soldiers down in combat. Poor, overly complex designs lead to a second serious problem: the equipment costs so much we cannot afford enough of it. This is the central equipment dilemma for the navy and the air force as well as for our ground forces: we are getting neither quality nor quantity in many of our weapons.

The general qualities that make a weapon effective in combat are small size, reliability and ease of maintenance, ease of operation, ability to achieve kills quickly, and affordability in sufficient numbers. However, in the case of each particular kind of weapon, careful analysis is needed to answer the question, "What characteristics does this weapon need to be effective in combat?" That analysis cannot be a shopping trip to the technology store. It must be based on research into what happened in past combat, and as closely as we can replicate it in peacetime tests, what will happen in combat today. Instead, what we usually get is sloppy thinking, which manifests itself in poor designs.

One variety of sloppy thinking is confusing peacetime with wartime quality. A good example of this failure is our latest tank, the M-1.

The army sometimes cites the M-1 as a case where the reformers, many of whom strongly opposed the tank from the beginning, were wrong. The troops in the field like the M-1 tank. They believe it is a great improvement over its predecessor, the M-60. They are happy to tell visitors about its fast acceleration, good ride at high speed over rough terrain, and ease of operation—all of which are important qualities. They say they would be happy to go into combat with it.

This means the M-I is a good peacetime tank. But combat is very different from peacetime training and life in garrison. Qualities that are vitally important in combat often do not stand out much in peacetime. Many reformers, acknowledging that the M-I is well-liked by those who use it in peacetime, still have doubts about its combat qualities.

What makes a tank a good tank in combat? One of the members of the reform group, Pierre Sprey, has done an exhaustive study of this question. Sprey begins by asking: What is a tank for? Is it for fighting other tanks? The army often says, "The best weapon against a tank is another tank." Or is a tank's purpose to shoot up the enemy's unprotected but vital rear area? That is how the Germans, the Israelis, and General George Patton used tanks. If we recognize that the second answer is the right one, we immediately see something surprising: a tank's main weapon is not its large cannon, but its machine guns. Most of the targets in an enemy's rear are soft targets—trucks, maintenance areas, ammunition dumps, and headquarters. They are generally best shot at with machine guns, not a large cannon. The cannon is important for helping the tank get to where it can lay waste with its machine guns. Unfortunately, two of the M-I's three machine guns are difficult to operate.

Sprey's combat-based study of tanks goes on to show that in many other respects the most important characteristics of a tank are not what the army thinks they are. In 1941, 4,000 German tanks advanced 1,000 miles in three months against 23,000 Russian tanks, some of which were technically superior. They were able to do so because tactics, unit cohesion, and training are more important in combat than many of the technical characteristics of tanks. However, technical characteristics that affect tactics, cohesion, or training are important. Tanks that are cheap to run mean more training time than tanks that cost a lot to run. The M-I's expensive spare parts and high fuel consumption make training costly; the M-I uses 9.3 gallons of fuel per mile, compared to 2.4 for the M-60.

The army stresses that its new M-I tank is faster than the old

M-60. But in the most critical aspect of speed in combat, the M-1 is slower. Speed is most important in terms of operational mobility: how fast can a tank unit, a battalion or brigade, suddenly pick up and move 100 kilometers, often over dirt roads, to take advantage of a gap leading into the enemy's rear? The M-1 has some serious disadvantages here. Its high fuel consumption makes frequent refueling necessary, and a tank battalion can easily take two or three hours to refuel. The army plans to equip the M-1 with a small auxiliary engine to save fuel while idling, which will help somewhat. But not all M-1s will get the auxiliary engine, and fuel consumption on the move will still be higher than that of the M-60. In addition, the M-1 weighs five tons more than an M-60. So there will be more bridges it can't cross, and its operational mobility will be further restricted.

Another highly important factor in combat is the number of tanks available on the battlefield. One billion dollars buys 1,100 M-60 tanks but only 360 M-1s. Even if the M-1 eventually proves as, or more, reliable than the M-60, the higher cost of the M-1 is likely to mean we will have fewer tanks.

The modern battlefield is full of light, hand-held antitank weapons. The thirty-year-old Russian RPG-7 is very effective, and every Russian infantry squad has one. The M-1's armor on the front of the tank is much better than that of the M-60 against RPG-7s and similar antitank weapons. But it is no better in back. Further, to survive against infantry armed with RPG-7s, tanks need to be able to bring machine-gun fire to bear quickly on any hostile infantry — especially infantry close to the tanks. The M-1 has serious problems with its machine guns. The tank commander's gun is almost unusable because of a complex, difficult-to-use mount. The loader's gun has a mount that tends to break or jam when he uses the gun. Only the gun in the turret works well, and it takes time to rotate the turret. The M-1's large, flat turret also obscures the crew's view of close-in enemy infantry. The M-60 also had serious problems with its machine guns, although these have been partially fixed. This is a classic case of not thinking through what is important in combat. All the attention goes to the tank's cannon, not its machine guns. The Israelis, who have had a great deal of recent experience in tank combat, are a notable contrast. Their tanks carry four machine guns, and they are quick and easy to aim and fire.

Other areas show similar problems. In designing the M-1, the army did not carefully ask the question, "What qualities do tanks most need *in combat?*" When the Israelis designed their excellent tank, the *Merkava,* the design team spent many hours talking to combat-experienced tank crews and asking them exactly that question. Not surprisingly, the *Merkava* showed an unusual ability to keep its crews alive in combat in Lebanon.

What do we need to do to give our troops a better tank? The M-1 has already been bought in large quantities, and its production is likely to continue, whatever its faults. So our first priority must be to fix what is fixable on it. We can, for instance, give the machine guns better mounts, so they can be aimed more quickly.

We should also act to improve the M-60. Large numbers of M-60 tanks will remain in our inventory well into the next century. The Israelis, who also use the M-60, have developed a package of improvements that do a great deal to keep the crew alive in combat. The package includes strap-on armor, better machine guns, removal of the vulnerable commander's "cupola," his little turret on top of the main turret, and a series of measures designed to prevent the tank's catching fire. The latter are especially important. In the 1973 Middle East War, the M-60 proved so flammable that it occasioned a bitter joke among Israeli soldiers: "What is the difference between a Zippo lighter and an M-60 tank? The M-60 lights every time."

Lastly, we can begin now to design a new tank, one based on the criteria set by Mr. Sprey's research. Not only would such a tank prove individually superior to both the M-60 and the M-1, but it would also cost less than either to build, which means we could buy more tanks.

A second common failure in thinking about weapons occurs when someone gets a new idea, which is a bad idea, but it gets reflected in new equipment anyway. We have a prize case of this in the army's new Bradley Infantry Fighting Vehicle. In the 1930s, a new variety of infantry was developed to work together with tanks:

motorized infantry. Motorized infantry rode in vehicles so that it could move faster than regular marching infantry. When it came upon a battle, it dismounted from its vehicles and fought on foot, like any other infantry. Originally, its vehicles were usually trucks. During World War II, both the Germans and the Allies mounted some of their motorized infantry in specially designed tracked or half-tracked carriers, called armored personnel carriers. The armor was light, just enough to give some protection from stray bullets or shell fragments. Infantry with these special carriers became known as armored or mechanized infantry.

In the 1960s, the Soviets and the Germans came up with a new idea: the infantry fighting vehicle. The big change was that the infantry was expected to stay in the vehicle much of the time in combat and fight from it. The vehicle itself did not change much. It acquired a light cannon—much lighter than that of a tank—and some firing ports in the side through which the infantry could fire their rifles. In some cases, including that of the Soviet BMP, it also got an antitank missile. The armor was still thin.

Unfortunately, the idea was a bad one. Why? The reason tanks have heavy armor is to keep the crew alive in battle. With the infantry fighting vehicle, a larger number of men can be sent into the same battle, staying in their vehicle, but with very thin armor around them. Most modern armies have a large number of highly effective light weapons designed to kill vehicles, including tanks. The heavy armor of the tank will stop some of these weapons. But they will, without exception, all go through an infantry fighting vehicle with ease. What will happen to infantry who stay in their fighting vehicle with all these weapons around? They will die.

When our army decided it had to have an infantry fighting vehicle because the Russians had one, it came up with the Bradley. The Bradley takes a bad idea and makes it worse. It is a very large vehicle. Its height is much greater than that of the BMP or the Germany infantry fighting vehicle, the Marder, making it easier for the enemy to see.

The Bradley is armed with a light cannon and an antitank missile. The army says this makes it better than its predecessor, the M-113 armored personnel carrier, which is armed only with machine guns. But the highly explosive ammunition for the cannon and the missile is stored in with the crew, behind the thin armor, making the Bradley a rolling powder keg.

American troops in Vietnam and Israeli troops in their various wars learned that it's usually safer to ride on top of their personnel carriers than in them. If they are inside and the carrier hits a mine, they are thrown against the roof and killed. On top, they are thrown off but live. Because of the turret for the cannon and the missile, the troops cannot ride on top of the Bradley.

To top it all off, the Bradley is built of aluminum. Light antitank weapons, like the Soviet RPG-7, have what are called "shaped-charge" warheads that burn their way through armor. When a shaped-charge warhead hits aluminum, the aluminum it hits is vaporized and burns, increasing the effect of the warhead.

The army recognized the Bradley's flaws well enough to try to rig its operational tests. They doused the dummies on board it with water so they wouldn't burn from the fireball, and when they burned anyway, they discounted that test. They were careful to shoot at only one small section of the vehicle so they wouldn't explode the ammunition stored on board. Fortunately, a courageous air force colonel in the Pentagon's development testing office blew the whistle on these phony tests, and the army is now doing some honest ones. They should be interesting. How much are we paying for this wonder weapon? Ten times as much as the M-113 personnel carrier it replaces—$1.5 million.

Where should we have started to get a different, better result?[5] We should have recognized that there are three basic tasks for infantry, which result in three different kinds of infantry. Tanks need some infantry, mechanized infantry, to accompany them and make possible armor-infantry combined arms tactics. For example, the infantry flushes out hidden enemy soldiers armed with antitank weapons, while the tanks provide firepower to knock out machine guns and bunkers that stop the infantry. These infantry units, since they are going to be up with the tanks, need a carrier with at least enough armor to stop light antitank weapons like the RPG-7. It should have a top that can be opened to protect the soldiers in it from mines, and it should be easy to get out of quickly. Infantry soldiers find safety by hiding in the ground, not by staying in their vehicle, and they must be able to get out of the carrier quickly when an enemy is encountered.

Then, there is motorized infantry. It does just what it did in World War II. It needs a fast, reliable carrier, which may be wheeled or tracked; it may differ little from a standard truck. It should be made of steel, not aluminum; the worst weakness of our current carrier, the M-113, is that it is made of aluminum. The carrier should be simple, reliable, and fast on the road, where it will spend most of its time, even in combat. It should be easy to get out of quickly. An effective personnel carrier may look rather strange, as do the infantry carriers South Africa has developed to keep its troops alive in Namibia. The military bureaucracy's desire for nice-looking vehicles should not be allowed to stand in the way of combat effectiveness.

Finally, there is true light infantry,[6] infantry that moves, as well as fights, on foot. In mountains, forests, swamps and jungles, infantry can often move faster on its feet than in a vehicle. The key to equipment for light infantry is simple: keep it light. A light infantryman cannot carry more than about forty pounds in combat, including dry socks and toothbrush, without suffering courage-sapping fatigue.[7] Light equipment is a light infantryman's best friend.

Another common failing in thinking about weapons is falling in love with new technology that whirrs, blinks, and beeps impressively but is inappropriate for combat. The best example is the infamous DIVAD self-propelled, radar-directed antiaircraft gun, a weapon so bad that the secretary of defense last year finally killed the program.

DIVAD made its sponsors' lives somewhat difficult. In one incident, a senator went out to an army base to take a look at a DIVAD. The army put the senator in it and let him shoot the cannon. After the third round, the cannon jammed, and it wouldn't unjam. The senator allowed that he didn't think he was going to vote for DIVAD. In another demonstration, a DIVAD's radar reportedly mistook a nearby fan in a latrine for a helicopter and aimed the cannon at it.

As usual, however, the real problems lay deeper. Even if all these deficiencies had been fixed, DIVAD would still not have been an effective weapon. Why? Because it is radar controlled. In World War II, most antiaircraft guns were visually controlled. The operator aimed the gun through sights. But now we have new technology in the form of radar. So the army thinks antiaircraft guns need to be radar controlled. A radar-controlled antiaircraft gun works fine as long as the aircraft the gun is trying to shoot down flies straight. But in combat, pilots quickly learn to "jink." Jinking means constantly twisting and turning the aircraft. Pilots who fly straight, even for a short time, get killed. In World War II, one German pilot, Hans Ulrich Rudel, destroyed more than five hundred Russian tanks with a cannon-armed Stuka. How did he survive all the fire from the Russian antiaircraft guns and machine guns? He practiced his attacks until he cut down the time he had to fly straight and level to no more than a second and a half. Most other pilots usually took just one second more, but that one second was enough to keep him alive while they got killed.

A radar-guided gun does poorly against aircraft that jink or that appear suddenly and unexpectedly. Its radar takes too long to react to a target that appears without warning. With a target that jinks, the radar is always aiming the cannon straight in front of the aircraft, while the aircraft is turning. Jinking aircraft or aircraft that appear suddenly are difficult targets for visually guided antiaircraft guns as well. But a well-trained gunner with a visually aimed gun can predict from the way the aircraft banks which way it is going to turn and aim the cannon accordingly. Men are still smarter than machines.

Unfortunately, the secretary of defense did not kill DIVAD because he realized radar control was inappropriate for an antiaircraft gun. The reason he gave was that Soviet antitank helicopters will soon have missiles that outrange DIVAD's cannon. In actual combat, the long range of such missiles means little, because the men in the helicopter usually cannot even find, much less identify, enemy tanks at more than 1,000 yards—well within DIVAD's range.

Because DIVAD was not canceled for the right reasons, its replacement is likely to be as bad or worse: a different radar-controlled antiaircraft gun or radar-controlled antiaircraft missiles, which have the same problem with jinking aircraft. There is a better answer: simple, visually controlled antiaircraft guns. But as long as the fascination with technology itself continues, we are not likely to buy them.

Still another common mistake is overlooking weapons that don't cost much money but are vital for keeping our soldiers alive in combat. Perhaps the worst example is our neglect of the need for an effective light antitank weapon. The Soviets have a very good light antitank weapon, the RPG-7, and they have it in large quantities. Every Soviet infantry squad has one. On the battlefield, tanks and other enemy vehicles can appear anywhere. If the Soviets use their tanks correctly, they will often be found in our rear area, among our headquarters, supply services, and artillery. Our soldiers in the rear, as well as at the front, need an effective light antitank weapon. Today they don't have one.

The remarkable thing about this critical deficiency is that it has endured for over forty years. In World War II, both the Germans and the Americans developed and fielded the first light antitank weapons based on the shaped-charge principle, which all such weapons now use. The American weapon was the bazooka. Unfortunately, the bazooka had a critical deficiency: the warhead was too small to penetrate the armor of most German tanks. General James M. Gavin wrote in his book *On to Berlin:*

> I looked into the situation after the war. One of the scientists advising the Ordnance Corps, Dr. Charles Lauritsen, Sr., of Cal Tech, had resigned because of the way in which the explosive was being made and out of the conviction that the weapon was too small. Nevertheless, we manufactured the weapon in large numbers and placed it in the hands of our troops for the Sicily battle. It could have been tested against German tanks captured in North Africa, but it evidently was not.
>
> Ironically, after many lives had been lost, in mid-August

1943 we received a War Department bulletin telling us that the bazooka would not penetrate the frontplate of the Tiger tank—as though we didn't know it already. More sadly, we still had not obtained a larger bazooka by the time General MacArthur sent the first troops to Korea seven years later to meet the Soviet T-34 tanks in the summer of 1950. The American infantry combat team there was overrun by Soviet armor.[8]

In contrast, the main German light antitank weapon of World War II, the *Panzerfaust,* had a huge warhead. It was large enough, at 150 mm, to kill almost any tank it hit. The size and weight of the warhead meant it had a significantly shorter range than the American bazooka. Despite this, it was by far the more effective weapon. Our best combat units in World War II in Europe, the airborne divisions, paid the Germans the supreme compliment of throwing away the bazooka and equipping themselves with captured *Panzerfausts,* even translating the operating manuals into English.

The Soviet RPG-7, like the *Panzerfaust,* has a large warhead. In contrast, our current light antitank weapon, the LAW, has a warhead too small to be effective, just like the bazooka. Even if it can penetrate a tank, it just makes a tiny hole that does little to kill the tank unless it happens to hit fuel, ammunition, or the hydraulic system.

The army recently designed a replacement for the LAW called the Viper. Viper performed badly in tests, and when the poor test results came to the attention of Senator Warren Rudman of New Hampshire, he led a fight against Viper. And he succeeded: for once we actually canceled a weapon because it didn't work. The Congress demanded a competition to choose a new light antitank weapon, a competition that would include foreign-designed weapons.

Unfortunately, the congressionally ordered competition was structured poorly. The weapons were strapped to benches to be fired, instead of being held by infantrymen as they would be in combat. Then, instead of shooting at real tanks, they fired at sections of armor plate. This makes a critical difference. Only if you fire at real tanks filled with fuel, ammunition, and hydraulic fluid, do you see not only whether the weapon can penetrate armor, but also whether it can cause an explosion behind the armor that destroys the tank.

The competition was won by a Swedish weapon, the AT-4. After further tests, which still did not involve firing at real tanks loaded with fuel and ammunition, the army decided to buy large numbers of AT-4s to replace the LAW. The Swedes claim AT-4 does heavy damage after it penetrates a tank's armor; if this is true, the AT-4 may at last give us the effective light antitank weapon we need. But the army's tests don't tell us whether the Swedish claims are true or not. We won't know unless we have to use the weapon in real combat. If the claims are not true, many American soldiers will pay with their lives.

All of these pathologies of weapons design—confusing peacetime with wartime quality; grabbing bad ideas and running with them (the attack helicopter, on which the army is spending billions of dollars, is another one); buying technology irrelevant or dysfunctional in combat; and taking insufficient care in selecting small, less expensive weapons that often determine whether our soldiers will survive in combat or not—add up to a dismal picture of the weapons situation. As much as military reformers should applaud and support the army for its reforms in other areas, they must also point out that its behavior in the field of weapons design remains totally unacceptable. If it were just a matter of money being wasted, the American people would rightly be concerned, but less so. The real problem is that current practices will waste lives. About 75,000 American infantrymen will ultimately ride in the Bradley if its procurement continues. Every American soldier, in the rear areas as well as near the front, will depend on light antitank weapons. The defense establishment's failure to design effective, affordable weapons and to test them thoroughly and honestly is a failure in its responsibility to its soldiers. That is a moral failure, not just a management failure.

Weapons are the most visible and the most important equipment the army buys for its soldiers. But other kinds of equipment also play very important roles in determining who wins or loses in combat. One type of equipment we are spending billions of dollars on is command and control equipment: radios and other devices soldiers use to talk to each other in combat.

This is another case of diving headfirst into technology without first thinking through the question, "Just what do we want to be able to do?" John Boyd has recently done some novel and interesting research in this area. His findings are something of a surprise.

The most surprising conclusion is that, if we really think about it, we don't *want* command and control in combat. We want something quite different: leadership and monitoring. Command means telling somebody else what to do. Control means keeping pressure on him to do it and to do nothing else. Both engender that most fatal battlefield disease: rigidity. If subordinates must wait until their commanders tell them exactly what to do, then act in constant fear of departing in any way from the instructions, we will have a rigid army, one that adapts slowly and clumsily to change on the battlefield. It will not be able to conduct maneuver warfare.

Leadership and monitoring are very different. Leadership conveys the commander's intent to his subordinates, and it also does more than that. It provides them the encouragement, support, and inspiration they need to carry out his intent in the face of the tremendous stress and obstacles combat presents. Monitoring, unlike control, is discreet. It does not demand constant reports to verify that the subordinate is doing what he is supposed to. It requires listening and watching, but only interfering when something is going wrong. It operates on the principle "silence is consent."

Colonel Boyd's briefing on command and control points out another surprising fact. In a healthy institution, most communication is implicit. Think of a family: the family members know each other and how each one thinks; therefore, most things happen automatically, without constant discussion. A military unit should be like a family. Each officer should know the others well enough to know how they think, what their individual strengths and weaknesses are, and where each needs help and where he is best left alone.

The billions of dollars worth of fancy radios and other communications equipment we are buying make more and more communication explicit. American units are notorious for constantly being "on the air," talking back and forth on the radio about everything. What does all this explicit communication do? It slows everything down, including the Boyd Cycle. It increases confusion, because the few important messages get overlooked in the constant chatter. It makes the commander spend all his time on the radio, worrying about what is happening within his unit, instead of what is happening in the outside world—what the enemy is doing. Our commanders spend so much time with all this message traffic that they have little time left to think about tactics or the enemy.

Several years ago, a visitor to the army's Ninth Infantry Division, the so-called High Tech Division, was briefed on the command and control system being developed for it. The plan was for a vast, elaborate system, with multiple "fusion centers" where all the messages would come together, be sorted, and be passed out for further distribution; lots of equipment for feeding information and direction from outside to commanders at different levels; and plenty of places where a roving division commander could "plug in" to see and hear what was going on in the division. Even company commanders were to have their own battlefield data terminals, where they could sit with their eyes riveted on a cathode-ray tube as the battle went on around them.

The visitor pointed out that what this equipment would ensure was "reflective blitzkrieg." One way blitzkrieg shatters its opponents is by doing so many things at once that they cannot see what is really going on as they try to follow everything. This fancy command and control system would enable the Ninth Division to "blitz" itself. Even if the enemy wasn't doing very much, the system would generate so much noise, so many reports about virtually everything, that the commanders would be unable to figure out what was going on. The enemy wouldn't have to paralyze them. They would quickly paralyze themselves.

Leadership requires personal, face-to-face meetings between leaders and led, not teletyped messages printed on computer paper. Monitoring demands simple selective listening systems, not volumes of reports. Implicit communications rely on a shared way of thinking among officers, developed through the officer education process, not fusion centers and cathode-ray tubes. The expensive communications equipment we are buying works against the things we need for success in combat. The best thing a combat unit could do with most of it is to kick it off the back of the truck when they move out to fight.[9]

Personnel

Equipment is the most visible part of the superstructure of our ground forces, but it is not the most important part. If our armies are to be able to make good use of their equipment, if they are to be able to conduct maneuver warfare, one of the most basic requirements is unit cohesion.

What is unit cohesion? It is the psychological and social bonding that occurs in small units: in squads, fire teams, and platoons. It is what makes the individuals in those small units a team. It is very important in war. Without it, many soldiers won't fight.

It is tremendously difficult for anyone to be active in combat. What everyone wants to do, quite naturally, is to hide, to remain as inconspicuous as possible. As soon as you fire a weapon at the enemy, he sees you, and he shoots back. Reading this book in a comfortable chair in front of the fire, that does not seem so terrifying. In combat, it is. The bloody remains of others who got shot are all around you. The smell of death is in the air. You want to live! You want to crawl as deeply into mother earth as you can and hide there until the shooting stops. You never wanted to do anything so badly in your life.

Unit cohesion is what overcomes a person's passionate desire to hide. The people around him are his friends. He knows they are depending on him to keep them alive. He knows he can depend on them. Some of them are shooting at the enemy. He doesn't want to let them down. He knows he has to face them that night. He cares deeply what they think of him. So he fights.

If a unit is to have cohesion, the people in it have to know each other well. It takes time for a group of men, men who have not known each other before, to become friends, to become a team. If they do not know each other, they do not feel they can count on each other's support. They do not trust each other. No one cares much what the others think about him.

Today most of the units in our two armies do not have good unit cohesion, because military people are moved around so frequently they don't have time to get to know each other. The average personnel turnover in a combat company can easily be 25 percent per quarter—a complete turnover each year. In combat, when people get killed and replacements must be sent in, we send individual men instead of whole units. In World War II, this practice was disastrous. Nobody knew the new guy, so nobody looked out for him. A high percentage of the replacements did not live beyond their first firefight.

The army has recently begun a praiseworthy effort to stabilize units and increase cohesion. Called the "New Manning System," it includes the COHORT program and the adoption of a regimental system. COHORT stands for Cohesion, Operations, Readiness, and Training. Applied originally to companies, it now also includes battalions. In both cases, COHORT keeps the same group of enlisted men together for three years—through basic and advanced training and on through the full term of enlistment of many of the soldiers. The men meet the officers and noncommissioned officers (NCOs) who will lead them during the last two weeks of their advanced training, and in the COHORT companies (less so in the battalions), the officers also are stabilized in the same jobs for three years. The program is still in its early stages—only about 10 percent of the people in the combat arms are currently in COHORT units, and the first COHORT units for support troops are only now forming —but the army plans to push forward steadily to bring more soldiers into COHORT. By 1991, it hopes to have 62 percent of the infantry, 58 percent of the artillery, and 47 percent of the armor units under COHORT.

The improved unit cohesion COHORT is sure to bring will be reinforced by a new regimental system. As in many foreign armies, a soldier will be affiliated with a regiment when he joins the army. If he leaves the service after the usual two, three, or four years, he will probably have served only one tour of duty, all in his regiment. If he stays for a longer career, the personnel system will attempt to keep him in the same regiment as he changes jobs and units and moves up in rank. If he must leave the regiment to go to school, serve as a recruiter, or accept a special assignment, it will try to send him back to his old regiment. In a twenty-year career, an NCO would probably serve three or four tours in his regiment, or between nine and sixteen years. The regiment will be the soldier's home, a home he will leave on occasion, but to which he will probably return. With its flag, regimental colonel and sergeant major, and long tradition (the new regiments will be assigned the numbers and histories of regiments we disestablished in earlier years), the regiment will complement COHORT in strengthening cohesion, morale, and esprit de corps. To date, only about 25,000 soldiers serve in fifteen regiments, but twelve more regiments are currently being established, and the program is to continue to expand.

The only real flaw in the COHORT and regimental programs is that their futures are not entirely certain. Bureaucratic pressures threaten to limit their expansion or broad application. There is as yet no firm plan to expand both systems until they include the whole army. Because of the concerns of career NCOs and officers about "punching their tickets" for promotion, both are stabilized less in the newer COHORT battalions than in the original COHORT companies. The army has itself found that NCO stability in the COHORT battalions is not sufficient as NCOs get promoted into new jobs. And although officers are in theory supposed to remain in their COHORT battalion for three or four years, they may be promoted out of it sooner or may move around a good deal within it, which means the troops may still get new platoon and company commanders so often they do not really come to know them. At the regimental level, returning troops to their regiment will be a "primary consideration" for the personnel system; however, it will just be one consideration among many for officers—which may mean it proves less important than moving officers from job to job to "punch their tickets." Perhaps most important, although the army is seriously looking at extending the COHORT system to wartime so that we have a unit rather than an individual replacement system in combat, it has not yet decided to do so. Yet it is precisely during wartime that cohesion is most important and that individual replacements suffer most.

Despite these potential problems, both COHORT and the regimental systems constitute real progress in a very important area—more important, on the whole, than equipment. The fact that the army is moving this way is testimony to the genuineness of its internal reform movement. The future task will be to keep both programs on course until they include every soldier.

The Marine Corps has also had a serious, enduring unit cohesion problem. In recognition of the problem, it several years ago established a system called PREPASS, for Precise Personnel Assignment System. PREPASS was intended both to reduce personnel turbulence and to match a marine's skills with his assignments. Although it has reduced personnel instability to some extent—according to one Marine Corps study, the time a marine remains under the same commander has improved about 20 percent—PREPASS does not go nearly far enough. Overall turbulence remains high—as high as 100 percent annually in a marine division if transfers among units within the division are included.

Within marine battalions, which are the basic combat units, there are other cohesion problems largely unaffected by PREPASS. Because of them, the corps' battalions are hollow. Personnel strength is generally significantly below what it is supposed to be. Troops are constantly farmed out for special duties, such as base cleanup projects and lifeguarding at the base swimming pools. The strength of a platoon, which should be forty-two marines, is often as low as twelve men. Battalions are supposed to be built up to full strength before deploying overseas, but the buildup is seldom complete and only occurs a few months before the deployment, which provides too little time to build cohesion or provide adequate training.

The root problem is not with PREPASS itself, but with the priorities PREPASS was designed to reflect. As one marine lieutenant colonel recently wrote, "None of these problems . . . can be blamed on the [PREPASS] computer models. The system is performing as intended. The models have been a great help in implementing policy. If some of their effects appear irrational, it is because the leaders have not faced up to the tough choices. Remember, we have three large special interests in the USMC: the ground combat arms community, the combat service support community [Installations & Logistics], and the air community. Each is headed by a three-star [general]. The 'referee' is a two-star in Requirements & Programs. Everybody wins, at the expense of the whole. You could almost argue that the Marine Corps is a paradigm of the federal government at large."

What needs to be done differently? The Marine Corps always likes to say that its first priority is the marine infantryman. It needs to put its money where its mouth is by making the combat battalions its first priority for people. Providing lifeguards and stable attendants is all very nice, but it must not be done by drawing people away from the combat battalions. Keeping those battalions at full strength, so they can train effectively and become cohesive, must become the first priority. As the marine officer quoted above said, "We don't need more lifeguards, we need more fighters."

PREPASS should either be modified as necessary to further reduce turbulence by a substantial amount, or it should be scrapped in favor of the army's COHORT and regimental systems. It is probably beneficial to have two competing approaches to the problem of improving unit cohesion. If PREPASS can be made to work, it should be retained. But the Marine Corps must make the requirement for strong unit cohesion and personnel stability, not PREPASS, its highest priority. If PREPASS cannot do the job, it should be junked.

Unit cohesion is one serious personnel problem. Another is our habit of assigning the best recruits to the technical services and sending the worst into the infantry. Again, we did this in World War II, with unfortunate results. In his excellent book on the Normandy campaign, *Overlord,* military historian Max Hastings talks about its effect there.

In this first battle in north-west Europe, the American army was given cause to regret the poor priority that it had given to infantry recruitment since the great mobilization of American manpower began in 1940. All nations in the Second World War diverted some of their fittest and best-educated recruits to the air forces and technical branches. But no other nation allowed the rifle companies of its armies to become a wastebin for men considered unsuitable for any other occupation. The infantry suffered in the services' attempts to allow men to follow specializations of their choice—of the 1942 volunteers, only 5 percent chose infantry or armour. "By the end of 1943," confessed the official history of the training and procurement of U.S. Army ground forces, "the operations of this priority and a number of other factors had reduced to a dangerously low level the number of men allotted to the ground forces who seemed likely to perform effectively in combat."[10]

Today both the army and the Marine Corps still do the same thing. They justify it on the grounds that the new equipment is so complex, it takes the smartest troops to maintain it. That is another good argument for buying simpler equipment. The Israelis have effective equipment, and they do just the opposite. The smartest recruits go into the infantry squads and the tank crews. Why? Because the Israelis recognize that nothing requires more ability to think and to react quickly than combat. Infantry soldiering, in particular, is extremely challenging. A thinking enemy is a far greater challenge than any piece of equipment.

Perhaps our single greatest personnel problem is in the officer corps. Quite simply, we have far too many officers above the company grades—from major on up through general. Edward Luttwak talks about this problem in his very thoughtful book, *The Pentagon and the Art of War: The Question of Military Reform.*[11] He notes that in 1945, the ratio of middle-rank officers to enlisted men was 1.3 to 100. By 1956 it stood at 4 to 100. Today it is 5.3 to 100.

At more senior levels the problem is worse. At the end of World War II, in all the armed forces we had 2,068 generals and admirals commanding 10,795,755 enlisted personnel. Today we have 1,073 flag-rank officers for just 1,831,079 enlisted personnel.

If this oversupply of officers only meant some unnecessary pay, it would be a small problem. Unfortunately, its effects on military competence are severe. The large number of officers must share a comparatively small number of real jobs—jobs that actually need to be done. For example, the Marine Corps has 1,636 lieutenant colonels but only 356 command positions for lieutenant colonels.

What do the surplus officers do? They take responsibilities that should constitute one job and break them up to constitute many, which means more and more decisions require a committee. They generate paper, which descends on unit commanders as requirements for volumes of reports. They create unnecessary staff positions. Every decision takes long committee meetings, which usually produce decisions that are both poor and late. The surplus officers also push decisions to ever higher levels: decisions that should be made by captains, and are made by captains in foreign armies, are reserved in our armies for colonels so the colonels have something to do.

The surplus of generals and admirals has similar results. The Marine Corps, supposedly a "lean and mean" organization, provides a good example: it has just three divisions and three air wings, but sixty-five generals. What do they all do? They get in each other's way, they push more and more decisions up to their level, and they succeed each other in the few desirable and useful jobs at such a rapid rate that few have time to become expert at anything other than promotion and assignment politics. Even simple decisions take endless meetings and memorandums.

The surplus of officers is what drives the constant rotation of officers from one assignment to another. Each gets only a short turn at command because behind him stands a long line of fellow officers waiting eagerly for a command position. Tactical expertise suffers greatly, because commanders, especially at the brigade level and above, have often been away from troop units for as much as ten years before they get their command. Those years were seldom spent doing anything related to war. They were spent in personnel offices, research and development and procurement programs, management schools, and similar assignments. What they learned about tactics and leadership as company and battalion commanders has largely been forgotten.

What led us to have this huge officer surplus? In both world wars, we had to expand our armed forces quickly. After World War II, we made a conscious decision to keep on active duty far more officers than the comparatively small peacetime forces required, as a base for expansion. The theory was that the next time we needed to expand the forces, we would have enough trained officers to command all the new combat units we would raise.

It was an understandable decision at the time.[12] But further time has rendered it obsolete. If a major war broke out today, we could draft millions of men, as we did before. But we could not equip them. Our complex weapons take years to build: an M-I tank takes twenty-four months to build, a fighter plane thirty-seven months, a submarine five years. Nor do we have much surplus production capacity for most weapons. Because they depend so heavily on fancy electronics, the rates at which we could build them would be limited by a multitude of production bottlenecks for high-technology components.

We need armed forces that can be expanded quickly in wartime. But our force expansion must be based on reserve units, fully equipped in peacetime, not on plans for drafting millions of new soldiers to raise new units. This is how many other nations now plan to expand their forces. The Soviet Union has 119 so-called category three divisions, which in peacetime have their equipment but only a small cadre of manpower. In time of war, they are filled out by mobilized reservists.

The officer surplus is the origin of a number of our superstructure problems, as well as being a superstructure problem itself. Solving it will be difficult. We need a relatively rapid reduction in the strength of the officer corps above the level of captain, and we need a large reduction: at least 50 percent. We cannot hope to accomplish it by reviewing each officer billet and determining whether it is really necessary, and if so, at what rank; the bureaucracy would delay that indefinitely. We need to make the cut and make it quickly, so that unnecessary and counterproductive jobs are eliminated by the simple means of not having enough officers to fill them.

We should not undertake a reduction in the strength of the officer corps by abruptly tossing people out on the street. That would have disastrous effects on officer morale, including the morale of those who remained. Just as society now does in many civilian industries when people are rendered redundant, we need to provide appropriate compensation to the officers who are forced out. The easiest way to do this would simply be to allow those individuals to retire early, before they have served twenty years.

A final personnel problem that must be tackled is retention of noncommissioned officers. NCOs are the repository of a military service's technical expertise. They are the people who must make the system function on a daily basis. Today we have serious short-falls among NCOs. The army is short ten thousand of these people, the Marine Corps, sixty-four hundred. The navy and the air force have similar shortages.

In the past, there were major differences in pay, benefits, housing, and social status between troops and NCOs. In recent years, those distinctions have eroded. A look at current pay scales shows that instead of having sharp breaks between troops and NCOs there is a gradual rise. NCOs have also lost many social distinctions.

We must restructure both pay and social benefits that symbolize prestige so as to re-create the clear distinctions of the past. The added pay and, perhaps even more important, improved social status of NCOs would help make continued service sufficiently attractive to retain the noncommissioned officers we need for a truly professional NCO corps.[13]

Training

Another major superstructure issue is training. Well-trained troops and units are essential for combat effectiveness. Today our ground forces have some serious training deficiencies. Reports show that performance is often inadequate. In 1982, the army put together a report on the results of its training exercises at its new National Training Center at Fort Irwin, California, which stated:

All echelons rarely understand the intent of the commander.
. . . The result is confusion and poor execution of missions.
Without the clear understanding by subordinate commanders,
command and control is complicated and degraded during the
heat of battle. Command nets become cluttered with detailed
instructions. . . . The massing of sufficient combat power at the
decisive point and time is often degraded and teams end up
fighting independent battles. . . . Task organization expressing
the combined arms concept remains a problem. . . . Both land
navigation and map reading are performed poorly at the NTC.
. . . Units do not habitually dispatch patrols, particularly at the
company/team level, to locate information critical to the accom-
plishment of the mission. . . . Orders are issued late and are
insufficient in detail. . . . Units undergoing training at the NTC
have displayed a complete lack of knowledge and understanding
of the threat posed by Soviet Radio Electronic Combat. . . .
Habitually, once contact is made, momentum ceases and heavy
casualties are experienced.[14]

A marine colonel who recently watched the marines' annual
"supersquad" competition in which the best infantry squads from
throughout the corps compete, commented, "None of them were
very good. Skill in the most basic tasks, like patrolling, was clearly
lacking. And these are the cream of the crop. I shudder to think
what the average squad is like."

Why is training not adequate to produce highly competent
soldiers, marines, and combat units? A principal reason is the
constant rotation of personnel. With his people turning over at a
rate of as much as 25 percent per quarter, a unit commander is
always faced with the fact that a significant number of his people
are untrained. Most have come to him straight from the training
establishment, usually with just the most rudimentary skills. The
new people must be taught the basics, which means the unit can
seldom get beyond practicing the basics. As soon as it begins to do
so, it has to start all over again to train more new people.

The army's COHORT and regimental programs should help
here. Commanders of COHORT companies report they have a far
better training environment than they have ever had before. They

have two to three months in which to start with the basics and work on up, from individual to unit training and from techniques to tactics. Through the remaining thirty-three to thirty-four months the company is together, they have a well-trained unit, at least compared with what they were previously used to.

But even with personnel stabilized, there will still be some major training problems. These include:

• Inadequate training time. A British Royal Marine receives two to three times as much training as his American counterpart. We need to provide the funding for at least a doubling of training time. Equally important, we need to insulate the combat units from the voracious demands of higher level staffs and headquarters for troops for post and garrison duties. Units that have many of their soldiers or marines detached as sentries, lifeguards, and base cleanup crews cannot train effectively.
• Insufficient training ammunition. Weapons like the TOW antitank missile are very expensive to fire in training. A single TOW round costs almost $10,000. To a limited extent, the army can use simulators for training: devices that operate like the weapon but use a small bullet or an electronic or laser beam as a substitute for the actual missile or shell. But simulators can easily mislead. Often they do not replicate some of the critical qualities of the weapon, such as back blast, noise, and recoil. In one experiment, the army trained a number of Dragon antitank missile gunners with simulators, then tested them with real missiles. They all failed, because the noise and the blast of the missile, not present with the simulator, threw their aim off. Ultimately, there is no adequate substitute for shooting real weapons with live warheads in training. The weapons we have selected make this expensive, but there is no short-run alternative. In the future we should keep in mind the cost of live-fire training with a weapon when we are making up our minds whether or not to buy it.
• Inadequate space for realistic training. While a few of our army and marine divisions are stationed on large bases like Fort Hood, Texas, where they have plenty of space in which to carry out realistic field exercises, most are not. Units like the Second Marine Division at Camp LeJeune, North Carolina, the army's First Infantry Division at Fort Riley, Kansas, and the Fifth Infantry Division at Fort Polk, Louisiana, do not have enough space in which to maneuver. Everyone quickly becomes familiar with each trail, gulley, and swamp, far more familiar than they are likely to

be with a real battlefield. This detracts from training realism. Environmental restrictions also sometimes severely hurt training. For example, Camp LeJeune is a nesting ground for the red cockaded woodpecker, which is listed as an endangered species. To avoid the nests, tanks have to stay on a few designated trails, which makes it very hard for them to do what tanks are supposed to do in combat: slip around the enemy and attack his rear. Training suffers as a result.

These are not easy problems to deal with. For example, buying more real estate around the existing bases is often not only expensive, but also, in the face of resistance from civilians who live there, impossible. What can be done to at least ameliorate these training problems?

The army has taken one imaginative step forward with the establishment of the National Training Center at Fort Irwin. Here, units come from all over the United States to maneuver through vast areas of the California desert. Equipment similar to their own is stockpiled there for them, greatly reducing the cost of bringing the unit out. They first go through a live-fire exercise, where they get to shoot real ammunition. Then they have to maneuver against an opposing unit that is trained in Soviet tactics. The maneuvering and shooting are recorded by special instruments on the vehicles that can tell who did what, who got shot, and who stayed alive.[15] At the end of the exercise, everyone sits down, and a replay of the exercise is run on a screen. The participants then get a critique. Although the critiques have so far been a weak point, focusing more on technical minutiae than tactics, and the exercise as a whole is too "set piece" and predictable, the overall approach is a good one. Commanders and troops get to practice combat in unfamiliar terrain, against a live opponent, with plenty of room in which to maneuver.

The Marine Corps has for at least a decade experimented with a similar approach at another huge desert site, their base at 29 Palms, California. Unfortunately, they haven't done much with its potential. Seldom do marine units who go there for training attempt more than what is called a Combined Arms Exercise, a live-fire drill that uses only a small portion of the available area. The drill never varies much, so everyone knows what to expect. It is run at a very slow pace. And there is no second phase of maneuvering against a real opponent. The result is mediocre training, or worse, negative learning: people learn tactical "lessons" that reflect the unrealistically slow pace and "canned" nature of the exercise, lessons that may get them killed in real combat.

Beyond programs like that available at the National Training Center, we may be able to improve training realism with a practice widely used by the Europeans. Every year, usually in the fall after the crops are in, European armies head off across the civilian-owned countryside for major exercises. Large tracts of land are used, where there are villages, ditches, streams and rivers, civilians, and all the other things that complicate real battlefields. Naturally, with tanks and troops maneuvering, some damage is done to civilian property. The damage is paid for by the government as a cost of realistic training. There is no reason why similar exercises cannot be done in the United States. There will be inconveniences to civilians, some damage to civilian property, and some cost to the government for the damage. But the citizens of our allies accept these costs as a necessary contribution to an effective defense. American citizens should be willing to do the same.

Environmental restrictions, including those related to protected or endangered species, must be eased in the isolated instances when they result in unrealistic military training. We share the concern of many citizens with protecting the environment. But unrealistic training endangers the lives of our soldiers in combat, and that means that in selected situations the need for realistic training must take priority. The military has complied with existing restrictions and would continue to work with environmentalists to provide as much protection as can be made consistent with training realism. In turn, environmentalists must accept the fact that our soldiers' and marines' lives come first.

• Insufficient unit training. Of the total available training time, comparatively little goes to the training of companies, battalions, brigades, divisions, and corps to act as units. Most training time is devoted to training the individual soldier or marine at individual skills. Individual skills are important, but unit skills are more than just an agglomeration of individual skills. For example, the fact that the infantrymen in a battalion all know how to use their weapons effectively and how to prepare fighting positions does not mean the battalion can suddenly break bivouac in the middle of the night and move out quickly without chaos. We need a proper balance between unit and individual training, which means more unit training.

Beyond these specific problems, one more general problem afflicts our training. Although combat is characterized above all by the unexpected, most of our training exercises follow rigid scripts, called "scenarios." Everyone knows long in advance what will

65

happen, and what his unit is to do when. Detailed operations orders of great length— orders so long they would be useless or worse in combat—are written up, with units often judged by how long their "op order" is. Most of the big exercises that make the newspapers, like "Solid Shield" in the United States, "Reforger" in Europe, and "Team Spirit" in Korea, are scenario exercises. They are better training for putting on an opera than for combat.

We need to scrap these stage-managed drills and make most training "free-play" training. In free-play exercises, two units are put together in one area, and each is told simply, "Destroy the other unit." All the actions that are allowed in combat are permitted in a free-play exercise, except using live ammunition. The atmosphere quickly becomes one of surprise, uncertainty, rapid change, short verbal orders, and initiative on the part of junior commanders—just like real war.

A free-play exercise undertaken several years ago by the marines' First Tank Battalion showed the good results this type of training can bring. The battalion went to the field and broke up into its companies. The rule was "Any other company you encounter is hostile," and the battalion commander gave orders that insured that companies would cross paths unexpectedly. The result was a series of surprises and countersurprises—just as in combat. Junior-level initiative was given a chance to flourish, and it did, aided by the use of mission-type orders. One participant said, "It was mass confusion, just like real war. We quickly learned not to be alarmed by disorder, but to use our commander's intent as a reference point and make our own decisions. We didn't shut down when things got confused. We just did what we thought we should to support the intent. And it worked."

An adequate amount of realistic training is an absolute requirement for military success. All the weapons anyone can envision are useless if troops and units are not well trained. Because training is less glamorous than weapons, because it is not built in any congressman's district or senator's state, because it seldom results in overpriced hammers, wrenches, or toilet seats, it tends to be overlooked, especially by Congress. This must change. On the whole, training is more important than equipment for winning in combat.

We must give it the attention and the resources that its importance demands.

Organization

Victory in combat does not always go to the larger force. Many of history's greatest military victories—Cannae, Agincourt, Austerlitz—were won by an outnumbered army. But numbers are still very important in war. The force with the greater number of combat soldiers has a very real advantage. At a certain point, the numerical balance overshadows everything else. No matter how fine its army—how good its tactics and strategy, how well designed its weapons, how cohesive its units and how realistic its training—Luxembourg could not defeat France or Germany. But numbers can, as always, be misleading. The number that counts is not the total number of soldiers in an army, but the number of combat soldiers. An army may be strong in total numbers, but weak in combat soldiers.

There are a number of different ways to count combat soldiers. In order to have an international yardstick, we have chosen to count divisions. Division sizes vary throughout the world. An American armored division, as an example, has 18,300 men, a Soviet tank division, 11,000. But the Soviet division has 335 tanks to only 324 for the American. By rough calculations, a Soviet and an American division can be said to have equivalent combat power.

Even a quick comparison between our two armies and the Soviet army shows our basic organizational problem: we don't obtain very many combat soldiers from our total army and Marine Corps manpower, or, as it is sometimes phrased, we have a low "tooth-to-tail" ratio. The United States Army today has 785,000 personnel, from which it obtains 17 divisions and nine separate combat units, which put together would amount to a bit more than another two divisions. The Marine Corps gets only three divisions from 198,000 men, although it also has its own air force. In comparison, the Soviet army gets 193 divisions from 1,840,000 personnel, which means we require more than four times as many people to get an equivalent combat unit.[16]

Our relative scarcity of combat troops is one of our military weaknesses. It was one cause of our defeat in Vietnam. As noted, out of a total of around 550,000 men at our peak strength, we fielded a maximum of 80,000 infantry combat troops.

Many of our allies share our organizational problem. In Europe today, NATO is outnumbered in divisions forty-four to seventy-three. In Korea, the United States and its ally, South Korea, field twenty-three divisions, while North Korea fields thirty-nine. In none of these cases is total resources a problem. Our resources were vastly greater than North Vietnam's. NATO has a larger population and a much larger and more powerful economy than the Warsaw Pact. NATO spends more for defense than the pact by most estimates, and NATO actually has *larger* ground forces, in numbers of personnel, than the pact. The pact deploys slightly more ground troops in Europe than NATO, but not nearly enough to explain its heavy advantage in divisions. South Korea has a population more than twice as large as North Korea's and a GNP four times larger. North Korea has 700,000 men in its army, compared to 540,000 for South Korea—not enough to explain the disparity in divisions.

Our low "tooth-to-tail" ratio has another major drawback beyond the deficiency of too few combat soldiers. Our tail is so large it is clumsy and unwieldy. With so many people in headquarters, maintenance units, and the like, they get in each other's way and in the way of our combat forces. The headquarters of a single division can contain hundreds of people, including 92 officers. A corps headquarters (a corps generally commands two divisions) has 151 officers (in addition to the 184 in the two division headquarters). As noted in the Introduction, our army in Europe today has more soldiers whose job is communications—keeping all these vast headquarters talking to each other—than it has infantrymen.

The root of this problem lies in our long-standing belief in firepower/attrition warfare. Despite our huge tail, if you talk to many of our officers in Europe, they will tell you the tail is too small: they need more support units for their few combat forces. What they are really saying is that the structure of the army does not yet reflect the army's change in 1982 from a firepower/attrition doctrine to maneuver warfare.

In firepower/attrition warfare, the support units must be very numerous, because the doctrine leads to situations where almost all the combat units are right up front, engaging the enemy in prolonged exchanges of fire—as in World War I. But maneuver warfare leads to very different situations. Usually, only a comparatively small portion of the combat forces are engaged. Most are in reserve, ready to maneuver. Their need for support is very much less. This is the assumption that lies behind the organization of the Soviet army, and it is the main reason their army has a much more favorable tooth-to-tail ratio than ours.

We need to restructure the army to reflect its new doctrine of maneuver warfare. By doing so, we should be able to get about two-and-one-half times the number of combat soldiers we have now, without adding any additional people. Without adding expensive manpower, we will be able to form the new combat units we need to provide stronger reserves.[17] As part of its effort at self-reform, the army is beginning to create more combat units. In 1985, it formed one new division, and plans call for one more in 1986, all without adding to the army's total manpower strength. This is a good beginning. As the army grasps more fully the implications of maneuver warfare, further steps in this direction should be forthcoming. Unfortunately, as usual, the Marine Corps is giving the need for more combat troops little thought and plans no changes.

Reforming NATO

The military reform movement recognizes that reform must be applied to policies and practices in specific theaters, such as NATO, Korea, and Southeast Asia, including the policies and practices of our allies. Dr. Steven Canby is preparing a book that discusses reform proposals for these theaters in detail.[18] To illustrate reform approaches to specific theaters, it is useful to examine one: NATO.

NATO's military strategic center of gravity is its central front: the inter-German border. Its greatest military weakness, which is most likely to lead to its defeat, is the lack of operational reserves on the central front. A thin cordon defense, such as the one NATO now has under the label of "forward defense," is very vulnerable.[19] Once an enemy makes a major penetration, the campaign is probably lost. Only by increasing operational reserves can NATO address this potentially fatal flaw. Operational reserves take on enemy penetrations and counterattack into their flanks or rear.

How can military reform create more operational reserves on NATO's central front? Dr. Canby outlines a possible new structure for the U.S. Army in Europe where, instead of about five divisions, we would have seven. Two of those could go into the reserve without weakening the forward defense cordon. In addition, we can identify at least three possible reforms of the armies of our European allies that would permit the strengthening of NATO's operational reserves.

• First, adopting the Dutch RIM system. Currently, most countries' reserve systems assign reservists to units as individuals. Naturally, in view of the small training time reserve units get, cohesion is poor, and the units are not very effective. The Dutch have developed a new approach that yields cohesive, high-quality reserve formations. Entire companies pass out of active service together, first into a five-month "leave" period, then into the reserve for a further fifteen months. All the cohesion and skills that were developed during active service carry over. Exercises have shown that RIM reserve units perform at least as well as regulars, so that they could be used to form high-quality operational reserves or to release regular units for that role. Steven Canby and David Greenwood, a British defense analyst, have shown how a RIM system, if developed by more countries than Holland, could be used to permit NATO to place five army corps in operational reserve while maintaining the forward defense cordon.[20]
• A second possible reform is putting new emphasis on light infantry. Much of Germany, including about half the inter-German border area, is heavily forested, mountainous, or both. In such terrain, as well as in cities and in towns, light infantry is more effective than road-bound tanks or mechanized infantry formations. Such light infantry must be very high quality, since its tactics depend on initiative at the fire team, squad, and platoon level. This means most of them would have to be regulars, although RIM-type reserve units might also be usable. But even if

expensive regular troops must be used, they need not be equipped with even more expensive tanks or armored fighting vehicles, which means NATO could afford more such units. By manning much of the forward defense, the light infantry would permit existing armored units to be moved into operational reserve.

• A third possible approach is making greater use of territorials —a militia, like that of the Swiss army— especially in Germany. If much of the forward defense cordon could be manned by territorial units, then many higher quality regular units could be moved into operational reserve. This appears feasible. As noted, much of the inter-German border region is close terrain, which favors units made up from local people who know the area well. Further, the German countryside is dotted with villages built out of stone houses. These villages make excellent strong points, which, held by territorials, can block all but the strongest enemy thrusts. They can also set up those enemy units that do penetrate for counterattacks by operational reserves. This solution is one of the least costly, because both equipment and manpower expenses are low.

With the strengthening of NATO's operational reserve must come a change in NATO policy. Current policy says that even after a possible Warsaw Pact attack into West Germany, NATO would continue to respect the border between West and East Germany. NATO would not counterattack across it. This is not a viable policy. It makes the whole of Eastern Europe a sanctuary for the Soviets, where their support services and rear echelons can operate safely and securely, except from air attack.

A successful defense requires room to maneuver, to strike into the flanks and rear of Warsaw Pact forces. That can only be done if NATO is willing to counterattack into Eastern Europe. Strong operational reserves would provide the combat units for such counterattacks. NATO's policy must make it clear that it will undertake them. A policy of cross-border counterattacks is consistent with the purpose of forward defense, which is to minimize combat on Western European soil. It also would substantially strengthen the deterrent value of NATO's conventional forces, because instead of just failing to conquer Western Europe, the Soviets could also lose Eastern Europe. Some specialists on Eastern Europe believe that if a Soviet attack on the west were stopped and NATO forces appeared in Eastern Europe, anti-Soviet revolts would break out in the satellite nations, revolts that might see substantial elements of the Eastern European armies change sides.

These would not be the only changes military reform would bring to NATO, of course. Improvements in weapons, unit cohesion, and training would all work to make the American contribution to NATO much more effective in combat. Some of these reforms might well spread to our European allies. While they have generally done better than the United States in areas such as style of warfare and unit cohesion, their weapons designers have also in many cases fallen victim to the delusion of overly complex technology, and training time is sometimes even less than that in the U.S. forces. Shortages of spare parts, ammunition, and war reserves are generally greater than our own. Military reform is not just applicable to American forces; it applies to our friends across the Atlantic as well.

Reserves and National Guard

The United States currently has a strong Army Reserve, Marine Corps Reserve, and Army National Guard—at least on paper. Together, 749,000 personnel are serving in reserve and guard units. They form three Army Reserve brigades (the equivalent of one division) with another to be formed in 1986, one Marine Reserve division, and fourteen and one-third National Guard divisions.

Both the reserve and the guard will take on greater roles and importance with military reform. The nation can no longer plan on increasing its forces in wartime through a massive draft, as we did in both world wars, because we would not be able to equip the new forces. Our ability to expand our forces in wartime must rest on the reserve and the guard, which are equipped in peacetime.

The ability to maintain a large reserve and guard has traditionally been a product of a draft. Men who were drafted served several years in the active forces, then were obligated to serve in the reserve for some additional years. The draft also supported the guard indirectly, because many young men who faced the prospect of being drafted chose instead to enlist in the National Guard.

Without a draft, which does not appear to be likely in the foreseeable future, it is improbable that we will be able to increase the size of either the reserve or the guard. Indeed, both the Army Reserve and the Army National Guard are today slightly below their authorized manpower strengths, by about fifteen thousand personnel in the case of the Army Reserve, and by about thirty-three thousand in the National Guard.

We can, however, improve their quality. Some reserve and guard units, particularly some of those in the southeastern and western parts of the United States, are very good indeed. At the other end of the scale, some units perform miserably. In one recent training exercise, elements of a National Guard division broke and ran, despite the fact that no real bullets or shells were being fired. A foreign officer, watching an exercise by another National Guard unit, commented that "sending troops into battle under those officers would be murder."

Fortunately, this is a situation where strong reform efforts are underway from within. In 1982, a group of fifteen National Guard generals, including some from both the Army and the Air National Guard, published an excellent, comprehensive plan for reform of the guard, titled *VISTA 1999*. This plan calls for, among other things, the adoption of a doctrine of maneuver warfare, integration of ground and air forces, and simple, effective equipment. *VISTA 1999* provides a basis for self-reform by the National Guard, and by extension of its recommendations, the reserve. The secretary of defense should form a panel of the authors of *VISTA 1999*, and empower it to carry out the study's recommendations. The panel should also be tasked with the job of accurately assessing the performance of guard and reserve units and identifying the steps necessary to make those that do not measure up combat effective. Units that will not take the necessary remedial steps should be disbanded. If war comes, we will need to send guard and reserve units into combat with little time for additional training. Units that perform poorly will get their men killed. We should not be willing to continue to maintain substandard or unprepared units in peacetime, regardless of the political influence they may have in their home states.

Summary

Style of warfare; weapons and other equipment; personnel policies with special emphasis on unit cohesion and the officer surplus; training; and organization: in each area, military reformers see the need for substantial changes from current policies and practices if our ground forces are to be effective in combat. None of these changes can be brought about by increasing the defense budget a few percent or cutting it a few percent. Few can be dealt with at all through the budget process, except for equipment and training time. Unless we refocus the defense debate on the real issues, we are certain to perpetuate our current weaknesses.

2

The Navy

EVERY NATION MUST FACE the fact of its geography. The vast size of the Russian Empire and its Soviet successor, its 20,619 kilometers of land borders, and a shortage of warm-water ports have molded Russia into the world's greatest land power. Germany's traditional excellence at land warfare was in part a product of her geography: without a strong army of her own, her position in the center of Europe would make her everyone else's battleground. The Royal Navy ruled the waves and waved the rules from its island home.

The geography of the United States makes us, like Britain, a maritime nation. Our overland economic, political, and cultural relations with Canada and Mexico are, of course, important; Canada is our largest trading partner, and Mexico today supplies about 18 percent of our oil imports. But our ties to Europe, Asia, and Africa, ties that have shaped us as a nation, all stretch across the seas. Overseas trade today constitutes about 14 percent of our gross national product. About one out of every eight manufacturing jobs depends on exports. The 18 percent drop in U.S. exports between 1980 and 1983 cost 1.5 million jobs.[1] Our culture remains closely bound to that of Europe, whence most of our population originally came.

Not surprisingly, our geography has given us a strong maritime and naval tradition. In both the Revolutionary War and the War of 1812, our navy was heavily overmatched by the Royal Navy. But in both of those conflicts, and especially the latter, we made our mark. When our navy sank or captured about thirteen thousand tons of British shipping in the War of 1812, the USS *Constitution,* "Old Ironsides," alone capturing three enemy frigates, the British stopped joking about our "fir-built ships." The first American merchant ship reached China in 1784, and the famous clipper ships of the first half of the nineteenth century, along with our extensive whaling fleets, quickly made our young republic a respected maritime nation. The Civil War saw us build a powerful force of highly innovative steam-powered iron warships, the monitors, at a time when the rest of the world's navies were largely built of wood. Both our navy and our merchant marine declined after the Civil War, but the navy revived dramatically in the latter years of the nineteenth century. Our fleet of steel battleships and cruisers handily beat the Spanish in 1898. An American naval officer, Alfred Thayer Mahan, became the world's most respected naval theorist through his book *The Influence of Sea Power Upon History 1660–1783.* By 1914, we were hotly contesting Germany for the rank of number two naval power in the world. The 1920s saw our navy accepted by Great Britain as an equal, a status made official by the Five Power Treaty of 1922. We emerged from the Second World War the unchallenged sovereign of the seas, with a navy of more than five thousand ships, including over one hundred aircraft carriers.

The seas are also important to our ground forces. The only way to move large American armies to the Eurasian continent and supply them and our allies is by sea. Both world wars showed this clearly. Had the German U-boats succeeded in severing the transatlantic sea link—as they twice came close to doing—Great Britain would have been starved into surrender, along with whatever land forces we had in Europe. Without command of the sea, without clear naval superiority, the only significant countries our armies can fight are Canada and Mexico. Geography is inescapable.

Today our mastery of the seas is being challenged. Beginning in the 1960s, the Soviet Union has built a modern, powerful, blue-water navy, already superior in some respects to our own. Its most important component is submarines. The Soviet navy includes the most powerful submarine fleet in the world; almost half the world's submarines fly the Soviet naval ensign. Our own submarine force is outnumbered by the Soviet's by almost three to one.

Starting in the late 1970s, in a belated response to the Soviet naval challenge, the United States began a major program of naval expansion. The naval shipbuilding budget increased, in constant 1986 dollars, from $7.5 billion in 1979 to $12.1 billion in 1985 (with a peak at $18.5 billion in Fiscal Year 1983). The size of the fleet has grown from 479 ships in FY 1980 to 543 in FY 1985. The Reagan administration has proclaimed the goal of a 600-ship fleet.

Unfortunately, a 600-ship navy by itself means little. This expensive shipbuilding program is in fact making us weaker, not stronger, because the kinds of ships the navy is buying and the type of fleet it is attempting to create are wrong. Guided by little more than intraservice bureaucratic politics, memories of a war that ended more than forty years ago, and unwarranted faith in complex technology, we are today building, not a navy, but the world's largest and most expensive naval museum. In view of our geography, nothing could be more dangerous (other than a failure of strategic nuclear deterrence) than an ineffective navy. Yet that, increasingly, is what we have.

Concepts

Unlike the army, the navy today shows few signs of creative thinking. As is so often the case, riches have brought complacency. Large and increasing shipbuilding budgets, routinely approved by Congress with little consideration of their content, have made the navy smug and self-satisfied. Why should it change when the money just keeps pouring in?

The navy's conceptual problems begin with its loudly proclaimed "maritime strategy." For the past five or six years, the navy has explained its need for more money and more ships by saying it is following a maritime strategy. Unfortunately, what the navy refers to when it says "maritime strategy" is precisely the *opposite* of what that term has traditionally meant. Through this terminological inversion, the navy has effectively reduced much of the naval debate to babel.

The concept of a maritime strategy goes back at least as far as

William Pitt, the British prime minister at the time of the wars of the French Revolution. Traditionally, it is a strategy whereby a nation isolated from the European continent by water—as both we and Britain are—preserves its own security by maintaining control of the sea. As long as an island nation controls the sea, an opponent on the Continent, however powerful his armies, cannot decisively defeat it. It was said of Napoleon that his power stopped when the water reached the bellies of his horses.

A maritime strategy has two necessary corollaries. The first is that a nation following a maritime strategy does not risk its continued existence in a battle on or for the Continent. It may commit an army to the Continent, as Britain has often done. But it neither builds that army at the expense of adequate naval power, nor risks its naval dominance in a sea battle intended to support its army. During the Napoleonic Wars and during World War II, Britain saw her allies defeated and her armies driven from the Continent. But because she maintained a superior navy, those defeats were never decisive. Britain lived to fight again another day and eventually to win.

The second corollary is that a nation with a maritime strategy is strategically cautious at sea. It does not willingly risk a potentially decisive naval defeat. In World War I, Admiral John Jellicoe, the commander of the British Grand Fleet, was sometimes criticized for his caution. But his defenders rightly pointed out that he was the only man in Britain who could lose the war in the course of an afternoon. Had Germany defeated France and driven the British Expeditionary Force from Europe, as it did in 1940, Britain would still have been able to go on fighting. But had the German High Seas Fleet decisively defeated the Grand Fleet, Britain would have lost the war. Either starvation through a German blockade or a German invasion would have been unavoidable.

A cautious strategy does not rule out tactical or operational boldness. Nelson, as well as other British admirals, exemplified both during the Napoleonic Wars. But even then, Britain's naval *strategy* was cautious. It was based on preventing the French navy, which was divided between the ports of Brest and Toulon, from joining into one united fleet, and later on preventing allied navies,

78

such as that of Spain, from joining into a united fleet with the French. Britain avoided, rather than sought, a great battle with an overpowering enemy fleet—a strategy of caution and prudence.

Today the U.S. Navy couples what it calls a "maritime strategy" with a high-risk "forward strategy." The forward strategy calls for throwing our navy against the Soviet navy, in the Soviet's own home waters, early in a war. The navy hopes, thereby, to influence the initial land battle for the continent of Europe in our favor, although many rightly question what effect even the greatest naval victory would have on that early land battle. Some elements in the navy's leadership envision throwing the bulk of the aircraft carrier force forward in this early battle; others visualize sending in most of the submarine force instead. The latter is strategically riskier, since, as will be discussed below, the submarine, not the carrier, is today the capital ship.

This forward strategy is contradictory to a true maritime strategy. It does what a follower of a maritime strategy tries to avoid: it voluntarily risks our continued control of the sea, early in the war, at least in part in an attempt to support the army in Europe.[2] By following this forward strategy, the navy's maritime strategy really becomes the naval component of a continental strategy—the precise *opposite* of a maritime strategy. In a continental strategy, a nation does stake its existence on the battle for the European continent. This is what we would do if we threw the bulk of our fleet forward against the Soviets—against them where they are strongest, in their own home waters—at the beginning of a conflict. If we lost that naval battle we would probably lose the war.

The result of calling the naval component of a continental strategy a maritime strategy is to obfuscate the debate over basic naval concepts to the point of total confusion. A debate over whether we should follow a maritime strategy— defined in traditional terms— or a continental strategy is legitimate, and military reformers are to be found on both sides of that debate. But it is not legitimate to reduce such an important debate to chaos by reversing the meaning of basic terms. The navy's eagerness to do so is a testimony to either the sloppiness of its thinking or its desire to attach a maritime strategy label to its search for a bigger share of the budget or both. As for the disservice it does to sound thinking about national defense, it is inexcusable.

The navy's conceptual thinking is further degraded by its insistence on justifying and defending the current force structure. Anyone within the navy who questions the wisdom of continuing to build our fleet around a small number of large aircraft carriers immediately puts his career in jeopardy. Anyone outside the navy who does so is immediately labeled an "enemy" by the navy.

Intelligent thinking about naval concepts is rendered virtually impossible when all thinking is imprisoned in the straitjacket of the current force structure. The basic problem is simple. Our only serious naval opponent is the Soviet navy.[3] The Soviet navy is primarily a submarine navy. Our current navy, built around big aircraft carriers, is largely irrelevant to the task of fighting submarines. Quite simply, it is much easier to fight our aircraft carriers with submarines than it is to fight submarines with our aircraft carriers.[4] The contradiction between our force structure and the task we may face — defeating the Soviet navy—means that to develop effective strategic, operational, and to some degree even tactical concepts, we must face the need for change. This the navy attempts to forbid.

As a result, the operational art, the art of planning naval campaigns, has largely been forgotten. It is difficult to make sensible plans for naval campaigns if the force structure cannot support them. Attrition warfare, an all-too-common substitute for the operational art, has become the accepted norm, and most thought is driven down to the level of technique—how to sink a Soviet submarine or shoot down Soviet naval bombers.[5]

What do we need to do differently? First, we must make fundamental changes in our naval force structure to create a navy appropriate to fight the Soviet submarine navy, not the aircraft carrier navy of Imperial Japan. Once we have such a navy, a strategy of blockading or destroying the Soviet navy in its own home waters (in which, if it follows its own announced strategy, the majority of its fleet is likely to remain) may be practicable. But in view of the implications that destroying Soviet strategic missile submarines may have for igniting a nuclear war, a strategy of blockade rather than destruction may be preferable. And even a strategy that has as its ultimate goal the destruction of the Soviet navy must be cautious. It must proceed from the realization that a naval defeat for us means a national defeat. Any decision to deploy the bulk of our capital ships into Soviet home waters must wait until we have enough combat experience to judge Soviet competence. We cannot judge it adequately in peacetime.

We also need to revive the naval operational art. It, along with naval strategy and tactics, must center on maneuver warfare. Maneuver warfare has as honorable a history at sea as on land. The British navy decisively outmaneuvered the German navy on the strategic level during World War I. The Germans counted on the British maintaining a close-in blockade of German ports. German torpedo boats and submarines would whittle down the British superiority in dreadnoughts until the German battle fleet could engage the British on sufficiently equal terms to have a chance for success. But the British instead maintained a distant blockade, where their dreadnoughts did not have to expose themselves to German torpedo boats and U-boats. The Germans had no answer to this British strategic maneuver, and their fleet of battleships— the building of which helped propel the British into an alliance against them (a strategic disaster for Germany) —was rendered useless.

On the tactical level, in the one major naval battle that occurred in World War I, Jutland, the Germans survived (the most they could hope to do against the British superiority in numbers) by outmaneuvering the British with the famous *Gefechtskehrtwendung,* or Battle Turn, where their fleet twice did what the British thought impossible by having all their battleships reverse course simultaneously.

One of the greatest naval practitioners of maneuver warfare was Lord Nelson. He made his name as a captain when he captured one Spanish warship by boarding her across the deck of another at the battle of Cape St. Vincent in 1797. At the battle of the Nile in 1798, he destroyed the French fleet by maneuvering around it and enveloping it on both sides. In his greatest victory, Trafalgar, he broke all the rules of naval warfare of his time and attacked in two columns at right angles to the Franco-Spanish fleet. The resulting envelopment of the enemy ships resulted in their destruction.[6]

With the focus shifted to maneuver warfare, further invigoration of the tactical debate must be pressed. This has begun at Newport, in the pages of our principal naval journal, the *U.S. Naval Institute Proceedings,* and elsewhere. Tactics must not be sacrificed to overconcern with engineering or other technical matters. The tactician must take his rightful place ahead of the technician. Tactical training must be adequate and realistic, which means free-play training and adequate live ordnance to use in training. Rules such as those that usually prevent submarines from showing their full power in exercises must be set aside.

The effects of new technologies on naval tactics must be studied. For example, radar enables a ship to find an airplane at a considerable distance; however, an enemy ship or aircraft can "hear" that radar and find and identify the ship using it at an even longer range. Modern communications technology provides a fleet commander with information much more rapidly than in the past, but it can also flood him with so much information that his decision process and his Boyd Cycle are slowed rather than accelerated.

Countering enemy high-technology systems puts a new and even higher premium on innovative tactics, on doing the unexpected and avoiding predictable patterns (such as our aircraft carrier's rigid flight operations cycles), because the electronic minds of complex technology systems are inflexible and cannot deal with situations not envisioned by their designers. Surprise is disastrous for these systems and for those who depend too heavily on them.

If concepts were unshackled from overconcern with technical and bureaucratic matters, from misuse of terms to confuse instead of illuminate, and above all from the deadweight of the institutional imperative to justify the perpetuation of the big carriers, there is no question that our naval officers could be as imaginative and innovative as their predecessors. Our navy has a rich history of innovation. The navy's current poverty is of its own making.

Equipment

A navy, much more than an army, is defined and shaped by its
equipment—by what kinds of ships it has. Certain types of ships
(and aircraft) can do only certain kinds of things. The central ship
in our navy today, the ship around which the rest of the navy
revolves, is the large aircraft carrier.

Aircraft Carriers

Viewed as monuments of naval architecture and engineering and
as examples of human organization, our aircraft carriers are stu-
pendous achievements. Few can spend any time on one and not
come away impressed. At ninety-five thousand tons, our most
modern carriers, those of the Nimitz class, are the largest warships
ever built, more than twice as large as the biggest ship in the Soviet
navy.[7] More impressive still is the tight teamwork of the more than
five thousand men on board. Operating high-performance jet aircraft, fighters and bombers, from a rolling, pitching airfield, sur-
rounded by water, and doing it by night as well as by day, in bad
weather as well as in good, is second only to combat itself in the
challenge it presents. Every man on board the ship knows he plays
an important role. Many of them, not just the pilots of the aircraft,
have jobs that, if not done rightly, put others' lives at risk. Their
skill and their seriousness are quickly evident to any observer.

But in the harsh world of war, neither size nor technical skill
nor even dedication are enough. The day of the large aircraft carrier, so large it is very expensive, and so expensive we can afford
only a handful—fifteen, even if the current naval building program
is completed—has passed. Like the battleship the carrier replaced,
its magnificence cannot nullify basic changes in the nature of war
at sea. The development of the nuclear-powered submarine, the
proliferation of powerful antiship missiles, and improvements in
ocean reconnaissance have made a navy built around a small number of large aircraft carriers an anachronism.

Carrier Weakness I

The carrier's weaknesses are, in essence, three. The first is the
vulnerability of each individual carrier. The navy argues that its

big carriers are its least vulnerable surface warships. This is probably true. Their size makes them difficult—although certainly not impossible—to sink. They are the only warships we now build that have any armor worth mentioning. Their hulls are designed to withstand torpedoes and mines.[8] Their magazines, a surface warship's most vulnerable point, are protected, although by no means perfectly so.

But the statement that the carriers are the least vulnerable of all our surface warships must be seen within the context of the increasing vulnerability of *all* surface warships. There are several reasons for this trend, which has been evident for at least the last twenty-five years. The first is the improvement in ocean reconnaissance brought about by satellites and also by long-range radio direction-finding. Finding the enemy's ships has always been one of the most difficult tasks in naval warfare. Nelson had much more difficulty finding French fleets than beating them. Even in World War II, the carrier task forces of both the Americans and the Japanese frequently had great difficulty locating each other. The greatest challenge faced by the German U-boats for much of the war was not sinking Allied merchant ships but finding allied convoys.

The task is still by no means easy, nor will it ever be something that can be taken for granted.[9] But the trend is clearly toward making detection of ships at sea easier. Ocean reconnaissance satellites are one of the reasons, for those nations that can afford them —still just the United States and the Soviet Union. But the Soviets, our only serious naval challenger, have an extensive ocean reconnaissance satellite system. They have three different types of ocean reconnaissance satellites, some of which take photographs, some of which listen for the radar and radio emissions of our ships, and some of which carry their own radars. They are linked into an elaborate communications system through which the satellite's information can (when the system works) quickly be retrieved, analyzed, and passed to Soviet surface ships, naval bombers, and submarines.

The Soviets back up their reconnaissance satellites with strategic radio direction-finding. This may, in wartime, prove more important than satellites, which can be shot down or jammed. Our ships, especially our aircraft carriers, emit radar and radio signals most of the time, although in many cases they do so because of long-ingrained habits not because of real necessity. The Soviets have systems for hearing these emissions and pinpointing their location on the ocean. Sometimes our carriers stop emitting, and this increases the Soviet's reconnaissance problems significantly. But, with most of our current equipment, we need to turn on our radars and radios once potentially hostile ships or aircraft come into the carrier's neighborhood. As soon as the carrier and its escorting cruisers and destroyers turn on their radios and radars, the Soviets are likely to hear them.

Another common and, in peacetime, effective reconnaissance tool the Soviets use is the "tattletail." These are Soviet ships that follow our carriers wherever they go. They give the Soviet navy an immediate, up-to-date picture of our fleet dispositions. In wartime, we would of course sink these "tattletails" very quickly. But they would help ensure that, at the outbreak of hostilities, the Soviets would have accurate pictures of the locations of our carriers, pictures they could use to launch an immediate, possibly preemptive, torpedo and antiship missile strike with surface ships, submarines, and naval bombers. This is, in fact, exactly what Soviet naval doctrine calls for. They call it "the battle for the first salvo."

Again, this does not mean reconnaissance is automatic or even easy. Especially if they turn off their radios and radars, surface ships can still be difficult to locate. But it is easier to find them today than it was forty years ago, when we last fought a naval war. And while our opponent would have had to find more than one hundred aircraft carriers in that war to target our whole carrier fleet, today he has to find just thirteen.

The second reason surface ship vulnerability is increasing is the development and proliferation of antiship missiles. Before these missiles existed, for a ship to throw a large shell (one of, say, one or two thousand pounds for twenty miles) it had to have a large cannon—a twelve-to-sixteen-inch gun for a shell of that weight. Such guns were themselves so heavy only the largest ships—battleships and battle cruisers—could carry them.[10]

Today even a large patrol boat can fire a shell of about that weight, if it is the warhead of an antiship missile. A Soviet Osa-class fast patrol boat carries four SSN-2 "Styx" antiship missiles, each with a warhead of eleven hundred pounds of explosives. The Osa itself displaces only 240 tons—about 1/250 the displacement of a battleship. In calm water, it is as fast as a battleship or faster, with a speed of thirty-five knots. Because it is small, it is cheap and can be built in large numbers. The Soviets have built for their own navy, as well as for export, hundreds of Osa missile boats, plus more missile boats of other classes. Although the Osa-class boats are too small to use in the open ocean, missile ships of fewer than one thousand tons do have oceangoing capability.

The antiship missile has another advantage: it has a guidance system that lets it home in on its target.[11] Unlike land warfare, the environment of naval warfare is relatively "clean." Ships stand out against the sea, rather than disappearing into vegetation, smoke, and folds in the terrain. Nor does an antiship missile have to find its target amid a plethora of rocks, buildings, fires, trucks, and other false targets, as do guided missiles on land.

The record compiled by antiship missiles in combat indicates that, unlike their counterparts in ground warfare, they do work. In the Falklands War, the French-built Exocet antiship missiles used by Argentina achieved three hits out of six missiles fired.

Surface ships have a number of different defenses against antiship missiles. Some are designed to shoot down the missiles with guns or other missiles. Others attempt to fool the antiship missile's guidance system into attacking a false target. Although no antiship missiles have yet been shot down in combat, some have been fooled successfully. In the Falklands War, a combination of chaff and electronic deception equipment mounted in helicopters seems to have been successful in decoying two Exocet missiles fired at the British carriers HMS *Hermes* and HMS *Invincible,* although one missile went on to hit the merchant ship *Atlantic Conveyor.* [12]

Antiship missiles are carried by about 175 Soviet surface warships, including about 30 major warships; approximately 350 Soviet naval bombers; and 64 Soviet submarines. Seven countries build antiship missiles, and many more build warships to carry them. More than fifty nations worldwide have antiship missiles in their naval arsenals.

The implication is clear: our surface warships, of whatever size and type, face a much higher probability of being hit by a weapon that can do serious damage than they did before antiship missiles existed. The more widely these missiles proliferate, and the more accurate and destructive they become, the more the vulnerability of surface ships will increase.

The third reason for the increase in surface ship vulnerability, and the most important, is the improvement in submarines. Although both submarines and surface ships have improved in the past forty years, submarines have improved more. The submarine, which almost won World Wars I and II for Germany, is a greater threat today than it was then.

These developments serve to put the carrier's status as the least vulnerable surface ship into perspective. So does a look at its specific vulnerabilities. Because of its size, armor, and compartmentation, carriers are almost certainly harder to sink than smaller surface ships.[13] But an enemy may not need to sink our carriers. It may suffice for him merely to knock them out of action. Carriers are quite vulnerable to this. They are especially vulnerable to fire. They must carry large quantities of fuel, bombs, rockets, and shells for their aircraft. Most of these are carried deep within the ship, but if the carrier is engaged in combat operations, some ordnance is also with the aircraft on the flight deck and on the hanger deck, where a missile can ignite it. Although explosions or fires on the flight deck are usually not tremendously damaging, a major explosion or fire on the hanger deck is another story. It can at least force the carrier to return to port for substantial repairs to its aircraft maintenance facilities, and it can easily do major structural damage that would require months in port to fix.

Missile hits on the flight deck can also put a quick end to air operations by blowing holes in the runways or knocking out the catapults that launch the aircraft. The navy claims this is harder than it looks. They say that in 1969, when several five-hundred-pound bombs that were stacked on the flight deck of the carrier USS *Enterprise* went off, the ship could have resumed flight operations in a few hours. But five-hundred-pound bombs just sitting on the deck are substantially less effective in blowing a hole in that deck than a single twenty-two-hundred-pound, armor-piercing warhead on a Soviet antiship missile hitting the deck at the speed of sound or faster. Repairs from such a missile hit could easily require shipyard repair, which means the carrier would be out of action for weeks, possibly months.[14]

Another danger is torpedoes. Even if torpedoes do not sink a carrier, which they certainly can do, they can force it to slow down or cause it to list, making continued flight operations impossible. A carrier sustaining torpedo damage would almost certainly have to be dry-docked to make repairs.

Carrier Weakness II

The individual carrier's vulnerability is compounded by the carrier force's second major problem: the small number of carriers. As noted, we have just thirteen deployable aircraft carriers. Even after the current shipbuilding program is finished, we will have only fifteen. A nuclear-powered carrier of the Nimitz class costs more than $3 billion. Its aircraft, escorts, and support ships boost the cost of a single carrier "battle group" to at least $15 billion. At that price, we cannot afford more than fifteen.

Nor are all the carriers always available. At any given time, about one-third of the carrier fleet is on station, one-third is "working up"—training so the ship and the aircraft can work as a team —and one-third is in port. Some of those in port are in overhaul and would take months to put to sea. Others could put to sea quickly but not with a well-trained crew.

With so few carriers, an enemy does not have to disable or sink very many before he cripples virtually our whole sea-based naval aviation. Senior admirals have repeatedly testified that our sea-based aviation is our principal superiority over the Soviet navy.

If we sail into battle against the Soviets depending on just fifteen ships, we will, like the Spanish Armada, sail in expectation of a miracle. Perhaps we will get one, although the precedent is not encouraging. Perhaps the opponent, despite numerous submarines and aircraft, will prove incompetent. But our survival, as a navy

and a nation, would depend on incompetence on the enemy's part
—massive incompetence—not our own strength.

Carrier Weakness III

The carrier fleet's third major weakness is a product of the specific
aircraft the ships now carry. We will look at those aircraft and
their deficiencies in the next chapter, when we look at all our air
forces. Here we will just note the fundamental problem: while the
carrier's aircraft may contribute to its defense against attack by
enemy bombers or cruise missiles, they face serious problems if
they must either engage an enemy tactical air force—enemy
fighters and fighter-bombers— or attempt to support ground
troops fighting ashore. The problems are sufficiently severe to raise
the question of whether the carriers can do anything more than
just survive at sea—if they can do that.

What this all adds up to is a dangerously fragile navy. Whenever we build another big carrier or more of the expensive escort
ships the big carriers require, we increase the fragility because we
perpetuate the current force structure.

But the most damaging effect the big carrier policy has on our
naval strength is indirect. It is, simply, that we spend so much
money on the big carriers and their "battle groups" that there is
little money left to build submarines.

Submarines

The most probable cause of a future American defeat at sea is the
navy leadership's continued underestimation of the submarine.
The submarine is today the capital ship, just as the battleship was
the capital ship at the beginning of the century, and the aircraft
carrier was the capital ship in World War II in the Pacific. This
is to say, whoever wins the submarine war wins the naval war. If
the Soviet navy were to win a submarine war, if the Soviets were
to wipe out our submarine force with much of their own still
intact, our surface ships, including the carriers, would be confined
to port. The danger of being sunk by a submarine would be too
great to put to sea. This is precisely what happened to the Argentine navy in the Falklands War. Once the Argentine cruiser *Gen-*

eral Belgrano was sunk by a British submarine, the rest of the Argentine surface fleet, including Argentina's aircraft carrier, did not dare leave port for the remainder of the war. Conversely, if we sink or drive into port the entire Soviet surface navy, or they do the same to us, the submarine fleets would still be able to go to sea with their effectiveness largely intact.

These characteristics define a capital ship: if the capital ships are beaten, the rest of the navy is beaten. But if the rest of the navy is beaten, the capital ships can still operate.

Another characteristic that defines capital ships is that their main opponent is each other. This appears to be true of submarines today. Submariners say the opponents they fear are other submarines, antisubmarine aircraft, and surface ships, in that order. Surface ships they fear very little, except those that carry antisubmarine helicopters. Helicopters and other antisubmarine aircraft are a problem to a submarine. But the submariners' greatest fear is another submarine. What will actually happen in combat is still an open question, since submerged submarines have never been pitted against each other in actual combat. But if the submariners' expectations are correct—and we have built our whole submarine fleet (except for the ballistic missile submarines) in the belief that they are—the submarine's status as the capital ship will be confirmed.

The most critical weakness of our submarine force is numbers. We currently have ninety-nine attack submarines, which are designed to sink other submarines and surface ships. The Soviet navy has about three hundred.[15] The Soviets have built so many submarines because they recognize that the submarine is today the capital ship. As early as 1963, the commander of the Soviet navy, Admiral S.G. Gorshkov, said, "submarines are the main force of the Navy." Later, in the 1970s, he stated that the "basis of our navy is nuclear-powered submarines of various types."

As military reformers continually point out, numbers are important in war. Being outnumbered by almost three to one is being outnumbered very badly. The reasons for our severe numerical disadvantage are two: the bulk of the navy's procurement money is drained away by the big carriers, their aircraft, their escorts, and their support ships; and the submarines we build are, by world standards, inordinately expensive.

The first problem is evident if one looks at the navy's budgets over the past five years. About 30 percent of the shipbuilding budget has been spent for carriers, carrier escorts, and support ships such as oilers and ammunition ships. Only 6 percent of the shipbuilding budget and 2.3 percent of the overall procurement budget have gone to build attack submarines.

Our submarines are badly outnumbered also because the navy chooses to build only very expensive submarines. Currently, an American nuclear-powered attack submarine costs $671 million. The next attack submarine design the navy wants, the SSN-21, is projected to cost $1.6 billion for the first four units, falling to $1 billion thereafter (an unlikely event)—with all costs in today's dollars. By way of comparison, a British nuclear-powered attack submarine costs $263.3 million, and a French nuclear boat costs $212 million. A modern, European-built conventional attack submarine, one with diesel engines that charge batteries to drive electric motors instead of a nuclear propulsion plant, costs between $100 and $200 million. We could buy up to sixteen of the latter for what the first SSN-21 is projected to cost.

The navy argues that only very expensive submarines have the capability it needs. Not only does this say capability is unrelated to numbers, but it also implies that none of the European navies, including the Royal Navy, knows what it is doing. The unfortunate fact is that the United States Navy consistently misdefines what constitutes quality in a submarine, and the way it misdefines quality leads to overly large, overly expensive submarines.

One person has largely defined what capability means for U.S. submarines: Admiral Hyman G. Rickover. When Admiral Rickover became head of the U.S. Nuclear Propulsion Program in the early 1950s, all submarines used diesel-electric propulsion. That is not inherently a bad thing. But conventional, diesel-electric submarines must periodically stick a tube called a snorkel up above the water's surface so they can run their diesel engines to recharge their batteries. In some situations, this can enable an enemy to find them.

More important, conventional submarines cannot go at high speeds underwater for more than about an hour or so—so many surface ships can outrun them. Nuclear submarines, Admiral Rickover realized, would have neither of these disadvantages. They would never have to poke anything up out of the water if they did not want to, and they could run at a high underwater speed indefinitely.

Under Rickover's ironfisted direction, the U.S. Navy built both nuclear submarines and nuclear surface ships. He was given the cream of the navy's officers and enlisted men, and he trained, harassed, and welded them into a technically proficient team. In doing so, he did the nation a tremendous service. But then he did something innovators who succeed are prone to do: he froze in the pattern of his original success. The last major change in U.S. submarine design was in 1959, when a nuclear power plant was put in a high-speed "Albacore" hull originally developed for conventional submarines. Since then, the navy's approach to submarine design, largely dictated by Admiral Rickover, has amounted to taking the previous submarine design and blowing it up in size. As a result, the navy now builds very large attack submarines. Our current SSN-688 class displaces 6,927 tons, and the projected SSN-21 will displace 9,000 tons or more, compared to 4,500 tons for the latest British nuclear submarine, 2,670 tons for a French nuclear boat, and about 2,200 tons for a modern, oceangoing conventional submarine. Cost has grown with size, as it usually does in warships.[16]

The large size of our submarines, coupled with intense work by Admiral Rickover and his protégés, has given us one advantage: our nuclear submarines are comparatively quiet. Unfortunately, their quietness has led the navy to argue that quietness is by far the most important characteristic in a nuclear submarine. Like most bureaucracies, the navy has proclaimed as most important the thing it is best at doing.

But the real situation is different. To destroy an enemy submarine, antisubmarine forces (including other submarines) must go through a four-step process. First, they have to detect it: to discover that a submarine is present. Then, they have to pinpoint its location—to "localize" it, as the navy says. Third, they have to hit it with an antisubmarine weapon. Fourth, the weapon actually has to sink or disable the submarine. If any step in the process fails, the whole process fails. If, for example, the antisubmarine forces detect and localize an enemy submarine but are unable to hit it with a weapon, they fail.

Quietness is useful and desirable, but it relates to just one fraction of one part of this process. One means of detecting a submarine is to listen for the noise it makes with its engines, its propeller, and its hull moving through the water. This "passive detection" is an important means of finding submarines. It generally has been the best means of finding them at long range. The quietness of our submarines makes it difficult for enemies to find them with passive detection.

But passive detection is not the only way to find a submarine. "Active detection" uses sonars that "ping" a beam of sound off a submarine and find it through the echo. In addition, both the Soviet Union and the United States are doing extensive research into "nonacoustic" techniques of detecting submarines, such as looking for the wakes they leave and for the "glow" from their nuclear propulsion plants, if they are nuclear powered. If any of these techniques prove viable, a submarine's quietness will help it not one bit. Indeed, the bigger the submarine, the more likely are nonacoustic techniques and active sonars to work against it.

Submarines can be designed with a philosophy that in effect says, "I don't want the enemy to find me. But if he does, and I can prevent him from localizing me, from hitting me with a weapon, or, if I am hit, from being destroyed or put out of action by the hit, I still survive and keep fighting." This seems to be in part the Soviet philosophy. Their nuclear-powered submarines have generally been noisier than ours, often substantially so —although some have been getting significantly quieter of late. Soviet nuclear subs are also generally faster, dive deeper, carry more torpedo tubes, have rubber "coatings" that to some degree protect them from the small active sonars our homing torpedoes depend on, and sometimes have double hulls that may enable them to survive a torpedo hit. They have also, until very recently, been smaller than our submarines, making them harder to detect with active sonars or future nonacoustic techniques. The Soviets have sought to counter our antisubmarine warfare through the whole process of detection, localization, hit, and kill, while we have tried to counter theirs only by avoiding passive detection.

Further, the Soviets have built a large number of very quiet submarines: conventional, diesel-electric submarines. A modern conventional submarine, when running on its batteries, is quieter than even the quietest nuclear submarine. It does make noise when it runs its diesel engines to charge its batteries, but when on patrol at low speeds, it only has to do that for about two hours out of each twenty-four.[17] While the "Washington Navy" disparages diesel submarines, the fleet admirals—those commanding battle groups at sea— often say they worry less about Soviet nuclear submarines than about the conventional boats, because the latter are so small and quiet they sneak up on them undetected.

The Soviet philosophy has given them a highly capable submarine fleet. (Its employment in combat may, of course, prove inept.) It has also kept the cost of the average submarine down sufficiently so that they have been able to afford submarines in large numbers. They build some individually very expensive submarines, but they build enough inexpensive ones so that, by buying a mix, they can afford a large force. Interestingly, of the five nations that build nuclear-powered submarines—the United States, the Soviet Union, Great Britain, France, and the People's Republic of China — only the United States now builds no conventional submarines. All the other countries build a mix of nuclear and conventional boats.[18]

Two further problems in U.S. submarine policy must be mentioned. First, although U.S. nuclear attack submarines are very quiet, they also have some major deficiencies. As noted, the large size of our submarines increases their vulnerability to active sonars and, possibly more important for the future, nonacoustic means of detection. In addition, our submarines have very few torpedo tubes —just four in all our current boats, although the SSN-21 is to have more. If a submarine-versus-submarine "dogfight" developed, the small number of torpedo tubes could prove a major deficiency.[19] While our submarines are quiet for nuclear subs, our torpedoes are noisy. As soon as it fires a torpedo, a U.S. submarine can be detected with passive acoustics. The large size of our submarines also makes them unsuitable for operations in shallow waters, which include some important parts of the world's oceans. Overall, in submarines as elsewhere, we are not buying quality instead of quantity. We are buying just one quality, quietness, at the expense of many others, including quantity.

Another problem is torpedoes. We have only one type of submarine torpedo, the Mark-48. When World War II began, five of the nations involved in it had large, active submarine fleets: Great Britain, Germany, Japan, Italy, and the United States. Three of those nations, Britain, Germany, and the U.S., found their torpedoes had serious defects and frequently malfunctioned. More recently, in the Falklands War, both sides reportedly had torpedo failures. The British ended up using torpedoes designed in the 1920s and built in the 1930s to sink the *General Belgrano* after two of their modern Tigerfish torpedoes failed. If our Mark-48s fail as the Tigerfish did, our submarines will be helpless.[20]

Further, presuming the Mark-48 works, we do not have enough of them. We have so few Mark-48 torpedoes in our inventory that if each submarine goes out with a full load, shoots all it has, and comes back to port for more, we do not have enough to give it a full reload. After that, we are out of torpedoes. Our submarines tie up at the docks for the rest of the war. We will build only 123 Mark-48s in FY 1986—a piddling supply for a war—and we cannot raise that production rate quickly to a wartime level.

What all these problems add up to is serious trouble. Our submarine fleet is heavily outnumbered, it has no overall equipment quality advantage over its main opponent, and it is dangerously short of ammunition. The current shipbuilding program does nothing to address these problems. The navy's stated goal is an attack submarine force of just one hundred boats. If the planned SSN-21 is allowed to go forward, the problems will get worse. The SSN-21 costs about twice as much as the SSN-688 we are building now, which means we will probably build half as many—two per year.[21] That in turn means an eventual fleet of just forty to sixty submarines. The vulnerabilities that accompany large size will be accentuated, because the SSN-21 is substantially bigger than the already overlarge SSN-688. The navy has no plans to acquire a second type of submarine torpedo nor to remedy adequately the torpedo shortage.[22]

Surface Combatants

The bulk of the navy's fighting ships are neither aircraft carriers nor submarines, but what are called "surface combatants." We currently have 200 surface combatants: 2 battleships, 30 cruisers, 68 destroyers, and 100 frigates. Surface combatants take up a major portion of the naval shipbuilding budget: about 32 percent of the ship construction budget went for surface combatants over the past five years. Surface combatants are the "worker bees" that serve the queen—the aircraft carrier. Their primary purpose is to protect other ships—primarily aircraft carriers, the carrier's supply ships, amphibious ships, and merchant ships—from submarines and from hostile aircraft.

Unfortunately, they aren't very good at either task. The classic picture of the battle between a submarine and a destroyer, as played out so often in World War II movies, is out of date. Today the advantage in such a fight belongs to the submarine. It can almost always detect the surface ship before it is detected itself, its weapons have longer range and more destructive power, and it is usually almost as fast and sometimes faster than the destroyer.

Destroyers, along with cruisers and frigates, have sought to counter improvements in submarines by carrying antisubmarine helicopters. The ship detects the submarine, then sends a helicopter to attack it while it tries to stay out of the submarine's range. Helicopters appear to be reasonably good antisubmarine systems, certainly better than the surface combatant itself.

Unfortunately, multipurpose surface combatants are a very expensive way of putting helicopters to sea. An American frigate costs $420 million and carries only two helicopters. Our latest destroyers, the ships of the Arleigh Burke (DDG-51) class, cost about $700 million. And they carry *no* helicopters![23] Only two countries in the world are today building destroyers that carry no helicopters: the United States and the People's Republic of China. Without helicopters, these destroyers are easy kills for any submarine they encounter. In fact, the navy has testified before Congress that they will have to be escorted by helicopter-equipped destroyers. The CG-47-class cruisers now being built can carry two helicopters, but each ship costs $913 million.

However, fighting submarines is not the main reason the U.S. Navy builds surface combatants. Here, as elsewhere, the navy underestimates the submarine threat. Both of the surface combatants the navy now builds, the CG-47-class cruisers and the DDG-51-class destroyers, are designed primarily to defend our big carriers from air attack. Their main weapon is an antiaircraft system called Aegis. Aegis uses radars and radar-guided antiaircraft missiles to try to shoot down attacking bombers and antiship missiles.

These ships are extraordinarily costly by world standards. As previously noted, a DDG-51-class destroyer costs about $700 million. In comparison, a modern British destroyer of the Type 42 class costs about $150 million. The navy traces most of the expense to Aegis. It argues it must have Aegis ships regardless of their cost because its carriers must be defended from air attack.

Unfortunately, Aegis may not work very well. The system underwent three major operational tests in 1983 and 1984. In the 1983 tests it hit only five out of twenty-one targets. In the 1984 test, the navy claimed success: Aegis supposedly shot down ten out of eleven targets. But serious questions surround the last test. Aegis was facing some potentially severe congressional questioning because of its failures in the first two tests. To protect its budget, the navy badly needed to show that the system worked. Reportedly, the test was rigged. The aircraft launching the target "drones"— small, radio-controlled airplanes used to simulate antiship missiles —flew high enough to make them detectable, giving long-range warning of the drones' arrival.

We still do not know whether Aegis works. The only way to find out is to have tests controlled by the independent Office of Operational Testing and Evaluation and insist these tests be tough and truly independent.

Further, although Aegis may not do much to stop a Soviet attack with antiship missiles, it may do a good deal to help the Soviets carry out such an attack. Aegis has a very powerful radar to find and track enemy aircraft and missiles. But the enemy can also use this radar to track the Aegis ships with radio direction-finding. Aegis is the most powerful radar on any ship afloat, and it has unique characteristics by which anyone hearing it can tell he is listening to an Aegis ship. Hostile aircraft and missiles can home on its radar, and they can do so without turning on their own radars, which would in turn tell us where they are. The Aegis ship can avoid serving as a beacon for the enemy by turning the radar off. But then the whole Aegis system is shut off, and the billion-dollar cruiser or destroyer might as well be carrying a load of scrap iron for its main armament.[24]

A Military Reform Navy

These criticisms of the navy's present structure and ships suggest massive changes are needed. That is indeed the case. Fortunately, some basic changes in the naval environment and in naval technology offer some interesting ways to solve our fleet's problems.

The most urgently needed changes are in our submarine policies. We must recognize that the attack submarine is the capital ship. Submarines must receive first priority in our shipbuilding program. The United States cannot permit itself to be outnumbered in capital ships by its principal opponent, the Soviet Union. The argument often advanced by the navy's leadership that our NATO allies' 144 submarines will be enough to make up the difference does not stand up to examination. If a conflict between the United States and the Soviet Union were to begin in, for example, the Middle East, how many of the NATO nations would actually join us? Are we realistically to expect West Germany, Holland, Denmark, Norway, Italy, Greece, or Turkey to declare war on the Soviet Union in a conflict that does not directly involve Europe? Britain, with her 28 attack submarines, might be expected to come to our aid in such a situation, and possibly France, with her 17. But who else?

If we are to have reasonable confidence in our ability to win at sea, we must seek rough numerical parity in submarines with the Soviet Union. The navy should set a force-level goal of 300 attack submarines, up from the current goal of 100. This will require a massive and expensive submarine building program. To create and sustain a 300-boat force, we must build 10 attack submarines per year, more than double the current rate of 4 per year. A construction rate of 10 attack submarines annually would give us a 300-boat force by about the year 2015. If it should prove possible to provide the necessary crews and base support more rapidly than that, it may be desirable to build at a higher rate so that the 300-boat-force level can be reached sooner.

The force should be a mix of nuclear and nonnuclear submarines, not only to make a construction rate of 10 or more submarines annually affordable but also because small, quiet conventional submarines are generally preferable for barrier operations and missions in coastal waters and closed seas, such as the Mediterranean. The final mix of nuclear and nonnuclear boats should be left open at this time, because developments in nonnuclear submarine propulsion are somewhat unpredictable.

Our diesel submarines should initially be built to a foreign design. No conventional submarine has been designed in the United States for thirty years. Over that period there have been many advances in conventional submarine design and technology. A number of allied and friendly nations today build effective, modern diesel submarines, including Great Britain, the Netherlands, West Germany, Italy, Sweden, and Japan. The navy should hold a design competition among their existing designs and build the winner under license in the United States.

Our current nuclear submarines of the SSN-688 class are overly large and overly expensive. We should return immediately to the construction of an improved version of their predecessor, the SSN-637 class, with better computers and updated reactors. The result would be a better submarine at lower cost. The SSN-637 class is smaller than the SSN-688 class by about 2,260 tons, handles better, and dives deeper. It is slightly slower and noisier. It costs about two-thirds as much as the SSN-688 class to construct.

Simultaneously, the navy should begin a high-priority, wide-ranging research and development program to design not one but several new classes of nuclear-powered attack submarines. The first act of the new program should be to unshackle nuclear submarine research and development from the restraints Admiral Rickover laid on it. Future submarines should not merely be larger versions of their predecessors. One innovation that could bring major payoffs is nuclear-electric propulsion that would allow shutting down the reactor to operate on ultra-quiet battery power, possibly using nuclear power plants similar to those in nuclear-powered satellites. Other areas for innovation include liquid metal reactors, modularity, automation to reduce crew size, innovative propulsors, and new hull materials.[25]

It is very important that we design and build more than one class of nuclear attack submarine. Our last new submarine design, the design for the SSN-688 class, went into production in 1970. It is not due to be succeeded until 1991. The Soviet Union has put four new classes of nuclear attack submarine to sea since 1980.[26] This is alarming for what it suggests each nation is learning in the field of submarine design. Each new design should improve on its predecessor, and the more designs a nation can afford to produce and test in service, the more it is likely to learn.

The navy should also begin a major research program to design a conventional submarine that would use a system other than diesel engines driving generators to charge batteries that in turn feed electric motors. The goal should be a conventional submarine that, like a nuclear boat, would be completely independent of the atmosphere. A number of technologies, most prominently fuel cells and the Stirling engine, offer promise. If the effort is successful, it may prove desirable to build a substantial number of submarines of this new type in lieu of both some planned diesel-electric and some projected nuclear submarines.

One further reform relating to submarines must be undertaken at once. We must greatly increase our inventory of submarine torpedoes, and we must put a second torpedo design into production. Few "savings" are more foolish than that by which we build far too few torpedoes to support even our existing submarine force in a major conflict. We must have enough torpedoes in stock to supply our submarines adequately until torpedo production can be increased to support wartime levels of consumption. This will mean roughly a ten-fold increase in torpedo production. Half of the new torpedoes should be built to a new design with no parts in common with the Mark-48, to guard against catastrophic torpedo failure. The new design should be selected from among foreign designs already in production, and foreign entries into competitions for future torpedo designs should be welcomed. The more design competition we have, the better the designs are likely to be.

What will all this cost? A good deal. A modern diesel-electric attack submarine, built in this country to a foreign design, should cost about $200 million. Nuclear attack submarines of the SSN-637 class would cost about $450 million apiece. The initial building program of ten boats per year, five of each type, would, therefore, cost about $3.25 billion. This is an increase of about $1.2 billion above what we are now spending to build attack submarines. Submarine research and development costs would at least double. The proposed increase in torpedo production would cost about $1.1 billion.

Those who see military reform as simply a way to save money will be disappointed here. But military reformers make no such promise. Their goal is an effective military, not just a cheap one. Military reform will give us a vastly improved return for our defense dollars. In the case of the navy, most of what we are now spending contributes to ineffectiveness, while the program proposed here would yield genuine strength. And there will be savings as programs that build ineffective weapons are canceled. But, as is the case with submarines, there will also be areas where spending increases.

As for aircraft carriers, we need to supplement and eventually replace our few large aircraft carriers with a significantly larger number of smaller carriers. These "light carriers," along with virtually all new surface combatants, should be varieties of a single, radically different, new type of ship: the High Adaptability Surface Combatant (HASC).

The HASC reflects two major, and in this country largely unremarked, changes in the field of ship design. The first is that, for the first time since the fifteenth century, the hulls and propulsion plants of merchant ships and those of warships have about the same capabilities.

Since the evolution of the purpose-built sailing warship in the sixteenth century, warships have been distinguished from merchant ships by two basic characteristics beyond the fact that warships were armed. First, warships were generally designed to sail faster than merchantmen. As recently as World War II, the average speed of a merchant ship was about ten knots. In contrast, a World War II destroyer could steam between thirty and forty knots, as could most cruisers and some battleships and aircraft carriers.

Today merchantmen can be as fast as warships. The U.S. Navy recently acquired as fast transports a class of merchantmen called SL-7, designed to steam at thirty-three knots. The navy's Perry-class frigates, the workhorses of its surface combatant fleet, have a top speed of about twenty-eight knots.

The warship's other traditional advantage was armor. The only ships we build today with any armor, beyond some protection for the magazines and some plastic linings in some topside spaces, are the big aircraft carriers. The Aegis cruisers are almost completely unarmored, as are the DDG-51-class Aegis destroyers and the Perry-class frigates. Foreign practice is generally similar.

The vulnerability of these unarmored warships was shown in the Falklands War. The modern destroyer HMS *Sheffield* was sunk by a single Exocet antiship missile, the warhead of which did not explode. Just the impact of the missile and fire caused by the burning of its unspent fuel were enough to destroy the ship.

Merchant ships are no more vulnerable than these modern warships proved to be. In fact, merchant ships hit by Exocet missiles fired by the Iraqis in the Persian Gulf war have seldom been sunk and often not seriously damaged.[27]

Reflecting these two basic changes in the relationship between merchant ships and warships and the resulting equivalence in speed and protection, the HASCs would all be built on merchant ship hulls and with standard merchant ship propulsion plants.

Although the hull and propulsion plant of a warship are not the major components of its cost, these changes would still result in substantial savings. A modern merchant ship of forty thousand tons costs only about $120–$150 million. At that price, we can afford a substantial number of warships built to merchant ship specifications.

The second major change upon which the HASC is based is the possibility of modularizing naval weapons and sensors. Thanks to developments in electronics, particularly microchips, weapons and sensors that used to take up a great deal of space and had to be built into a ship can now be packaged in standard-sized modules or containers. Ships can be designed with standard-sized openings to receive the modules.

This is not some high-technology fantasy. Ships built and equipped exactly this way are today in service with a number of navies—although not ours. They were built by the German shipyard of Blohm & Voss on what they call the MEKO system. Blohm & Voss developed MEKO to give a variety of foreign navies whatever weapons and sensors they wanted in a standard hull so that warship costs and development time could be cut. The current MEKO ships, built with what the shipyard calls "first generation" MEKO, are equipped with weapons and sensors at the time they are built and only reconfigured during major overhauls. This alone is a major step forward compared to U.S. Navy practice, in which everything is built into the ship and is, therefore, very expensive to change. But Blohm & Voss will soon begin building a new generation of MEKO ships in which the weapons and sensors can be changed quickly and easily to reflect changes in the ship's mission. A ship will carry one set for, say, antisubmarine warfare, and then can quickly be reequipped for antiair warfare. How quickly? A representative of the shipyard said that in a test, the shipyard completely reconfigured a ship from one mission to another, changing many of the weapons and sensors, in a weekend.[28]

The High Adaptability Surface Combatants will combine merchant hulls and propulsion plants with modular weapons and sensors. Beyond that, what will they look like, what size will they be, and how will they replace current carriers and surface combatants?

All the HASCs will look like aircraft carriers, so they can all serve as aircraft carriers when that is what the mission requires. They will have a flat top deck for a flight deck, an island superstructure (built on one side of the ship), and a big open deck under the top deck, with a large elevator running between the two. Built into the top deck at regular intervals will be hatches into which modular weapons and sensors can be inserted. The hatches will be of standard sizes, to which the weapon and sensor modules will be built. The HASCs will all have a merchantship Roll-on, Roll-off (RO-RO) bow or stern, so they can serve as amphibious ships. The sizes of these ships can vary almost infinitely.[29]

Normally, the bulk of the HASCs would serve as aircraft carriers. They would carry Vertical or Short Takeoff and Landing (VSTOL) aircraft, like the Harriers currently employed on British aircraft carriers, and also helicopters. Many HASCs would normally serve as carriers for antisubmarine aircraft, reflecting the fact that defeating the Soviet navy primarily means defeating the Soviet submarine fleet. Others would carry fighters or attack aircraft or a mix of both. The aircraft would change depending on the mission.

What about the surface combatants? Both roles for these ships are in question. In antisubmarine warfare, as noted, a cruiser, destroyer, or frigate is essentially a device for towing a sonar and providing a landing pad for some helicopters. A HASC can carry a sonar as well as a traditional surface combatant; both towed-array and dipping sonars could be modularized. An expensive surface combatant normally carries only two helicopters, but a comparatively cheap HASC of the same size could carry four to eight.

Before we configure any HASCs for antiair warfare, we must determine how well radar-guided antiaircraft missiles work. Indications thus far are that they do not work very well. If they can prove themselves in vigorous, realistic, honest operational tests, the missiles and their radars can be modularized and mounted in HASCs. If they fail the tests, long-range defense will depend on fighters. All HASCs would normally mount containerized antiaircraft guns.[30]

The aircraft, weapons, and sensors carried by the HASCs would themselves reflect reform ideas. In particular, heavy emphasis would be placed on passive electronics, which listen for enemy radars rather than depend on their own. HASCs with passive electronics would find it easier to hide from the enemy reconnaissance systems, because their merchant ship hulls and propulsion plants would help them blend in with normal sea traffic.

HASCs would be bought in large numbers, reflecting the military reformers' belief in the importance of numbers in war. A precise number cannot be set here, because it will depend on what sizes prove to be optimal and what roles will still be allocated to surface ships after the submarine is recognized as the capital ship.

But numbers should be emphasized in at least two major areas. The first is aircraft carriers. Our entire sea-based tactical aviation is today very fragile, depending as it does on thirteen carriers. The same number of aircraft (or more) carried by those thirteen ships should be spread around into approximately three times as many ships, that is, about forty HASCs serving in the strike-carrier role, in addition to whatever number were serving as antisubmarine carriers.[31]

The second critical aspect of numbers is having the numbers when they count: in wartime. In both world wars, we found we had to expand our naval strength very rapidly to meet the threats we faced. Almost everyone knows how our shipyards turned out tremendous numbers of ships, to the point where we had a navy of more than five thousand ships in 1945. What is not generally known is that the expansion came too late. In World War II, the decisive naval battles, the Battle of Midway in the Pacific and the U-boat Battle of the Atlantic, had to be fought and won with ships built or begun before the war began. Not a single large carrier ordered after Pearl Harbor joined the fleet until 1944. The first destroyer-escort antisubmarine ship ordered after we entered the war did not join the fleet until March 1943, the month the tide of the battle turned against the U-boats.

No navy can hope to have all the ships it needs, of every type, in service in peacetime. The cost would be far too high. Capital ships must generally be in commission in peacetime, but many other ships can be kept in reserve, costing little in time of peace but, unlike new construction, available quickly if war breaks out.

Today our naval reserve is small: 1 destroyer, 12 frigates, and 18 minesweepers make up the bulk of the naval reserve force. The HASCs would change that. A large number of HASCs would be in reserve in peacetime, not sitting at docks but serving as American flag merchant ships. Their design would enable them to serve well in merchant service. Today our merchant navy has shrunk to the point where we have just 517 ships. We rank tenth in the world listing of merchant fleets. The high cost of building and crewing American merchant ships makes it necessary to subsidize both their construction and their operation. Because many policymakers do not see much value in a large merchant fleet, such subsidies have been heavily cut back or eliminated.

But HASCs that were serving in time of peace as American merchant ships could quickly be converted in time of war into full-fledged, first-line warships, no different from those regularly in naval service. The aircraft and the modularized weapons and sensors could quickly be put abroad, crewed by naval reservists. This capability makes a strong case for a well-funded program to build HASCs for peacetime merchant service and to subsidize their operation. It also argues strongly for expanding the naval reserve to man their aircraft, weapons, and sensors in war. A condition of the operating subsidies should be that the crews also joined the naval reserve to help man the ship when it was mobilized for naval duty. In this way, we could quickly expand our navy in time of crisis or war, at relatively low peacetime cost. We would not depend on a slow naval expansion through construction of new warships. We would also revitalize our merchant marine, our shipyards, many of which face closure because of a lack of orders for new ships, and the profession of merchant seaman.[32]

The HASC represents a radical break from traditional warships. Those who visualize navies as long, sleek "greyhounds of the sea" will not identify readily with a ship that shares its hull and propulsion plant with merchantmen; that looks like an aircraft carrier (or worse, like an aircraft carrier with radars, missiles, and guns sprouting from its flight deck like mushrooms on a putting green); that changes its mission, weapons, and sensors as readily as a sailor changes his clothes to go on liberty; and that from afar is indistinguishable from ships in merchant service. But just as the graceful clipper ships eventually had to yield to squat, dirty, "smudge pots on scows," the steamships, so the day of the elegant traditional cruiser or destroyer and the massive supercarrier is passing. The big carrier is too expensive to build in large numbers, and in war, numbers count. Cruisers, destroyers, and frigates are fragile, underarmed, and overpriced. The submarine dominates all surface warships, as does the aircraft. Indeed, it is primarily as a platform for aircraft, a floating landing strip, that the surface ship continues to be viable.[33]

Personnel

Many of the personnel problems we discussed in relation to the army carry over to the navy. In particular, the overly large officer corps is a serious problem. At the end of World War II, we had a total of 3,380,817 people serving in the navy. We had 470 admirals and 30,094 officers with ranks between lieutenant commander and captain. For the navy's more than 5,000 ships, we had 3,877 captains.

Today we have just 543 ships and 560,000 navy personnel. But we have 252 admirals, 24,853 people ranking between lieutenant commander and captain, and 3,720 captains. The effects, as with the army, include dividing work into ever smaller pieces, pushing decisions further and further up the chain of command, doing business by committee, and constantly rotating people into new jobs. The solution is also the same as for the army: reduce by at least 50 percent the number of officers above the rank of lieutenant (the navy rank equivalent to captain in the army).

Also similar to the army is the shortage of noncommissioned officers, called petty officers in the navy. In 1985, the navy was short 5,775 petty officers. Both pay scales and special privileges must be increased to make a career as a petty officer sufficiently attractive to retain the number we need.

But in addition to these common problems, the navy has some particular problems of its own. One is that, in the officer corps, the identification with the service "branch" has gotten badly out of hand. The navy has three basic branches in its officers corps: aviation officers (those who fly aircraft), surface warfare officers (those who specialize in cruisers, destroyers, and frigates), and submariners. All have become very parochial. Officers seldom have tours with another branch. A submariner, for example, will seldom serve with an antisubmarine ship or air unit. A surface officer seldom serves a tour of duty with a submarine, even though a submarine is the greatest threat to his surface ship. We lose important knowledge through this failure to cross-train.

In addition, officers develop a bureaucratic myopia in which they think first about the needs and desires of their branch, not the total combat effectiveness of the navy. A former chief of naval operations, Admiral Elmo R. Zumwalt, wrote about this "union" problem in his book, *On Watch:*

> For the last quarter-century or more there have been three powerful "unions," as we call them, in the Navy—the aviators, the submariners, and the surface sailors—and their rivalry has played a large part in the way the Navy has been directed . . . The intense competition for resources and recognition among the three unions . . . almost inevitably breeds a set of mind that tends to skew the work of even the fairest, broadest-gauge commander if he is given enough time. Whichever union such a commander comes from, it is hard for him not to favor fellow members . . . It is hard for him not to think first of the needs of his branch, the needs he feels most deeply, when he works up a budget. It is hard for him not to stress the capability of his arm, for he has tested it himself, when he plans an action.[34]

The only way to eliminate this unionism is to require cross-branch training. At some point in his career, an officer should serve a tour with the branch that, in the Soviet navy, is his main opponent. Surface officers and antisubmarine aircraft aviators should do a tour in a submarine. Submariners should serve with antisubmarine air units or surface ships. Each could thereby see, on a day-to-day basis, how others will seek to hunt and destroy him. And each could learn what other branches can contribute to help him solve the problems facing his own branch.

Another navy personnel problem, again one that affects primarily the officer corps, is the domination of engineers. In response to the increasing complexity of naval equipment, especially the nuclear propulsion plants in almost all our current submarines and some surface ships as well, the navy has placed heavy emphasis on training officers to be engineers. The engineering emphasis begins at the Naval Academy, where about 40 percent of the midshipmen major in engineering. Fifty-six percent of all naval officers have engineering degrees. Before taking command of a ship, all officers must go through a twelve- to thirteen-week course in engineering.

Competent engineers are important for the navy, but the domination of the officer corps by engineers has some unfortunate effects. As one submariner put it, "The captain of a nuclear submarine spends 90 percent of his time thinking about the aft end of the boat (where the engine room is located)." But tactics, the operational art, strategy, leadership, and training are not simply subsets of engineering. They take a different type of training, a different type of thinking, and often people who may not be very good engineers. They all lose out to the dominance of engineering. Yet wars are won more by these qualities than by propulsion plants and other technical aspects of hardware.

Nuclear propulsion plants require a great deal of attention, because if something goes wrong, the result can be catastrophic, and not just for the specific ship in question. Therefore, the navy should have a designated "Nuclear Engineer Corps" to provide specialists for ships with such propulsion. But generally, ship captains, including captains of nuclear-powered ships, should be chosen for their abilities as tacticians, leaders and trainers, not engineers. Current policy that insists a captain of a nuclear-powered submarine be a nuclear engineer should be changed. Career opportunities for nonengineers should be greatly broadened. The education system, starting with Annapolis, should be modified to reflect the fact that naval commanders should know how to use engineers and engineering, but need not be engineers themselves.[35]

The unit cohesion problem that looms so large in ground forces is less of a problem in navies, because on cruise, ship crews are necessarily stable. It is not possible to dribble new people in and take trained people out at sea. However, if cruises are short and frequent, as sometimes happens depending on where a ship is assigned, crew turnover can be high. And when a ship sails on a cruise, most of the people on board are new to each other and cohesion is low. In war, a ship may be in action from the moment it leaves harbor, or even before if the harbor itself is attacked or has been mined.

Unit cohesion in the navy could be strengthened by adopting a practice followed by some foreign navies: as long as a person is in the navy, he is generally assigned to the same ship. This would make the ship analogous to an army regiment. It does not mean people would not have tours of duty away from the ship. But at the end of their shore tour, when it was again time to go to sea, they would usually go back to the same ship.

Because most sailors serve for only a four-year enlistment, they often have only one cruise in their career. But petty officers and officers, by returning to the same ship, would build a cohesion among themselves that would help keep the ship functioning smoothly even at the start of a cruise. There would always be some turnover as people leave the service, but there would be more cohesion than with the current system. Additionally, there would be a bond between the men and their ship that would strengthen morale and esprit de corps.

Training
Effective training is as important for a navy as for an army. Unfortunately, navy training today has some major deficiencies. In general, they parallel those of the army, although, again, a ship inherently has better cohesion than a ground unit and therefore

fewer training problems. While a ship's captain may start a cruise with an inadequately trained crew, he can train them up to a high level of performance during the cruise without constantly having to start over again as new people come in.

But just as in the ground forces, navy training is far too often "canned." Exercises frequently follow scripts and scenarios. Submarines in particular are restricted in what they can do—officially, so as to permit others to practice attacking them. However, in reality, they are limited to avoid the embarrassment of what usually happens if the restrictions are lifted. If the submarine is allowed to use its full capability, it often brings the exercise to a halt because it quickly sinks its opponents, and there is little they can do to stop it. Instead of realizing what this implies for the structure of its shipbuilding program, the navy usually hobbles the submarines during the exercises.

The navy's attempts to ignore the capabilities of the submarine carries over into the way the results of its exercises get reported. A dramatic example of this problem surfaced several years ago before the Senate Armed Services Committee. The navy briefed the committee on one of its major Atlantic Ocean fleet exercises, called "Ocean Venture." It said that the exercise had proved its big carriers could sail into waters where the Soviets were strong and survive.

But a junior naval officer disagreed. A lieutenant commander named Dean Knuth had served with the group of experts who had analyzed "Ocean Venture." According to his findings, both carriers had been sunk by submarines early in the exercise. The navy had simply ignored these sinkings in its final report. Knuth wrote up his findings on "Ocean Venture" as an article for the *U.S. Naval Institute Proceedings.* When the Navy discovered he had done so, it immediately classified his article "Secret."

It appears that the results of training exercises are systematically reported inaccurately by the navy. This leads to highly unrealistic training, which causes the navy to adopt practices that will not work in war. If something works in training only because what really happens is ignored, it is not likely to work in combat.

Organization

A navy is not organized into divisions like an army. Task forces or, as they have recently been named, "battle groups," are tailored to fit each situation, with differing numbers and kinds of ships. So the "tooth to tail" problem must be looked at somewhat differently.

Possibly the easiest way to look at it is to relate the number of ships in the navy to the number of people. If that is done on a historical basis, something interesting emerges. Today the navy has 543 ships and 560,000 people. In 1964, it had 873 ships and 668,000 people. In other words, over about the last twenty years, the navy has shrunk 37.8 percent in ships but only 16.2 percent in people.

During those twenty years, the navy took a number of actions that should have reduced, not raised, the ratio of men to ships. It replaced World War II ships with more modern vessels that usually carry smaller crews. For example, the converted World War II missile cruisers of the Cleveland class, which were still in service in 1964, displaced 13,755 tons and carried a crew of 1,077 men. The current CG-47 missile cruisers are smaller, at 9,530 tons, and have a crew of 353 men. Comparing ships of similar tonnage, the Juneau class light antiaircraft cruisers displaced 8,200 tons and had a crew of 579 men. The new DDG-51-class antiaircraft destroyers displace 8,300 tons and have a crew of just 303 men. In addition, many tasks performed in 1964 by sailors have been civilianized. Since 1964, the number of civilians employed by the navy has grown from 347,038 to 358,197. In fact, the navy's total manpower, uniformed and civilian, is today 918,000, compared with 1,015,000 in 1964.

Why? The basic answer is "Parkinson's Law." C. Northcote Parkinson observed that when the British Royal Navy declined in number of ships between 1914 and 1928, the number of people in various support jobs actually rose. He found this process so regular and so certain he made it one of his famous "laws": whenever the size of the fleet shrinks, the size of the shore establishment expands.

Parkinson's Law has been at work in our navy during its reduction from almost 900 ships to just over 500. Part of the expansion in the shore establishment is justifiable. With an all-volunteer force, the number of people assigned by the navy to recruiting duty

has risen, from 3,471 in 1964 to 5,769 today. The increased maintenance requirements of the complex, high-technology equipment
the navy has bought—which, whether it works in combat or not,
still has to be maintained—has driven up the size of the shore
establishment.

But most of the increased size of the shore establishment is due
purely to Parkinson's Law—that is, to bureaucracy. As the navy
shrinks in the number of ships, its bureaucracy seeks to build new
kingdoms on shore, kingdoms that can offer seemingly important
employment to all its surplus officers, provide new ground for
bureaucratic battles for money and prestige, and help justify the
navy's budget.

The military reform navy proposed here will be substantially
larger in the number of warships than the navy we have now. In
order to deal a blow to Mr. Parkinson, we should freeze navy
manpower at current levels as the expansion in the number of ships
goes forward, compelling the navy to man the ships by reducing the
shore establishment.

Summary

The changes military reform will bring to the navy will be even
more drastic than those it will bring to the army, especially in view
of the fact that, while the army is reforming itself, the current
leadership of the navy is bitterly opposed to military reform. The
new navy will be a new generation navy, one reflecting radical
advances in ship design and in the structure of the fleet. The
recognition that the submarine, not the aircraft carrier, is the
capital ship will mean a change greater than when the carrier
replaced the battleship in that role.

Can the changes be made in time? That is the most troubling
question. The Soviet navy has recognized the submarine as the
capital ship for the last thirty years and has built its navy accordingly. Our navy has not even begun to change yet, and it will not
until an administration and a Congress dedicated to military reform compel it to do so. If a major confrontation should occur
before the reform of the navy is at least partially completed, we
could be in very serious danger as a nation.

3

Air Forces

JUST AS THE UNITED STATES has more than one army, it also has more than one air force. In fact, it has four: the United States Air Force, naval aviation, army aviation, and Marine Corps air.[1] The official air force is the largest: it has 9,367 aircraft of all types, including 3,302 fighters, 1,059 attack aircraft (light bombers), 329 bombers, 1,219 transport aircraft, and 268 helicopters. The air force also has 600,795 people, 108,191 of whom are officers. Although smaller than the air force, naval aviation is also sizable. The navy owns 5,909 aircraft, including 1,023 fighters, 1,270 attack aircraft, 529 antisubmarine aircraft, and 1,351 helicopters. About 15,700 navy officers are aviators, and about 131,000 navy personnel work to support navy aircraft. Of these, 1,486 aircraft, 4,865 aviators, and 39,217 support personnel are part of Marine Corps aviation. Finally, there is the army. The army is forbidden by law from having fixed-wing combat aircraft, so most of the army's air force is helicopters. It has 5,343 of them. The army also has 403 fixed-wing noncombat aircraft, for a total of 5,746 aircraft.

Together, these four air forces make up the largest air force in the world. The navy alone has the fourth largest air force in the world, larger than that of Britain or of France. The Marine Corps has the world's tenth largest air force. The United States Army has more helicopters than Israel or West Germany have aircraft of all types. The army has more helicopters than the United States Air Force has combat aircraft.[2]

Conventional wisdom has long decried these four separate air forces, arguing it would be more efficient if we had just one, or, at most, perhaps two, to allow the navy its own shipboard aircraft. It probably would be more efficient in peacetime. But for military reformers, the goal is combat effectiveness, not peacetime efficiency. And from the standpoint of effectiveness, four air forces can give us something one cannot: competition.

However, not all competition is desirable. It can easily focus, not on finding ways to improve military effectiveness, but on budget size, political influence, or prestige. To make certain we get the right kinds of competition, we need to undertake some major changes.

First, we need to insure our four air forces really do compete. Like most bureaucracies, they do not enjoy competition. They enjoy comfortable, stable arrangements where each agrees to say the others need whatever they want.[3]

Second, once we get some competition going, we need to be able at some point to say that one service's approach to a given problem has won and make the others adopt it. Thus far, most efforts at doing this, at obtaining what is called "commonality," have been miserable failures. Each service wants whatever it has developed and bitterly resists adopting anything developed by another service. In the past, aircraft have been a partial exception to this rule. The famous Phantom (F-4) fighter-bomber was developed by the navy but bought by the marines and the air force as well. The air force also adopted the navy-developed A-7 attack aircraft.[4] But of late, commonality in aircraft has diminished. The navy now flies the F-14 and F-18 fighters, while the air force has the F-15 and F-16. The marines fly some F-18s, but they also have the British-developed Harrier VSTOL attack aircraft, which the navy refuses even to consider for itself.

The F-18 is a particularly good example of how we currently fail to benefit from competition. In the late 1970s, the air force held a competition between two prototype lightweight fighters, the F-16 and the F-17. The F-16 won, and the air force bought it. The navy then bought the F-17 and renumbered it the F-18. To get its own, unique airplane, the navy was willing to buy the fighter that lost the competition and then spend a fortune improving it.

Third, interservice competition in aviation and in other matters must be kept constructive. It can easily get out of hand and become destructive to military effectiveness. In World War II, interservice rivalry between the Imperial Japanese Army and Imperial Navy was so fierce that interservice cooperation became almost impossible. Ultimately, the Imperial Navy had to get its own army, while the army built its own navy, including its own submarines.

The civilian defense leadership should foster constructive interservice competition. But it should also be quick to penalize competition when the services sacrifice military effectiveness in squabbling over money or prestige.

Concepts

Just as in the case of the navy, equipment controls employment doctrine in air forces much more than it does in armies, because certain types of aircraft are best used in certain ways. Just as a navy's concepts are strongly influenced by whether it perceives the submarine or the aircraft carrier as the capital ship, so an air force equipped primarily for supporting an army differs in its thinking from one equipped primarily for strategic bombing. Because of this close integration of equipment and ideas, concepts will be examined here as they apply to different types of air force equipment.

Fighters

There are three basic concepts regarding air-to-air combat, each of which results in a different approach to fighter design. The first is what might be called the "close combat school." Adherents to this school believe most air combat will consist of surprise "bounces" or classic dogfights: one aircraft sighting another visually, then maneuvering against it for an advantageous firing position.[5] This school emphasizes that, since air combat began in World War I, 60 percent to 85 percent of all aircraft shot down in air battles were destroyed by an opponent they never saw. Thus, small size and relative invisibility are important in a fighter. Often, these surprises occurred in the midst of a general melee, in which an aircraft intent on shooting down another was ambushed from behind by a third. The close combat school believes the dogfight or "furball," where numerous aircraft engage in intensive maneuvering and countermaneuvering, will remain the dominant element in air combat for the foreseeable future.

The second school might be called the "missileer" school. Its proponents argue that new technology, in the form of radar-guided air-to-air missiles, has made the dogfight a thing of the past. Radar-guided air-to-air missiles are directed from a fighter to hit another aircraft by a radar in the fighter. These missiles have ranges that exceed those at which a pilot can see an enemy with his eyes; he "sees" them only with his radar before he shoots. According to this school, these missiles are so effective that few if any aircraft will survive long-range encounters with them to get in close enough to dogfight.

The third school, which might be called the "current design school," because three of the four fighters that the United States is currently procuring reflect its views, believes that most air combat will involve both long-range engagements with radar-guided missiles and dogfighting. The proportion will vary depending on circumstances.

Each of these schools propounds fighters that reflect its views. The close combat school favors lightweight, highly agile fighters, aircraft optimized for dogfighting. The ideal lightweight fighter would have the following characteristics:

• Small size, smaller than any fighter currently in production in the United States. The larger the fighter is, the easier it is for the enemy to see and shoot down. Small size is very important in a dogfight, if a fighter wants to remain unnoticed.
• Excellent maneuverability, including transient maneuverability: the ability to shift quickly from one maneuver to another. The ability to change maneuvers quickly gives a fighter agility and a rapid Boyd Cycle.
• The ability to cruise at supersonic speeds. Today most fighters can fly supersonically, but only for a few minutes, because supersonic speed burns so much fuel. All current fighters cruise at

subsonic speed. The first fighter that can cruise supersonically will have a major advantage, because it will continually be coming up behind enemy fighters and surprising them, while they will seldom do the same to it. The ability to cruise about a hundred knots faster than any other fighter helped make the German jet fighter of World War II, the Me-262, so potent and so feared as a surprise attacker.

• No radar-guided missiles. The ideal lightweight fighter would be armed with infrared guided missiles like the Sidewinder, which are fired within visual range, and cannon. However, it would also carry a new type of very long-range air-to-air missile: missiles that home in on the radar emissions from enemy aircraft.

• Mostly passive electronics. Just as with ships, aircraft can be found through the emissions from their radars and radios. An ideal lightweight fighter would rely mostly on electronics designed to hear the other aircraft's emissions without emitting signals itself, although it would, when necessary, use a very short "burst" of radar.

• Low cost, so it could be bought in adequate quantity. Lightweight fighter proponents believe a true lightweight fighter would cost about half as much as the F-16, the least expensive fighter we now buy.

The missileer school believes that because all the fighting can be done by radar-guided missiles, the aircraft itself need not be a fighter at all in the traditional sense. The aircraft does not need to maneuver. It just serves as a carrier for radars and missiles. A transport aircraft could serve quite adequately as a missileer fighter. The ideal missileer would have approximately these characteristics:

• Large size and weight, for large payload and long loiter time—time on station in the air.

• No combat maneuvering ability. No supersonic speed.

• Main, possibly sole, armament of radar-guided air-to-air missiles, such as the Sparrow and the Phoenix. Armament might include some infrared missiles for last-ditch self-defense.

• Heavy electronics suites, including powerful radars.

• Very high cost, possibly twice as high as our most expensive current fighter, the navy's F-14.

The current design school's views need not be described theoretically, because they are reflected in three of the fighters we now procure: the air force's F-15 and the navy's F-14 and F-18. In general, these are the characteristics:

• Large and heavy compared to other fighters around the world. The largest and heaviest, the F-14, is 3¼ times the weight of the world's most numerous fighter, the Soviet MiG-21. The smallest and lightest, the F-18, is still twice the weight of the MiG-21.
• Maneuverability ranges from marginal in the F-14 to fairly good in the F-15. The F-14's maneuverability is so marginal it is almost a missileer. It depends heavily on radar-guided missiles fired from beyond visual range. This is consistent with its mission, which is not really that of a fighter, but an interceptor: shooting down large enemy bombers that are attempting to attack our aircraft carriers.
• Supersonic speeds for short distances, but about the same subsonic speed as a Boeing 707 for cruising.
• Radar-guided missiles, infrared missiles, and guns.
• Mostly active electronics, i.e., they emit signals most of the time when flying tactically.
• High cost. The F-14 is the most expensive, at about $32 million per aircraft. The F-15 costs $27 million, and the F-18 $18.7 million.

One fighter currently in production does *not* reflect the current design school. It is the air force's F-16A, and it is an anomaly. As a prototype, its design was heavily influenced by two members of the military reform group, John Boyd and Pierre Sprey, and it reflects their belief in the lightweight fighter. It is the smallest of the four fighters we now procure; it has the best maneuverability of the four, including transient maneuverability; it is armed only with infrared missiles and guns, carrying no radar-guided missiles; and it is the least expensive, at a cost of $9.5 million.[6]

Which of these three contending schools is correct? The close combat/lightweight fighter school presents the most convincing case. It offers the following arguments:

• Although radar-guided missiles have been in development since the late 1940s, they have consistently performed poorly in combat. In the Vietnam War, our primary radar-guided missile, the Sparrow, had a probability of kill (Pk) of just .08 to .10; we had to fire more than ten Sparrows for each hit.[7] In contrast, the infrared Sidewinder had a probability of kill of .19, and guns had a Pk of .24. This came as a major surprise to the services. They had been so confident of the radar-guided Sparrow that the first four models of our primary fighter of the time, the Phantom, had been built without any guns. We quickly had to put guns on them.

In the Middle East, the story has been the same. Almost all Israeli air victories have been won with infrared missiles and guns. In the 1973 war, when Israeli fighters claimed to have shot down more than three hundred Arab aircraft, only one (and perhaps none) was shot down with radar-guided missiles; twelve such missiles were fired. In the Falklands War, the Argentines fired some radar-guided missiles, with no successes. In contrast, the latest model of the infrared Sidewinder, used by the British, had phenomenal success: nineteen of the twenty-six Sidewinders fired hit their targets.

• Beyond visual range, combat is generally not feasible, because it is not possible to tell whether the aircraft on the radar is friend or enemy. Military aircraft have what are called IFF systems: electronic devices designed to signal whether they are a friend or a foe. But the IFF is not reliable. Quite understandably, pilots don't like getting shot down by their own side, so rules of engagement almost always demand they identify the other aircraft visually before they shoot at it. Once they are close enough to do that, they are close enough to shoot infrared missiles or guns.

Between the IFF problem and the poor performance of radar-guided missiles in combat, it is clear the missileer concept, except possibly in special, limited circumstances, is not viable.

What of the current design school? Does it not represent the best of both worlds? Unfortunately, it may represent the worst of both. In combat among large numbers of fighters and fighter-bombers, such as we would face in a war in Europe, these fighters' radar-guided missiles are not likely to be effective or, in view of the IFF problem, even usable beyond visual range.

The possible exception is if the navy were to face Soviet naval bombers attacking our aircraft carriers. The direction from which the bombers would be coming and their radar, if they were foolish enough to leave it on, should enable us to identify them beyond visual range. A major reason why radar-guided missiles have performed poorly in combat is that they have been used against fighters and fighter-bombers, which can outmaneuver them. But large bombers, like the Soviet's Backfire, maneuver poorly. Therefore, the F-14 may make sense for the navy, as may a pure missileer —as an interceptor, not a fighter.[8]

In order to carry radar-guided missiles, current-design fighters pay major penalties in dogfight performance. The missiles require large, heavy radars—in the fighter—for guidance, which make the aircraft large and heavy: major disadvantages in a dogfight.[9] Having their radars on most of the time for the missiles gives their positions away to the enemy. And their size drives up their price, so we cannot afford the number we need. In the early 1950s, we bought more than five thousand fighters annually. Today, spending about the same amount of money in constant dollars, we buy only about three hundred fighters annually. In fighters, as elsewhere, numbers are important in war.

Current design school proponents counter with the argument that radar-guided missiles are necessary to shoot down enemy aircraft that attack at night or in bad weather. This is not true as regards night attacks in clear weather: in World War II, cannon-armed German and British night fighters were quite effective in clear weather. Further, the radar-homing missiles proposed by the lightweight fighter advocates would work well at night in any weather, since enemy bombers would have to use their radars to find their targets. More important, enemy bombers can only find fixed targets—cities or rail yards, for example—at night, and attacks against such targets have not been of much military value in past wars.

The problems that restrict beyond visual range combat to a few special situations, the poor performance of radar-guided missiles, and the penalties to dogfighting capability inherent in the current design school all suggest strongly that the lightweight fighter is the way to go. Without much long-range combat, the dogfight and the surprise "bounce" will continue to dominate air combat, and that is where the lightweight fighter excels. It is also the only fighter we can afford in adequate quantity. We should, of course, retain the existing F-15s, but future emphasis should be on the procurement of lightweight fighters.

Fighter-Bombers

Today heavy bombers are generally used only in nuclear or naval roles, or, as in Vietnam, for conventional bombing where there is little fighter opposition. Most bombing is done with light bombers, known as attack aircraft. One fundamental conceptual issue dominates any discussion of attack aircraft. It is so important that almost everything else flows from it. It is the issue of independent bombing versus integrated bombing.

Since airplanes began dropping or shooting things at targets on the ground, this issue has been central to air power. It involves a basic choice in all air-to-ground action. The question is, should air power act independently from what armies are doing on the ground, or should it be integrated with what those armies are doing?

Independence translates into what was called "strategic bombing" in World War II and is now called "deep interdiction." The concept is that the best way to defeat the enemy is to use air power to destroy his industry, bridges, roads, railroads, power plants, and sometimes his cities and civilian population. There are two variations of the concept. One argues that this sort of bombing will cut off the supply of weapons, ammunition, fuel, and food to the enemy's armies at the front, greatly weakening their ability to fight. The other variation says that if an enemy's cities and civilian population can be attacked heavily and repeatedly from the air, the enemy will surrender even if his armies at the front are still fighting effectively. In both variants, air power is seen as just a type of firepower, and it is used to achieve attrition.

In contrast, integrated bombing (including strafing) means using air power directly in support of an army, attacking the enemy's troops that are actually in combat (what is called "close air support"), and also blocking his movement of reserves (what is known as "battlefield interdiction"). Integrated bombing also has two variants. In one, aircraft are used as flying artillery to bomb the kinds of targets that would otherwise be hit with cannon shells. This approach is compatible with either firepower/attrition warfare or maneuver warfare on the part of the army. The other variant is more purely maneuver warfare: it uses air power to support the ground commander's scheme of maneuver. It must be closely integrated not just with the army, but with what the army is trying to do.

Today both the air force and the navy are almost wholly oriented toward and equipped and trained for independent bombing. Marine air emphasizes close air support in its rhetoric, although its equipment and procedures are not well suited for it.

But the history of air warfare argues conclusively against independent bombing. In World War I, Germany began independent bombing raids on Britain in January 1915, using not airplanes but airships: zeppelins. Germany conducted more than thirty zeppelin raids on Britain. Later in the war, German heavier-than-air bombers also joined in, conducting twenty-seven raids. Some of these bombers were enormous, with a wingspan only three feet shorter than that of a B-29.

About £83 million in damage was done, 1,414 people were killed, and 3,416 were injured. Few targets of any military value were hit, and zeppelins and bombers were lost at a disastrous rate. But the German independent bombing campaign nonetheless had significant long-term effects on the development of air power.[10] Convinced that independent bombing was a waste of effort, the Germans rebuilt their air force in the 1930s considerably more oriented toward integrated bombing.[11]

In contrast, the British had been badly shaken by the German air raids. Overlooking the fact that there was little real effect, they built their interwar air force primarily for independent bombing.

Independent bombing also received a big push forward in the inter-war period from several writers on air power, most notably an Italian general, Guilio Douhet. In his book *The Command of the Air,* published in 1921, Douhet argued that armies had been rendered obsolete by heavy bombers. The next war would not be decided by land battles, but by fleets of bombers attacking the enemy's cities.

Douhet's book had tremendous influence on air forces around the world, including in Britain and the United States. In the U.S., where the air corps was part of the army, aviators saw in Douhet not only a prophet but a potential liberator. If air power would win the next war, and if aircraft should be employed separately from what was happening in the land battle, then the air corps should become a separate service.

In World War II, the Royal Air Force and the American Army Air Corps put the theory of independent bombing into action with a vengeance. British air raids on German cities began early in the war. Contrary to the predictions of the bomber advocates, bombers quickly proved very vulnerable to fighters, which forced the British to bomb only at night. This meant doing away with any pretense of attacking only military targets, since night bombing was too inaccurate for that. Carpet bombing of German cities was the norm by 1942. The Americans joined in as soon as they could station enough B-17s in Britain, although the Americans persisted with daylight raids, taking very heavy losses until 1944, when sufficient fighter escort was available. The Americans also concentrated their air attacks in the Pacific on Japanese cities.

The physical destruction was extensive, but much less than had been predicted. At least two hundred fifty thousand Germans and one million Japanese, mostly civilians, were killed. A raid on Hamburg in the summer of 1943 destroyed sixteen thousand buildings and killed seventy thousand people. The firebomb raid on Tokyo in March 1945 killed more than one hundred thousand Japanese, more than were killed by the atomic bomb dropped on Nagasaki and almost as many as died at Hiroshima.[12]

Because independent bombing was the ticket to service independence (a separate U.S. Air Force was created in 1947), it has remained at the heart of air force thinking ever since. Its effectiveness is the air force's founding myth.

And myth it is. Independent bombing failed to accomplish what its advocates before the war had claimed it would. No Axis nation surrendered solely because of air bombardment of its cities. Germany did not surrender until the German army had been defeated on the ground and the country was occupied by Allied troops. The conventional bombing of Japanese cities did not defeat the Japanese armed forces, and although the atomic bombs played a major role in Japan's surrender, we now recognize that the use of nuclear weapons is an entirely different type of warfare.[13]

What about integrated bombing in World War II? When it reflected genuine integration of the armies on the ground with aviation, it was highly successful. The German Luftwaffe, designed for integrated bombing, was the main practitioner, and air power was an important element in the blitzkrieg. German aircraft contributed heavily to the success of Panzer divisions by serving as "air artillery" at key points, such as the German's crossing of the Meuse River at Sedan in France, and also by impeding the enemy's ability to shift operational reserves to meet the Panzer's attacks.

Allied air power also made a major contribution to the war effort when it was integrated with the ground forces in the battle of Normandy. It prevented the Germans from effectively undertaking the operational counterattacks with their Panzer divisions that were their forte. The integration of allied air power at Normandy was done only over the bitter objections of most of both the British and American air generals, who saw it as a wasteful diversion from the attacks on German cities.

The use of American air power in the Korean and Vietnam wars taught the same lessons.[14] In all these cases, there is strong evidence that bombing enemy civilians does not destroy civilian morale. Instead, it appears to harden the will to fight and thus may actually lengthen wars.

What all this means is simple: one of the most fundamental guiding concepts of the air force (and naval aviation) is wrong. We should be directing our energies toward the concept of integrated, not independent, bombing. This means we must make a substantial change in air force doctrine, and not just in the doctrine on paper, in manuals, but in practice, in planning air operations. Other changes will be needed to put the doctrine of integrated bombing into effect: changes in the commander who directs an air operation (often, it will be the ground commander); in air-to-ground communications (today the radios of ground troops in many cases cannot be received by the radios in our airplanes); in the types of aircraft we buy and their armament; in pilot training (pilots need a good understanding of ground combat if they are to support an army effectively); and perhaps most important, in the attitudes of both air force and navy aviators. Both must come to see themselves as soldiers first and fliers second if they are to work effectively with the soldiers on the ground.[15]

Transports

Although fighters and attack aircraft get most of the attention, transport aircraft make up a significant part of our total military aviation. The air force has 1,219 transport aircraft, which are intended to carry soldiers and their equipment from one place to another. Some of the aircraft are quite expensive: the air force's huge C-5B transport, the largest airplane in the Western world, costs $168.5 million apiece.

The basic conceptual issue facing transport aviation is what its job should be. Should it be to move ground combat units and their equipment, including tanks, armored personnel carriers, and artillery over very long distances and then keep them supplied once they get there—what is called "strategic airlift?" Or should it be "theater airlift": moving soldiers and the kinds of consumables often urgently needed in combat—ammunition, spare parts, fuses —*within* combat theaters?

Today we plan to do both, and we buy aircraft for both. Our most numerous and probably most useful transport aircraft, the venerable C-130, which first entered service in 1956, is designed for theater airlift. Our most expensive transport aircraft, the C-5, is designed for strategic airlift. The air force currently wants a new transport that is advertised as ideal for both, the C-17, which would cost $180 million per airplane. The C-17 is, in fact, too small for strategic airlift and much too expensive to risk on forward airfields doing the theater airlift job.

The problem with strategic airlift is that it cannot really be done. It is not possible to move and supply a large ground combat unit over intercontinental distances solely by air, unless it is only light infantry with no heavy equipment. Even then it is very difficult to lift and supply a force of more than a brigade or two. Even the largest strategic airlift aircraft carry comparatively little. The C-5 can carry only one M-1 tank.

The famous airlift to Israel during the 1973 Middle East War shows how little strategic airlift can actually do. Only 29 tanks were airlifted during the entire thirty days, and only 14 pieces of heavy equipment were delivered before the cease-fire. A GAO report on the airlift stated, "The quantities delivered were not significant enough to have affected the war's outcome .. . ." Seventy-four percent of the material sent to Israel went by sea. The first ship reached Israel twenty-two days after the airlift began with 3,321 tons of heavy equipment. By that date C-5 aircraft had delivered only 1,251 tons of heavy equipment. The army estimates it would today take *all* our military airlift capacity twelve and a half days to move a single mechanized division with 10 days' supplies from the United States to a transoceanic theater.

The only way to move large ground forces overseas with supplies is on the sea in ships. Personnel without their weapons can be moved in large numbers by air, but we do not need expensive military aircraft to do that. We can mobilize civilian airliners for that task, as we plan to do in an emergency under the Civilian Reserve Air Fleet (CRAF) program. Sometimes heavy equipment like tanks can be pre-positioned in overseas theaters, as we now do for army divisions in Europe and for two marine brigades in the Persian Gulf (where the equipment is pre-positioned afloat on ships). The troops can be flown in to join up with the equipment. In other cases, the only option is to put both troops and equipment on ships and sail them where they are needed. Airlift simply cannot do the job.

Fortunately, even a fraction of the money we spend for strategic airlift will buy a great deal of shipping. A modern merchant ship of forty thousand tons, which could carry about 500 tanks, costs about $150 million—less than a single C-5. Even if that C-5 can make twenty round-trips in the time it takes the ship to make one, the ship can carry a great deal more. The funds the air force plans to spend on future strategic airlift, including the C-17, should instead be used to improve our sealift capability, both by buying more transport ships for the navy and also by subsidizing an expansion of our merchant marine.

Theater airlift, the ability to move men and emergency consumables by air within a combat theater, has proved very valuable in past wars. The C-130, despite its age, is an excellent aircraft for this purpose. We should not only maintain but also increase the size of the C-130 force, primarily by acquiring more of them for the Air Reserve and Air National Guard. At a price of $18.75 million, the C-130 is one of the few things we now buy that is sufficiently inexpensive we can afford substantial numbers.

Helicopters

Our fourth air force, army aviation, is made up almost entirely of helicopters. The army today has 5,343 helicopters, and we are spending about $2 billion annually for more helicopters for the army. The Marine Corps is also a heavy user of helicopters, owning 740. The navy, as noted earlier, also uses them, primarily for antisubmarine warfare: it has 611. The air force has 268 more, for a total (active duty) U.S. helicopter force of 6,962 (the Army Reserve and Army National Guard have about 3,000 more).

The reason the army depends so heavily on helicopters is not any lessons gained from combat, but law. Service agreements that have the force of law forbid the army from having any fixed-wing combat aircraft. The army, however, has long realized that the air force is oriented toward independent, not integrated bombing, which means it is not interested in providing air support to the army. Because it needs air support, the army decided it had to have its own air force to provide it. And because it is not allowed to own fixed-wing combat aircraft, that air force had to be built around helicopters.

The conceptual issue about helicopters is whether they are simply transports for use in rear areas, or whether they can be effective combat aircraft as well. Their use as rear area transports and pilot rescue aircraft is not in question: past experience has proved they are useful in these roles. But the army (and the Marine Corps) also use helicopters heavily as combat aircraft, both to land troops and to provide close air support. The army has 1,333 attack helicopters, which are equipped with missiles, rockets, and guns intended to destroy enemy ground targets. It plans to acquire 675 Apache attack helicopters that cost $10.5 million apiece—more than an F-16A fighter. It also has 2,335 observation helicopters for use over the battlefield. Some of its transport helicopters are also intended for battlefield use, in so-called air assault tactics. One army division, the 101st Airborne (Airmobile), is built around the concept of using helicopters in combat, and it is equipped with 490 of them.

Unfortunately, the fate of helicopters in combat has thus far not been very encouraging. We lost at least 4,643 helicopters in Vietnam. On Grenada, we lost at least nine in just three days against a weak enemy.[16] Reportedly, the Soviets have suffered relatively heavy helicopter losses in Afghanistan, again fighting an enemy with little more than machine guns for air defense. The helicopter's disadvantages in combat are several:

• It is inherently fragile compared to a fixed-wing aircraft. A hit on the rotor will usually destroy a helicopter, while fixed-wing aircraft can usually survive a hit in the wing.
• It is very maintenance-intensive compared to fixed-wing aircraft. Operating costs show this clearly. The air force's A-10 close-support aircraft has a cost per flight hour of $1,702, compared to $3,714 for the AH-64 attack helicopter. The C-12 transport airplane costs $396 per hour to operate compared to $1,340 for the UH-60 Blackhawk transport helicopter.
• Most important, helicopters cannot outmaneuver antiaircraft fire or enemy radar-guided missiles. Most fixed-wing combat aircraft can do this; few helicopters can. Instead, the army says helicopters will avoid antiaircraft missiles by flying very low. But this puts them in range of enemy machine guns and antiaircraft cannon, which are also deadly.

In view of these inherent problems, it is appropriate to be skeptical about the use of helicopters as combat aircraft. The army is not to be blamed for what it has done. In the face of the law and the air force's disinterest in supporting the army, it has had little choice. But these bureaucratic problems should not compel the army to build its air force around helicopters. If, as should be done, the air force is reoriented from independent to integrated bombing, the army will not need its own combat aircraft. But if that is not done, then the mission of supporting ground troops should be taken from the air force and given to the army, with encouragement to acquire fixed-wing combat aircraft for the task.

Air Defenses

Over the last several decades, the Soviet Union and its allies have deployed extensive ground-based air defenses built around surface-to-air missiles and radar-guided antiaircraft guns. The Soviets currently have at least a dozen different types of air defense missiles in service.

The conceptual issue is whether these air defenses are effective or not. Currently, our air forces believe they are. This belief has two effects. First, we devote an increasing amount of resources to countering enemy air defenses. Second, our air forces plan to spend the early part of any conflict destroying enemy air defenses, so they can subsequently operate safely against the enemy's ground forces and deep interdiction targets.

Unfortunately, both of these policies make the enemy's air defenses effective, whether or not they are actually very good at shooting down our aircraft. Money devoted to air defense suppression and countermeasures is money unavailable for fighters, attack aircraft, and general purpose ordnance. In last year's defense budget, $573.5 million was spent for air defense suppression weapons.[17]

More important is the diversion of our aviation in the early stages of a conflict to a private war with enemy air defenses. The early stages of the ground campaign will certainly be important, possibly decisive. If our aviation is occupied in a private war against enemy air defenses, those defenses will have done their job. They will have kept our aviation off the back of enemy ground forces and deprived our ground forces of air support.

Our air forces reply, "But the high effectiveness of the air defenses leaves us no choice. If we try to go in and support our ground forces without first destroying the enemy's air defenses, we will be slaughtered." But what if the effectiveness of those air defenses is greatly overrated?

There is evidence it may be. Most of the Soviet air-defense missiles are radar guided. Just as with radar-guided air-to-air missiles, they have not proved very effective at shooting down fixed-wing combat aircraft because the aircraft can countermeasure or outmaneuver them. Because they use radar, a simple radar receiver in our aircraft warns the pilot when one has been fired at him, so that he can maneuver to avoid it and use countermeasures, such as chaff, against it. In Vietnam, the SA-2 Soviet-built air defense missiles used by the North Vietnamese had very poor probabilities of kill (Pks): just .002 to .005. In the 1973 Middle East War, the vaunted Soviet-built SA-6 had a Pk of just .01. In the Falklands War, British surface-to-air missiles did no better. The Rapier, which we recently bought at a cost of $464.1 million to defend our airfields in Britain, got just one kill. The British will not say how many Rapiers they fired, but the number is believed to be high—in the hundreds.

Infrared surface-to-air missiles have so far not done better. The hand-held Soviet SA-7 has proved quite poor against fixed-wing aircraft. In the 1973 Middle East War, about five thousand SA-7s were needed to shoot down between one and three Israeli aircraft.

Israeli aircraft have faced Soviet-designed surface-to-air missiles over Lebanon repeatedly, with very few losses. Simple countermeasures, such as dropping chaff and flares, have been effective against them, as was maneuver. (Of course, these missiles are dangerous to helicopters, which cannot outmaneuver them.) It appears our air forces' high regard for the effectiveness of air defenses may be the defenses' greatest strength. They certainly do not seem to shoot down many aircraft.

Air defenses have traditionally been fairly effective in protecting fixed targets, where the defenses can be carefully set up in large numbers, camouflaged, and netted together. But they have not been very effective in defending moving targets, such as tank columns, because the air defenses themselves are moving with the columns. This suggests air defenses will work better against our aircraft if we remain wedded to independent bombing, where most of the targets are fixed, but will be less effective if we go instead to integrated bombing where most targets and their air defenses are moving. History suggests this is true. Close air-support loss rates have traditionally been five to ten times lower than losses in interdiction bombing.

Further, if we look at the air defenses of a Soviet division in the field, we see they may actually have declined in effectiveness since World War II. By the end of that war, a Soviet motorized rifle division had fifty-two visually aimed antiaircraft guns. Today a Soviet motorized rifle division has just nineteen antiaircraft guns, radar-directed ZSU-23s, which performed poorly in tests done by the U.S. Army on several captured in the Middle East. The division also has 146 surface-to-air missile (SAM) launchers, 120 of which are SA-7s. But if the missiles perform as poorly in the future as they did in Vietnam and the Middle East, the total air defense capability of a Soviet division may have declined since World War II.[18]

The questionable capability of SAMs and radar-guided antiaircraft guns also has major implications for our own air defenses. Both the army and the marines rely heavily on missiles for air defense. Our only current antiaircraft gun is the seriously deficient 20-mm Vulcan. The poor performance of Soviet air defense missiles was always answered with, "But ours are much better, because Western technology is much better." The equally poor performance of British SAMs in the Falklands War brings that reply into question. We need not only to rethink our approach to Soviet air defenses but also to reconsider our own. Combat results suggest we should make a significant investment in visually aimed antiaircraft guns, at the expense of further investments in SAMs and radar-guided guns.

Equipment

Most equipment issues have been discussed in the concepts section. Here the specific implications of military reform for the aviation equipment of each service will be examined.

Air Force

With 834 F-15 s now in service or on order, we have a more than adequate number of radar-missile-equipped, current design school fighters. Production of the F-15 should be halted. The funds saved should be used to buy a larger number of F-16 s.

At the same time, the F-16 should be returned to what it originally was: a pure fighter. The air force leadership, which is less than enthusiastic about the F-16 because its design was influenced by "outsiders," has tried to convert it into a bomber and, more recently, has added substantial electronic "improvements" to it. Both have added large amounts of weight and complexity, which reduce fighter performance. We should return to the much lighter, "hotter" F-16 that won the lightweight fighter competition—thereby also reducing the price of the F-16 by at least a third, so that we could afford more of them.

An effort to develop the pure lightweight fighter described in the concepts section should be begun immediately. Several different prototypes should be developed, with a production aircraft selected through a competitive "fly-off."

The air force currently has six different types of attack aircraft (including fighter-bombers). All but one, the A-10, are optimized for independent bombing. No more aircraft for this mission should be bought. Instead, we should begin immediate development and procurement in large numbers—in the thousands— of a new integrated bombing aircraft, the Combined Arms Fighter.[19] Like the A-10, it would be built around a powerful cannon, the best weapon for attacking ground troops and enemy tank columns.[20] It would improve on the A-10 by being more survivable, much smaller, and vastly more agile. Selection would be by a competitive fly-off among several prototypes. The price would be kept under $5 million, to allow several thousand to be bought.

In transports we should continue production of the excellent C-130 indefinitely. The C-17 program should be canceled. We should also expand the Civilian Reserve Air Fleet (CRAF) program, which facilitates the conversion of civilian airliners to military use upon mobilization.

Navy

We have seen two of the big aircraft carrier's weaknesses: the vulnerability of each individual carrier and the vulnerability of the whole carrier fleet that derives from the small number of carriers. The carrier's aircraft are a third major weakness. Because of the kinds of aircraft the navy flies from its carriers, it is not clear that the big carrier is very useful even if it can survive. It is not clear that its aircraft can do much beyond protecting the carrier—if they can do that.

Our principal carrier-based fighter is the F-14. As noted, it is not really a fighter, but an interceptor. If its radar-guided missiles can hit bombers trying to attack our fleet, it may be a good interceptor. But its large size and marginal maneuverability make it a poor fighter.[21] This brings the carrier's utility for "power projection"—attacking targets ashore—into serious question. If the carrier attempts to project power against a nation that has an air force of its own, the F-14 is likely to be forced into air combat against land-based fighters. If those fighters are competently flown, the F-14 is likely to find itself in serious trouble. That in turn means that the fighter-bombers it would be escorting would become very vulnerable to enemy fighters.

The carriers also carry F/A-18 aircraft, which are intended to be true fighter-bombers: they are designed to perform both as pure fighters and as attack aircraft. They appear to be reasonably good fighters, certainly better than the sluggish F-14.[22] However, because the navy views it primarily as a bomber, the F-18's pilots are not likely to receive sufficient training in air-to-air combat to make them really competent at that highly demanding task. As a bomber, the F-18 (called the A-18, for Attack, when used in this role) is suitable only for independent bombing; it is too fast and too vulnerable to small-arms fire to be effective in integrated bombing. It should be reasonably effective for attacking enemy surface ships, but in most cases major surface ships are likely to be sunk by submarines before they get in range of the carrier's aircraft.

The carrier's other bomber, the A-6, is useful only for independent bombing because of its large size and poor maneuverability. In fact, it is so vulnerable even in this role, especially to enemy fighters, that the navy plans to use it primarily at night, when anything other than independent bombing is impossible because the aircraft crew can only find large, fixed targets. The A-6 is also inferior to smaller attack aircraft, like the A-18, for attacking enemy surface ships.

The remainder of the carrier's aircraft is a mix of antisubmarine aircraft (both fixed-wing airplanes and helicopters), radar-equipped early warning aircraft designed to find attacking enemy aircraft at long range, and support aircraft of various types. The antisubmarine aircraft are useful, reasonably effective, and relevant to the main threat, the Soviet submarine force. But they are too few in number to do much beyond protect the carrier, if they can do that; one of the navy's big carriers usually carries ten S-3 antisubmarine airplanes plus six antisubmarine helicopters, for a total of just sixteen antisubmarine aircraft out of more than ninety normally aboard.

The unsuitability of the F-14 for dogfighting, the inability to use the A-18 or the A-6 effectively in integrated bombing, and the small number of antisubmarine aircraft mean that the carrier faces not only a question of survival but also of relevance. Even if the F-14s can keep enemy bombers from sinking the carrier, if its antisubmarine aircraft can protect it from enemy submarines, and if its bombers can attack enemy surface ships that may get close enough to threaten it, what can it do beyond simply survive? It can conduct some independent bombing against land targets. But even if the targets are destroyed, history suggests that kind of bombing does not achieve much. The big carrier with its current air wing looks very much like a modern-day Maginot line: perhaps able to defend itself, but not useful for much else.

What should be done to give our carriers more effective and useful aircraft?

The F-14 should be subjected to rigorous, independent testing to determine if its radar-guided missiles, the Sparrow and the very long-range Phoenix, actually work against sluggishly maneuvering targets such as heavy bombers and also cruise missiles. If they do, we should keep the F-14 in service as an interceptor. If not, it should be scrapped and replaced with a real fighter.

The F-18 program should be terminated. We have bought enough to serve as fighters, and as an attack aircraft it is suitable only for independent bombing.

In order to get the kinds of aircraft the navy really needs for power projection, two new naval aircraft should be developed as quickly as possible: a naval lightweight fighter and a naval Combined Arms Fighter. To operate from the High Adaptability Surface Combatants (HASCs), these aircraft must either be Vertical or Short Takeoff and Landing (VSTOL) or Short Takeoff and Landing (STOL) aircraft. Because it is also desirable to free air force aircraft from dependence on long, vulnerable runways, these same characteristics may be appropriate for the air force's lightweight fighters and Combined Arms Fighters, in which case both services should use the same aircraft.

Because the Soviet navy is primarily a submarine navy, many of the HASCs (and possibly some of the existing big carriers as well, which would be retained in service) will serve primarily as carriers for antisubmarine aircraft. That means we will need a new antisubmarine aircraft, one that can fly from the HASCs. The Osprey, an aircraft-helicopter hybrid now being developed, may be a suitable choice for this if its cost can be kept down.

Another major and important component of naval aviation is our land-based antisubmarine aircraft, currently P-3s, of which we have 414. These are generally effective aircraft, or would be, if they had a better antisubmarine torpedo than the Mark-46. But they have one inherent disadvantage: they cannot do the first part of antisubmarine warfare, submarine detection, very well. Most detection equipment is too large and heavy for them to carry, and its use requires a platform that can stop or at least move slowly, which of course an aircraft cannot. But an air*ship* can. The next generation of land-based antisubmarine aircraft should be blimps. In World War II, 89,000 merchant ships were escorted by blimps; not one was lost to an enemy submarine. Blimps are also inexpensive; they can perform a mission at about 20 percent of what it costs an airplane to do the same mission. We should bring back the blimps.[23]

Marine Corps Aviation

The justification for marine aviation has been its supposed interest in integrated bombing, in supporting the troops on the ground. But marine air has gotten quite far afield from ground support, having its own fighters and interdiction bombers as well. In fact, the Marine Corps today does not have any aircraft that are well suited to providing close air support. Its F-18s, A-6 bombers, and F-4 Phantom fighter-bombers (slowly being replaced by the F-18s) are no different from those the navy owns and no better at providing close air support.[24]

The Marine Corps hangs its hat on the AV-8 Harrier as its close-support aircraft, but the claim does not stand up to examination. The Harrier is this country's only VSTOL aircraft— our only airplane that can take off and land vertically. That does provide one major advantage in close air support: the Harrier can be based just a short distance behind the front, flying from small "pads" instead of runways. Based so close to where the ground troops are fighting, it can get there quickly when they need air support.

But in other respects, the Harrier is much less well designed for close air support than the air force's A-10. Like almost all our other fighter-bombers, it is fast—and when pilots can go fast, they usually do, because it is usually safer. Unfortunately, it means they cannot see what is happening on the ground. The Harrier's 25-mm cannon is less effective for strafing than the A-10's 30-mm gun, because it cannot destroy tanks. Most important, the Harrier may be of all our aircraft the *most* vulnerable to ground fire, especially to machine-gun and small-arms fire. Most of our current aircraft are vulnerable to this kind of fire, but the Harrier is particularly so, because it carries much of its fuel in a tank wrapped right around the engine, and the fuel tanks are not self-sealing. (They do not automatically "plug" a bullet hole, as many combat aircraft fuel tanks do.) This creates a high likelihood that a shot from an enemy rifle or machine gun will cause a fuel leak in close proximity to the engine, with disastrous results.

Yet at the same time, the Marine Corps did the nation a great service when it bought the Harrier. Why? Although the Harrier is not very good for what the marines bought it for, close air support, it is a reasonable general purpose naval fighter-bomber. The Harrier reflects most of the limitations of "current design" aircraft, so it is no replacement for lightweight fighters and Combined Arms Fighters. But until they are ready, it gives us something we get from no other aircraft in any of our four air forces: an ability to fly from ships other than big carriers. Because it is a VSTOL aircraft, the Harrier can fly from virtually any ship that can carry a helicopter. With the Harrier, twelve of our amphibious ships can serve as small aircraft carriers. Thanks to the Harrier, we need not be completely dependent on just thirteen aircraft carriers for sea-based aviation. Should a naval conflict occur before the HASCs, naval lightweight fighters, and naval Combined Arms Fighters are ready, we can spread some of our naval aviation "eggs" into at least a few more "baskets." Thus, while the Harrier may not be a very good aircraft for the Marine Corps, it might turn out to be our most useful naval aircraft, at least for the present.

In the long run, with military reform reorienting both the air force and the navy from independent to integrated bombing, the traditional justification for separate marine aviation would no longer be valid. Should it then be abolished? As noted earlier, competition among several air forces can be very useful. Marine aviation has a history of being innovative, from its invention of dive-bombing in the interwar period, to its adoption of the first U.S. VSTOL combat aircraft, the Harrier, in the 1970s.[25] We should therefore keep marine aviation but put it "on probation." If it is innovative and imaginative, if it competes effectively with the air force and the navy in developing new ways to improve combat effectiveness in integrated bombing, it will be a good investment. If not, it should go.

Army Aviation

Army aviation, as noted, currently means helicopters. And combat results have brought the viability of helicopters as combat aircraft very much into question. But here as elsewhere, there may be new lessons to learn. We should scale back army combat helicopter aviation to a size suitable for continued experimentation, say, a single combat helicopter brigade. If the army can think its way around the helicopter's tactical fragility, the way the Germans thought their way around the tank's tactical fragility in the 1930s, something useful may come of it. If not, an army no longer dependent on helicopters for almost all its air support would not be endangered by failure. Army aviation should in any case continue to have helicopters for rear-area movement of troops and supplies.

Personnel

Unit cohesion is important in aviation units, just as in ground units. It is important that pilots in a unit know each other well. Air combat, like ground combat, is not a matter of "every man for himself." People must work together, and that means unit cohesion is important. Cohesion is also important in relation to the enlisted personnel who maintain the aircraft. They, too, must work as a team. They will be under heavy stress in combat from the high pace of operations and from the need to get aircraft repaired and back in combat quickly, often in the face of shortages of spare parts and of casualties caused by enemy air attacks on our air bases. Just as in the ground forces, personnel turnover in aviation units today is too high to allow adequate cohesion to develop. That means we need something like a regimental system in air units, where people belong permanently to a given unit, always returning to it after assignments at headquarters or time in schools.

The officer surplus is also a serious problem in air units. Ironically, it leads to its opposite, a retention problem: pilots' leaving the services in such numbers that we periodically experience severe pilot shortages. The navy is now facing a major retention crisis: it is short 1,232 pilots. In fact, it is now offering pilots a $36,000 lump-sum bonus if they will reenlist for six years.

How does the officer surplus feed this problem? As in the army and the Marine Corps, there is no surplus of junior officers, who make up most of the pilots. But there is a large surplus above the rank of air force captain (lieutenant in the navy), which means many senior pilots end up "flying desks," stuck in make-work staff jobs that just generate bureaucracy. Good pilots like to fly airplanes, not desks, and they see what the future holds for them while they are still junior officers. So when they reach the rank of air force captain or navy lieutenant, they leave the service and fly for an airline or join the Air Reserve or the Air National Guard, where they can keep on flying. As a result, the reserve and guard have many of our best pilots. Here and elsewhere, the only solution is a drastic reduction in the size of the mid- and upper-level officer corps. The pilot who wants to stay a pilot for his whole career should be allowed to do so.

We should also consider whether all pilots, except for some army helicopter pilots, should be officers, as they are today. A strong argument can be made that some, maybe most, pilots should be enlisted personnel: noncommissioned officers or warrant officers. The army warrant officer helicopter pilots are, by all accounts, superb. This is because they fly all the time, for their whole careers. They do not often get stuck in desk jobs. Their job is to fly, period.

If we adopted a policy providing for enlisted pilots, it might also help address a problem with our current officer pilots: too many do not think beyond the cockpit. If many or most pilots were enlisted, then officers, in addition to being proficient pilots, would also be expected to be leaders, thinkers, operations planners, tacticians, and trainers. An officer, after all, should never be only a technician. Today, with all pilots officers, we end up with few real aviation officers, leaders who can think about war as well as fly. Recognizing that flying is itself a technical task and making most fliers enlisted personnel might help create a true aviation officer corps.

Retention is a problem with skilled aviation technicians as well as with junior officers. The noncommissioned officers leave, in part, because the airlines pay much more than the military and also offer easier working conditions.[26] The services will never be able to compete fully in these respects. But the measures needed to improve retention of other noncommissioned officers will also help retain NCOs who serve as aviation technicians. Unit cohesion will offer psychological rewards that can make continued service attractive. Sharp gradations in pay among enlisted personnel, noncommissioned officers, and staff noncommissioned officers will also help, as will the restoration of special NCO social and prestige benefits.

Training

The single greatest aviation training problem is insufficient flight sorties. An average U.S. Air Force fighter pilot gets 12.7 flight sorties per month. In contrast, Israel, which provides some of the world's best combat pilots, has, until recently, scheduled about twice as many sorties per month.[27]

Flight time is the basis of pilot training, and there is no way around it. Simulators can be useful for practicing procedures, but practicing air combat in simulators is not sufficiently realistic. It can easily result in negative learning—learning things that are wrong and that will get pilots killed in combat. The first and most important step in improving aviation training is to double sorties per month. It is also important for improving pilot retention. Good pilots like to fly. Let them fly more, and more of them will stay in the service.

Aviation training also needs to be restructured. Today not enough of the flight time our pilots do get is spent tactically, train- ing for air combat. This is particularly true in the navy, where much flight time is devoted to the difficult skills of taking off from and landing on aircraft carriers, although the tactical training navy pilots do get is much less rigid and therefore better than what air force pilots receive. Interestingly, the adoption of VSTOL aircraft will greatly reduce the navy's problem. It is much easier to land a VSTOL aircraft on a ship than to land conventional aircraft, as was shown in the Falklands War when Royal Air Force Harriers, whose pilots had no previous shipboard experience, were based on British aircraft carriers. As one British pilot said, "It is much easier to stop and then land than to land and then try to stop." This is also a reason the navy's senior aviators so dislike VSTOL: if air force pilots can land on a ship as easily as navy pilots, naval aviation is bureaucratically threatened.

In addition, more training time needs to go to unit, as opposed to individual, training. Today most American air-combat training is one aircraft against one, or two against two. This does not reproduce the stress and chaos of real air combat. We do very little squadron-versus-squadron free-play air combat training. Just as with ground troops, unit skills are more than an agglomeration of individual skills. They are only acquired by unit-versus-unit free-play exercises, and such exercises must become the norm, not the exception.[28]

Both the air force and the navy have taken an innovative step forward by establishing special bases and squadrons for dissimilar air-combat training. In the past, aircraft trained against other similar aircraft. But wartime opponents often fly aircraft with very different characteristics, and they use different tactics. In Vietnam, our kill ratio in air-to-air combat deteriorated from the Korean War ratio of ten to one to just two to one; at one point we were down to one to one. Our aviators decided that the different characteristics of the Russian-built MiGs flown by the North Vietnamese and their different tactics were part of the reason. Our pilots flew as if they were flying against American aircraft; as a result, they got some nasty surprises.

The Vietnam experience led to the foundation of the navy's "Top Gun" and the air force's "Red Flag" programs. In these programs, aircraft engage in mock air combat with special training units that fly aircraft with characteristics as similar as possible to those of Soviet aircraft (the navy just leased some Israeli-built Kfir fighters to serve as its "aggressor aircraft"), and they use Soviet tactics, as best we know what they are. These programs deserve strong support. But at the same time, some rigidities have crept into them of late. They have become somewhat stereotyped, which makes events predictable and training unrealistic. Like much ground training, they have become something of a ballet. This must be changed; the training at Top Gun and Red Flag must be free play.

Organization
The problem in our air forces is the same as in our ground forces and in the navy: too much "tail" and too few "teeth." The air

force's many bureaucracies are notoriously large and lethargic. One of them, Air Force Systems Command, is well described by Dr. Edward Luttwak:

> Consider, for example, the role of the Air Force Systems Command, which has expanded and subdivided over the years to accommodate 10,524 officers, including no fewer than 34 generals, at last count. . . .
>
> The central headquarters of the Systems Command at Andrews Air Force Base, just outside the border of the District of Columbia, which supervises the various divisions and offices of the Command that do the final supervising, already forms a very large bureaucracy. Headed by a four-star full general (whose own inner-office executive group includes four colonels), with a three-star lieutenant general serving as vice commander, the headquarters is coordinated by a chief of staff who has his own well-staffed inner office. These officers supervise the sixty-eight "directorates" that divide the functions of the headquarters among them; mostly headed by colonels who report to eleven deputy chiefs of staff (who are mostly brigadier generals), these directorates cut the work into very fine slices indeed—and each slice provides employment for several officers. . . .
>
> And that is only the central headquarters. The actual work of the Systems Command is distributed among four major divisions, each headed by a three-star lieutenant general. . . . In addition there are eight other lesser divisions and "centers." Each of the divisions has its own headquarters (very large in the case of the four major divisions), which coordinates and supervises the different functional offices and directorates, which in turn supervise the contractors and in-house laboratories. Whatever else may be said, the acquisition of Air Force equipment does not suffer from a lack of supervision.[29]

Our air forces are simply too fat in people. In the air force's Tactical Air Command, the overall ratio of aircraft to people (military and civilian) is 1 to 170. Some foreign air forces offer a striking contrast. Israel gets a ratio of 1 aircraft to 30 people. Sweden gets 1 per 27. Our particular circumstances may require somewhat more people, but it seems doubtful that we need more than five times as many as Israel, which flies many American-made aircraft and performs superbly in combat.

As with the navy, our several air forces' overall personnel strength should be held constant as the number of aircraft is increased with the introduction of the new lightweight fighters and Combined Arms Fighters. The additional personnel needed by the new squadrons and wings should be taken from bloated bureaucracies like Air Force Systems Command.

The Air Reserve and the Air National Guard

Our Air National Guard and Air Reserve forces are not only good, they are in many cases better than the regulars. They often win competitions against the regular forces, despite (or perhaps in part because of) their older, less complex, supposedly inferior equipment.

A substantial portion of our overall air strength is found in the reserves of the army, navy, air force and marines and the Air and Army National Guard: 4,899 of our military aircraft belong to the reserve and guard. Many reserve and guard pilots have several thousand flight hours in the same type of aircraft, far more than the average active duty lieutenant or captain. Their maintenance personnel are long-term, often working on the same aircraft for decades, and they are true experts. Air Reserve and Air National Guard units are cohesive, with the same people serving together for many years, often with one maintenance crew serving the airplane of one pilot for years.

The air guard is also much more oriented toward integrated bombing than the regular air force. The air force, not much liking its one ground-support aircraft, the A-10, pushed many of them into the guard and reserve as quickly as possible. They could not have done the ground troops a greater service. The guard wants to support the soldier on the ground, and guard A-10 units provide the best air support any ground unit is going to find anywhere.

In return for its effectiveness and its efficiency, we should expand the Air Reserve and Air National Guard, relying on them even more heavily than we already do. Unlike the situation in Army Reserve and Guard units, recruiting is seldom a problem:

people fly airplanes and also work on them because they enjoy it. We can recruit the people to support additional missions for the guard and reserve, and we should listen to their opinions about the type of equipment they need to carry them out. We should let the Air National Guard control the selection of its own aircraft. And because of the guard's genuine commitment to integrated bombing, we should let it run the fly-off competition to select the Combined Arms Fighter—for the regular air force as well as for itself.

VISTA 1999, the excellent study of the future of the Air and Army National Guard written by a group of National Guard generals, should be the blueprint for the future of the Air National Guard and, by extension, the Air Reserve as well. The secretary of defense should simply give the authors of that study the directive, "Go to it!" And he should give them the money and the backing they would need against the inevitable resistance of the regular service bureaucracies.

Summary
The changes military reform will bring to the air forces are no less drastic than those it will mean for the navy. New basic concepts, new doctrine, very different equipment, increased and improved training, many more "teeth" for the amount of "tail," and a reserve and guard much stronger relative to the regular forces: these are not minor changes. Can they really be carried out? It won't be easy, but it will be easier than losing the next air war or losing the next ground war because our air force wasn't supporting our soldiers.

4

The Defense Budget

NEITHER HERE NOR ELSEWHERE will this book say how large the defense budget should be. There is no consensus within the military reform movement on the size of the defense budget, nor has there been any effort to get such a consensus. Some reformers favor a larger budget, some a smaller budget. Most recognize that, barring unforeseeable, major shifts in the international situation or domestic politics, cuts or increases in defense spending are likely to be a matter of a few percent either way.

Further, if history is any guide, a period of sustained growth in defense spending is usually followed by a period of sustained reductions and vice versa. Looked at over the long term, for example, from FY 1950 to FY 1985, the annual growth rate of the defense budget has been quite modest—discounting inflation, about 1 percent per year, on average. Since 1981, growth has been much higher, but it now seems clear that these large increases were a temporary phenomenon.

However, during that time some important changes took place. The real-dollar costs of buying and operating weapons have grown tremendously, with the result that the same amount of money buys a far smaller force than it used to. According to one recent air force study, today's lightweight fighter, the F-16, is 1.75 times more expensive than its 1954 counterpart, the F-104; the F-15 fighter is 14 times more expensive than its equivalent of 1951, the F-100; and the B-1 bomber will be about 11.5 times more expensive than the B-52 of 1951. In all these comparisons, inflation has been discounted; all prices in the air force study were in 1981 dollars.[1]

The following table puts this problem of cost growth into stunning perspective by comparing the budgets and quantities of aircraft procured for the air force and navy during the four-year periods of FY 1953–FY 1956 and FY 1982–FY 1985.

	PERIODS		
	FY53–FY56	FY82–FY85	Change
Cumulative Aircraft Procurement Budget of Air Force and Navy (FY86 Dollars)	$121 billion	$137 billion	+13%
Cumulative Aircraft Procured (Air Force and Navy):			
Fighter/Attack	10,644	1,284	−88%
Strategic Bombers	856	52	−94%
Transports, trainers, helicopters, etc.	6,181	485	−92%
Total	17,681	1,821	−91%

Notwithstanding a 13 percent increase in constant dollar budgets, total procurement is down by 91 percent. Clearly, this kind of cost growth must ultimately translate into involuntary unilateral disarmament.

Not surprisingly, the total size of our armed forces has shrunk. In 1957, we had a navy of around 1,200 ships, an army of twenty divisions, and an air force of 26,000 aircraft. Today we have 543 ships, seventeen army divisions, and 9,367 airplanes in the air force. Further, ammunition stocks, supplies of spare parts, and war reserves are generally low, often dangerously so. Training time is often inadequate. Readiness is low. Overall, our defense dollars don't buy nearly as much defense as they used to.

This is not because we have planned to get weaker. One administration after another, Republican and Democrat, has planned to increase the number of weapons we buy, improve the ammunition and spare parts situations, and increase readiness. But the realities have not matched the plans. We have planned to get stronger, but we have actually gotten weaker.

Why has this happened? What do we need to do to correct it? Regardless of what size defense budget someone supports, he does not want to find that when the money has been spent, he has gotten results exactly the opposite of what he wanted. The best work on this problem has been done by a defense department analyst named Franklin C. (Chuck) Spinney. Several years ago, a briefing he wrote called "Defense Facts of Life" got a great deal of attention when, over the objections of Secretary of Defense Harold Brown, it was presented to several congressional committees. He has since prepared a study titled *The Plans/Reality Mismatch* that goes into the problem in greater depth.[2]

According to Spinney, the roots of the mismatch problem lie in the internal decision process of the Department of Defense. The five-year plans produced by this process are plagued by a destructive pattern of optimistic assumptions. First, each year's decisions are based on the assumption of steadily rising budgets for the next five years. Second, notwithstanding the steady introduction of more complex equipment, the department's plans assume that operating budgets will grow at a slower rate than the overall budget. Third, by presuming slow future growth in the operating budget, planners can assume even higher future growth in the new equipment procurement budget. Finally, planners make the optimistic assumption that unit procurement costs will substantially decrease during the five-year planning period. This pattern of assumptions makes it possible—on paper—to pack the procurement budget with more programs.

The fifth year of the five-year plan looks rosy under these assumptions. However, we never get there, because the pressures created by the errors in the assumptions reinforce each other and unravel the plan. Overall budgets come in lower than predicted. Because high-complexity weapons prove more expensive to operate, there is continuing pressure to increase the operating budget —just to maintain low readiness. The net effect is to squeeze the procurement budget. Rising unit procurement costs magnify the squeeze. Compounding these basic pressures are, first, the historical fact that neither the Pentagon nor the Congress likes to relieve the pressure by canceling programs, and second, the fact that both the Pentagon and the Congress approve new programs with long-term consequences when budgets are increased in the short-term. This was clearly the case in FY 1982 and FY 1983.

This situation is similar to superheated steam that continues to be heated in a boiler—sooner or later, the boiler must blow off steam. Theoretically, there are four ways to do this.

First, we can increase the size of the defense budget. However, even proponents of increased defense spending have a problem here, because when costs grow unexpectedly, spending must increase more than they had planned. Second, we can further cut readiness or the size of our armed forces—reducing real defense strength. Third, we can buy fewer weapons, again weakening our defenses. Or fourth, we can simply cancel major weapons programs. Without weakening our defenses, we could cancel a number of programs today for weapons that don't work; however, future unexpected cost growth could force cancellations of programs for needed, effective weapons. Again, the result would be weaker defenses. Further, all these alternatives are just short-term adjustments. They do nothing to keep the same problems from reemerging.

In *The Plans/Reality Mismatch,* Spinney notes the role that weapons complexity plays in this pattern of mutually reinforcing pressures:

> In the short-term, we tried to hold down operating (i.e., personnel, Operations and Maintenance, and readiness related procurement) budgets while pumping growth into procurement (i.e., modernization) budgets. At the same time, we modernized with more complex equipment that is more expensive to buy, operate, and support . . . Over the long-term, the only way the operating budget could be held down was to maintain low readiness while shrinking the size of the force. However, the massive force reduc-

tions of the last 25 years were not able to offset the growth in the cost of low readiness; and consequently, it was also necessary, over the long-term, to shift the allocation of funds away from modernization and into the operating accounts. The fact that the overall defense budget has fluctuated up and down during this period tended to mask these internal dynamics.

The rising cost of even low readiness is relatively simple to understand. Over the past thirty years, weapons have grown steadily more complex. As we have seen in earlier chapters, that does not necessarily mean they have grown more effective. In many cases, simpler weapons would work better in combat. But wisely or not, the Pentagon has bought more complex weapons. An F-86 fighter of the Korean War had one engine, no search radar, and only four to eight major electronic components. An F-15 fighter of today has two engines, a complex radar, and approximately forty major electronic components. In tanks, ships, and other major pieces of equipment, the trend has been the same. Not surprisingly, these new weapons cost more to operate, fix, and train with than their predecessors. The relationship between increasing weapons complexity and rising operating costs is logical. Once the services decided to define capability largely in terms of increasing complexity, the increase in operating costs was unavoidable.

But what of the unexpected cost growth? Why has it persisted as *unexpected* growth? Since it has been occurring regularly for decades, why has it continued to take us by surprise? Why aren't the cost estimates for new weapons programs more accurate, since they have the experience of past programs to draw on?

There are two levels of answers to these questions. The first explains what happens to the early, overly optimistic cost estimates. The second looks at the reasons why we continue to make those early estimates so optimistic.

Chuck Spinney examines both sets of answers in *The Plans/ Reality Mismatch*. First, he notes that we still expect weapons costs to decline sharply as production rates rise. In the Five-Year Defense Program put forward in February of 1982, cost decreases (in terms of cost per unit) were projected for many major weapons between FY 1983 and FY 1987. The cost of the M-X was projected to decrease by 81 percent, the B-1 bomber by 78 percent, the AV-8B VSTOL attack plane by 65 percent, the AH-64 attack helicopter by 59 percent, the F-18 fighter by 39 percent, the SSN-688 attack submarine by 29 percent, and the F-15 fighter by 26 percent. All figures reflected real costs, adjusted for inflation.

Why does the Pentagon expect these cost decreases? The first reason is amortization of initial costs. According to Spinney, many of the programs for which the largest cost decreases were projected were in the early stages of production:

> For these programs, start-up costs . . . are high and production rates are low; and because the overhead is spread over few units, unit costs are very high. Later, as production rates increase, the overhead will be spread over more units and one-time costs will cease and consequently unit costs will decline. . . . If we over-estimate this decline, the program can be seriously underfunded, and *after* a significant sunk cost we will be faced with the unexpected options of increasing the budget, reducing production rates, or cancelling the program . . .
>
> Contrary to the economic theory of sunk cost being an irrelevant factor in future decisions, it is common knowledge in the defense business (and government in general) that such sunk costs establish constituent pressures—both in government and out of government—that strongly influence future decisions. Generally, in such situations, it becomes difficult to cancel programs and we are condemned to even higher cost low-rate production stretch-outs.

A second reason the Pentagon expects costs to decline is the production "learning curve." The learning curve suggests that as production increases, costs decline. According to *The Plans/Reality Mismatch,* this is possible up to a point. There are four basic reasons: workers become more familiar with their jobs, but it doesn't take very long for an experienced machinist to learn how to set up a jig; management does the same with the same limited effect; production techniques are improved with experience, but sooner or later production lines stabilize; and fixed overhead gets spread over more units.

Moreover, for these factors to have effect, four other conditions must be met: the design must be fixed; the work force must be stable; flows of parts and raw materials must be stable; and planned quantities of weapons and budgets must not change. However, Spinney states:

> If there is one thing that does *not* characterize defense planning, it is this kind of stability: designs continuously change; flows of parts and materials are interrupted constantly; production rates change, in part because of cost and budget changes; budgets change sharply from year to year; etc. Many of these instabilities are built-in to the political/bureaucratic/economic environment influencing our plans and decisions, and, therefore, cannot be eliminated.

Overoptimism about amortization of initial costs and the effect of the learning curve are reinforced by a problem called the "procurement bow-wave." The procurement bow-wave means that we tend to start a large number of expensive new programs in a short time, believing we can fund them in the future because the procurement share of the defense budget will grow, while the operating budget grows more slowly. However, as we have noted, the complexity of the new equipment actually drives up operating costs over time, creating pressure to reduce rather than increase the share of the budget available for procurement. The present administration has projected exactly this kind of "bow-wave," as have previous administrations of both parties.

Again, Spinney points out that reality is likely to be otherwise:

> Although the bow-wave has been a characteristic of our five-year plans for years, it has *never* materialized . . . Since the equipment coming into the inventory over the next five years continues to be more expensive to operate and support than the equipment being replaced, since force size is projected to grow in the future, and because readiness was allowed to atrophy during the 1970s

(in effect, running up a deferred readiness cost), there is strong reason to suspect that the operating budget will continue its upward trend—perhaps at a faster rate than planned. Whether or not we can sustain a procurement bow-wave in the presence of this increasing cost pressure is highly uncertain. The best that can be said about a modernization plan premised upon a bow-wave assumption is that it is an optimistic high-risk plan which relies on a historically discredited assumption.

When we put all these factors together—the dangers of overestimating the results of amortizing production costs, optimistic expectations about the production learning curve, and the bow-wave—we begin to see why our plans have repeatedly resulted in realities very different from what we expected or intended. Nor do recent plans look like an exception. Between FY 1983 and FY 1987, the M-X's cost was projected to decrease by 81 percent; by FY 1986, it had actually decreased by .9 percent. The B-1 was projected to decrease by 78 percent; the actual decrease was 5 percent. The F-15, 26 percent decrease projected, 16 percent *increase* achieved; AH-64 attack helicopter, 59 percent decrease projected, 52 percent achieved; F-18, 39 percent decrease projected, 2 percent increase achieved; SSN-688, 29 percent decrease projected, 1.8 percent increase achieved.

Further, overestimates of inflation through this period gave the Defense Department a $20- to $50-billion dollar slush fund (the General Accounting Office says $36 billion) in which to hide cost growth. The cost increases of these programs are therefore understated, and the cost decreases overstated.

And what has happened to recent plans for major force modernization? We can look at a four-year period, that from FY 1983 to FY 1986. In January 1982, the Defense Department projected that we would, in FY 1986, buy 96 F-15 fighters for the air force, 1,080 M-1 tanks for the army, 132 F-18 fighters for the navy, and 60 AV-8B attack aircraft for the marines. In the actual FY 1986 budget, the figures are 48 F-15s, 840 M-1s, 84 F-18s, and 46 AV-8Bs.

Why do we continue to make the same errors over and over

again? Who benefits? Those who want to reduce the defense budget find that they face pressures to increase it. Those who want to increase our military strength find we must buy fewer new weapons than we thought we could. What keeps a system going that produces results nobody wants?

The basic answer is that short-term political and economic pressures overwhelm long-term military considerations in our defense planning process. Short-term incentives to start new programs are very strong. A new program means a new sub-bureaucracy in whatever armed service starts it, with new jobs, new chances for advancement and promotion, and a new claim the service can use to increase its share of the overall defense budget. Defense contractors benefit from new start-ups. They cannot make money from a program that isn't there, but they almost always make money from an ongoing program, even if unit costs soar above those initially projected and production rates fall. This leads them to "buy in," to make an initial bid that is unrealistically low, which in turn is reinforced by the Pentagon's tendency to be optimistic about costs. Congress also plays a large role. A new production program means dollars and jobs for congressional districts and states. Members of Congress who support a defense contractor's efforts to start a new program may also benefit in campaign funds from the contractor's political action committee. In the short term, politicians, the uniformed bureaucrats, and the contractors benefit. But they benefit at the expense of the nation's long-term well-being.

In contrast, long-term considerations do not weigh very heavily in planning. Congress budgets one year at a time. The Defense Department has a five-year plan, but Spinney's analysis shows that future-year projections merely rationalize short-term decisions. The press focuses on this year's budget, not projections for future years. Congressmen, military officers, and Defense Department political appointees often serve only a couple years in positions that relate to a specific program.

Pressures to think long-term are as weak as short-term considerations are strong. The result is a decision-making system that rewards new program starts while exacting few penalties for failure to attain long-term goals—except, of course, the penalty of defense weakness. And nobody loses his job for that.

What do we need to do differently? First, we must project more realistic overall defense budgets. Second, we need to reprice the Five-Year Defense Program on a historically realistic basis. Long-term projected program costs must reflect past realities. Projected savings through initial cost amortization and the learning curve must reflect what has happened, not what we would like to have happen. The procurement bow-wave must get similar historically realistic treatment.

The one-time result will be a five-year plan that either reduces the number of weapons we plan to buy or raises the overall defense budget for conventional forces. Neither will be easy politically. Unless we can increase overall defense spending, assuming we want to maintain current readiness and economic production rates, we will have to cancel a number of programs outright. Jobs and money will be lost. Contractors, service bureaucracies, congressional districts, and states will all suffer, and they will all set up a howl. The alternative, a large increase in the defense budget, might be better if the nation could afford it. But with the deficit already hovering around $200 billion annually, it cannot. There should be no doubt in anyone's mind: facing up to historical reality in defense budgeting will result in a nasty shock.

But after that one-time shock, we will have a far better chance of matching plans and realities. We will be able to project future buys of ships, tanks, and fighters with far greater assurance that, when the future comes, we will be able to buy the number we had planned on. We will no longer have to choose between unplanned increases in defense spending or smaller buys of weapons we need. We will no longer have to choose between budgetary disaster or military weakness.

Assuming we can make the politically tough choice to reprice the defense budget on a historically realistic basis, how can we keep old habits from creeping back in? If all the short-term pressures stay as strong as they are and long-term considerations as weak as they are, why won't we just return to the practice of starting programs we can't pay for? Clearly, unless the balance between long- and short-term considerations is readjusted to give more weight to the former, we probably will. We need to change the system to give increased weight to long-term planning.

PART

TWO

The Reasons Why

A s we have seen, the defense superstructure is riddled with serious problems. Many concepts are outdated or poorly thought out; we wrongly define "quality" in weapons to mean the complexity of the technology they embody rather than how well they perform in combat; our navy is more a museum than a modern fighting force; training is inadequate and often too rigid; the officer surplus generates bureaucracy and centralization; and the way we budget for defense insures results precisely the opposite of those we intend. Each of these problems is serious. Any one of them, if left to fester further, could cause us to lose a battle, maybe a campaign or a war. Together, they suggest that we are in serious danger.

To provide for the common defense, we need to move swiftly and firmly to root out each superstructure deficiency. Saying that a problem is part of the superstructure does not mean it is unimportant. The superstructure is, after all, what the enemy encounters on the battlefield. A competent enemy will quickly find any weaknesses in it and exploit them ruthlessly—to our undoing.

But we cannot address superstructure problems successfully if we do not look beyond them. They tell us *what* is wrong in many important areas, but they leave unanswered the question, *why?* Why have we made so many blunders in the superstructure? Why have we not seen our errors and changed our ways long ago? What underlying problems have led to the deficiencies in the defense superstructure?

5

The Officer Corps

"THERE ARE NO BAD TROOPS—only bad officers." This old saw has some truth to it. In the early 1970s, when we first went to an all-volunteer military, the low quality of many enlistees did cause serious problems. Many of the people we took in had low levels of self-discipline, basic skills, and ability to learn, which created insoluble problems in training, leadership, and unit discipline. But today, almost any officer you talk with will be quick to praise the troops. Since the late 1970s, a combination of improved military pay and reduced job opportunities for young people in the civilian economy has brought in high-quality recruits. For example, in 1973 only 49.6 percent of the people joining the Marine Corps had high school diplomas. Today the figure is 95.8 percent. Anyone who encounters these young marines or their soldier, sailor, or airman counterparts is quickly impressed with their positive attitude, intelligence, and seriousness about their work. They are first-class troops, a credit to their services and their country.

This means our officers have high-quality raw material from which to build an effective military. But it also means that many of the deficiencies in our defense superstructure must be traced to problems in the officer corps. We cannot blame the troops. Civilians in the Defense Department and the Congress share the responsibility for our defense inadequacies. But a significant portion of our defense superstructure problems are traceable to deficiencies in the officer corps.

This does not mean most officers are individually to blame. The problems are systemic. For the most part, our officers are themselves victims of the current system. The problems are rooted in the officer surplus and in the way we educate and promote our officers —matters over which only the most senior officers have any control. That is why so many younger officers are themselves part of the military reform movement. They know the superstructure shortcomings are not due to laziness, disinterest, or lack of dedication on their part. Few other groups in our society put as much effort into their work as our military officers. Sixty- and even eighty-hour workweeks are common. Working conditions are often bad. Physical discomfort and danger, separation from family, and inadequacy of material with which to do the job are the rule, not the exception. Pay, although much improved in recent years, is still often low in relation to the responsibilities carried and the stress and hardships of the work itself. No one serves as a military officer to get rich.

But the problems in the officer corps are nonetheless real, as officers themselves are often the first to say. In 1984, the army conducted two surveys of its officers. The first was sent to 23,000 officers ranking from lieutenant through colonel, the second to 436 generals and colonels who had been selected for promotion to general. In the first survey, 14,046 officers replied; 333 responded to the second. Both surveys revealed some serious problems in the officer corps. Of the generals, 45 percent felt that "senior Army leaders behave too much like corporate executives and not enough like warriors." Of the younger officers, 49 percent (though only 25 percent of the generals) said that "the bold, original, creative officer cannot survive in today's Army." Of the younger officers, 68 percent (and a full third of the generals) agreed that "the officer corps is focused on personal gain rather than selflessness." A summary of the survey results sent to all army generals by the chief of staff added that

> Most [officers] feel that only half or less of their peers would make good wartime leaders . . . Thirty-two percent agree most officers are promoted before becoming competent at their exist-

ing grade level . . . General officers disagree with the statement that "the promotion system does not reward those officers who have the seasoning and potential to be the best wartime leaders"; commissioned officers (as a whole) tend to agree with that statement . . . General officers and commissioned officers tend to agree that the weakest areas of officer preparation tend to be warfighting, leadership, and critical thinking.[1]

The fact that the army undertook such surveys is greatly to its credit. It is another example of the army's own self-reform movement at work. Only by identifying problems such as those found in the surveys and moving to correct them can the services hope to restore combat effectiveness. It is a comment on the navy's, air force's, and Marine Corps' head-in-the-sand approach to their problems that they have made no move to follow the army's example and survey their own officers on similar questions.

Why do these problems exist? What needs to be changed in the officer corps to eliminate them? There are three basic answers: the officer surplus, the military education system, and the "up or out" promotion system.

The Officer Surplus

The problem of the officer surplus has already been noted. While there is no surplus of junior officers—indeed, there is generally a shortage of junior officers—there is a large surplus of officers in the ranks of major/lieutenant commander and above.[2] This surplus causes much of the bureaucratization and centralization that plague our armed services and reduce their military effectiveness. Since there are far fewer real jobs—those that actually need to be done—than there are middle- and senior-ranking officers, vast numbers of make-work jobs are created. To compete for promotion, officers must be very busy in these unnecessary jobs, and their activity results in the generation of paper, in pushing decisions to ever higher levels, and in doing everything by committee consensus.

What is to be done? In each service, the size of the officer corps from the level of major/lieutenant commander on up should be reduced by 50 percent. That may not ultimately prove to be a sufficient reduction, but it would make a good start. There would not be enough officers left to perform all the jobs that now exist. That is of course the idea—to eliminate many of those jobs. There would not be enough officers to rotate unit commanders frequently. Many decisions made by senior officers would have to be delegated to those less senior. Noncommissioned officers would have to be made responsible for many tasks now done by commissioned officers. The authority of individual officers remaining in such areas as manpower and weapons programs would have to be expanded to encompass the achievement of goals, not just filling out reports and attending committee meetings. Many of those committee meetings would have to be replaced with decisions made by one person and traceable to that one person. There would not be enough officers left to fill out or to read all the reports the system now requires. All of these changes are, in our view, highly desirable.

The 50 percent reduction in the number of middle- and senior-ranking officers should not be accomplished through a Reduction In Force (RIF), such as that which followed the end of the Korean and Vietnam Wars, in which officers were simply fired. Those RIFs severely hurt the morale of the officer corps, and reformers do not want to do that. The goal is to free officers from the tentacles of bureaucracy, not leave them wondering whether they will be able to feed their families. Therefore, the mechanism for reducing the size of the officer corps should be to allow those officers who are identified as surplus to retire early, whether or not they have completed the twenty years of service normally required to qualify for retired pay.[3]

The process of selecting which officers will be asked to retire early must be controlled by the kind of officers we need to retain: by tacticians, trainers, and leaders—by warriors, not by bureaucrats in uniform, office politicians, and courtiers. Just as promotion boards tend to clone themselves, so the boards that will identify officers for early retirement will tend to retain clones. We need to clone warriors, not milicrats. This does *not* mean the retirement boards should be made up exclusively of officers from the combat arms. Whether an officer is a warrior or a milicrat is not a function of his branch. Both can be found among officers from the combat arms, and both can be identified from among officers from fields such as logistics. It does mean the members of the boards must be chosen very carefully as individuals. Here as elsewhere, there is no "objective" or mechanical substitute for personal, subjective judgment.

Military Education

The second basic cause of problems in our officer corps is the current military education system. Most of our officers are not well educated in the art of war. That is not their fault. It is the result of the way we structure military education.

Throughout our society, not just in the military, the word "education" has lost a great deal of its meaning. People speak of a "high school education." They assume any college will automatically "provide an education." Virtually any sort of instruction is presumed to have "educational value."

But education is much more than the learning of skills or the acquisition of facts. Education means acquiring a broad understanding of our culture, our civilization. It means knowing our culture's basic ideas, principles, and values, not just as terms or buzzwords, but as tools for shaping thought. That knowledge must include history—how our culture came to be what it is and why. Education develops an ability to put immediate situations into a larger context built of history, philosophy, and an understanding of human nature. Inherent in true education is an ability to think logically and to approach problem solving methodically but without a predetermined set of solutions. True education is really what is called "classical education." It has changed little since Thomas Jefferson's day, and not all that much since the days of Thomas Aquinas.

True military education is a more specialized version of general education. It must give the student a thorough grounding in the art of war—the soldier's culture. He must come to understand the guiding concepts of his profession, why they are held to be true, and how they evolved. He must be able to put whatever military situation he faces into a larger context built of military history, military theory, and an understanding of how people behave in combat. He must come to understand why ethics are central to what it means to be an officer. His education must give him an ability to think logically and creatively about war and in war. It must teach *how* to think, not what to do or what to think.

That is not what our various military academies, schools, and colleges do today. For the most part, they teach little military history or theory. The curricula focus on engineering, management, staff processes and procedures, formats, forms, and terms. Instead of teaching creative thinking—how to think—they emphasize school solutions, set ways of doing things: what to do and what to think. There are exceptions to this in individual schools and in individual instructors in all schools. But the norm is illustrated by what one instructor recently told his students at the Marine Corps Command and Staff College: "Don't worry about the tactics, just get the format right."

The Military Academies

Most officers receive their undergraduate education from a civilian college. However, the military academies play an important role in forming our officer corps. Together, the three academies—the Military Academy at West Point, the Naval Academy at Annapolis, and the Air Force Academy at Colorado Springs—graduate about three thousand men and women annually. These graduates provide a large proportion of our senior officers. For example, only 15 percent of all army officers are West Point graduates, but 31 percent of all army generals entered the officer corps by graduating from the academy.

Unfortunately, the art of war has only a small place in the curricula of these schools. The focus is on science, math, and engineering. This made sense in the early days of our country, when West Point was founded. The country needed civil engineers more than it needed soldiers. Today we have many top-quality civilian engineering schools. Yet the curricula at the academies remain heavily focused on engineering and other scientific and mathematical subjects.

Military history is the basis of a military education. Yet West Point requires just two one-semester courses in military history— a recent increase from a single course. Annapolis requires just one semester, the Air Force Academy one, plus three-and-a-half semesters of "military studies." At no academy can a cadet spend most of his time studying the art of war.

There are some signs the academies are moving to give greater emphasis to warfare. The military history faculty at West Point is excellent, even though most cadets take only the required two semesters of military history. The military studies courses at the Air Force Academy, which were added to the required curriculum in 1980, introduce cadets to such subjects as air power theory and doctrine, combat leadership, and the writings of great military thinkers, such as Sun Tzu and von Clausewitz. These are positive developments, but they are not enough to produce well-educated officers.

Nor do the academies provide a classical education. In this they are no worse than the vast majority of civilian colleges and universities. But they are no better either. Few academy students graduate with more than a cursory overview of how the West came to be as it is, the ideas that define it, what its values are, and why we deem them valuable. History, literature, and philosophy are the bases of a classical education, but they all receive short shrift at the academies. On the whole, like most of their civilian counterparts, cadets and midshipmen are trained, not educated. They receive far less true education than students got at William and Mary two hundred years ago.

If we cannot say much in favor of the subjects taught at the academies, what about the method of teaching? Does it teach people how to think, or just how to absorb large numbers of facts and regurgitate them in tests? While some departments and individual instructors are exceptions, the academies are generally notorious for the latter. Midshipmen and cadets are subjected to such heavy work loads and tested so intensively for factual knowledge that they have very little time to think. In this the academies are markedly worse off than most civilian schools, where students do have more time to think, to pursue personal intellectual interests, and to give their minds time and opportunity to wander creatively.[4]

Measuring cadets' and midshipmen's performance by the ability to swallow, then spit back large quantities of facts at the expense of giving them time to think is not the way to produce officers who can think creatively in the stress and chaos of combat. It leads to mental rigidity, thinking in formulas, and looking for cookbook answers to problems.

What should we do instead? First, regardless of the subjects taught, the method should emphasize how to think, and cadets should be given time for thinking. Second, the curricula should be reformed drastically to emphasize general, classical education combined with the military art, the latter taught primarily through military history. The military needs some engineers, but they can be obtained at far less cost (to keep just one cadet at West Point for a year costs about $50,000) through Reserve Officers Training Corps programs at civilian colleges and universities. The academy graduate's primary distinction from other officers should not be an academy ring, but a much deeper understanding of the art of war, coupled with a true education. So educated, academy graduates could play a major role in shifting the officer corps' self-image to that of the warrior and the creative thinker.

What of the higher level schools and colleges for officers? A survey of some of each service's more important schools shows both problems and some prospects for positive change.

The Army

The army's most important schools are the branch schools—the Infantry School and the Armor School in particular—that officers attend as second lieutenants, at the beginning of their careers, and again later at the rank of captain; the relatively new Combined Arms Staff Service School at Fort Leavenworth, Kansas, which is bringing a major improvement in army staff skills; the Command and General Staff College, also at Fort Leavenworth, which is attended by about 45 percent of army majors; and the Army War College in Carlisle, Pennsylvania, where specially selected lieutenant colonels and colonels study. The courses at the branch schools run about twenty weeks; those at Fort Leavenworth and Carlisle, for a single academic year.

The branch schools have been intellectual backwaters for at least the past several decades. Learning has been mostly rote. Faculty selection, preparation, and reward have generally been weak, with most faculty little senior to or more knowledgeable than the students, and with a faculty tour looked on as "not career enhancing." Faculty have generally been expected to teach material prepared by others and have not been expected to have any real understanding of infantry warfare, armored warfare or whatever the school is focused on, except at the technique level. In the mid-1970s, a visitor to the Infantry School at Fort Benning, Georgia, attempted to discuss prospective future developments in infantry warfare. A meeting with selected faculty members ended when the senior officer present said, with regrettable accuracy, "We simply are not prepared to discuss infantry warfare at the Infantry School."

However, the army's own reform movement is beginning to touch these schools, with positive results. Both the Infantry School at Fort Benning, and the Armor School at Fort Knox, Kentucky, are beginning to grapple with the fundamental changes in officer education that must follow from the army's adoption of maneuver warfare as doctrine. Maneuver warfare requires junior as well as senior officers who can think creatively, who understand tactics, as well as techniques, and who can think "two levels up." For a lieutenant to command a platoon effectively in maneuver warfare, he must be able to understand what is happening and what his commander is thinking not just at the company level but also at the battalion level.

If they are to prepare officers effectively for maneuver warfare, the branch schools must become centers of thinking in whatever branch they teach. Teaching and thinking cannot be divorced; if a school tries to teach by having instructors merely read out of books prepared elsewhere, the teaching will be rote and oriented to teaching what to do, not how to think. This means faculty selection, preparation, and reward take on new importance. Not everyone can teach effectively. Not every competent company commander can think broadly enough about his branch of warfare to serve on a faculty. Many of those who have the potential to do both will still need substantial preparation time to do the reading and thinking about their warfare specialty that regular service seldom provides. A year's preparation for faculty would not be excessive, and it may be necessary to have some permanent faculty who teach the teachers. Career rewards for a successful tour as an instructor should be at least equal to those for successful completion of a command tour. The army is beginning to make some moves in these directions. Officer education is perhaps the single most important activity in a military, and it should not be shortchanged in any way. If that means more resources are needed, they will be a good investment.

The Command and General Staff College at Fort Leavenworth is currently the bright spot, not just in army education but in American military education generally. The yearlong regular course is still focused somewhat too much on procedures, too little on how to think tactically. But the army recently added a new, second-year course for a small number of outstanding students from the regular course. This new course is the finest educational program offered by any service, and it points the way to a bright new future for army education. The entire year is devoted to the art of warfare, not terminology or procedures. It is built around extensive historical study, campaign analysis, and war-gaming. The army chose one of its most outstanding military theoreticians, Colonel Huba Wass de Czege, the author of the new field manual *FM 100-5,* to design the course and serve as its first director, and he in turn chose faculty who knew how to think and how to teach others how to think. The instruction includes not just tactics but also the operational art: the art of the campaign, of using tactical events to strike at the enemy's strategic center of gravity. By order of the chief of staff of the army, graduates are guaranteed an "internship" on the staff of a division or corps, where they can both build their own knowledge further and work to improve the army's battle and campaign plans.

The second-year course is similar in many ways to the finest tactical and operational school in modern history: the famed German *Kriegsakademie* of the prewar period. The *Kriegsakademie* played the major role in preparing German officers to exhibit the tactical and operational excellence that so strongly marked the old German army. There is every reason to believe the Fort Leavenworth course can do the same for us, leading to true excellence in our army's thinking. It should be a model not only for other army schools but also for the schools of the other services as well.

Unfortunately, the revolution at Fort Leavenworth has not yet spread to the Army War College at Carlisle. Despite some excellent faculty, the Army War College remains something of a rest home, a place to send officers who have performed well for a nice, relaxing year. This is unfortunate because it leaves a major gap in the preparation of army officers for war. The gap is strategy. The Army War College should be preparing strategists the way the second-year course at Fort Leavenworth is preparing tacticians and practitioners of the operational art. The method should be largely the same: intensive study of military history, campaign analysis and war-gaming, with the emphasis on how to think. A follow-on assignment to an appropriate staff billet, one where strategic plans are prepared, should be guaranteed. If we emulate German excellence in educating officers at the tactical and operational levels but neglect the strategic level, we will have copied the Germans' greatest error.

The Navy

Until a naval officer attends the Naval War College at Newport, Rhode Island, almost all of his education is technical: how to fly an airplane, run a high-pressure steam- or gas-turbine propulsion plant, or operate the nuclear machinery of a submarine. In at least some of the technical schools, an effort is under way to put more emphasis on tactics and to teach how to think, not just what to do. The Surface Warfare School recently made some interesting changes along these lines, and they are to the good. But the bulk of the time in the Surface Warfare course, like that in counterpart navy schools, is devoted to the technical side.

That unfortunately puts the Naval War College in an essentially impossible position, because it is both the first navy school an officer will attend that looks beyond the technical level, and the last: it is the highest navy school. There are two courses at the War College, the junior and the senior, but few students attend both, and the course material is largely the same.

The yearlong course is the best that is offered by any of our war colleges. It is divided into trimesters: one on strategy and policy, one on defense decision making, and one on naval operations. The first is heavily historical. It begins with the Peloponnesian Wars and brings the student to the present through a series of case studies of national policy and strategy, with the emphasis on policy. It is well structured, well taught, and does as much as can be done in fourteen weeks.

Unfortunately, fourteen weeks is not enough to produce a strategist. One faculty member recently said, "Our goal is to have the students leave the course saying to themselves, 'The world is a lot more complicated than I thought.' " That is a worthwhile achievement, but again, hardly enough to give the navy competent strategists.

The same is true for the defense decision making and naval operations courses. Because of time constraints, they are necessarily broadbrush. Naval operations is especially important, because previous schools have spent little time on tactics or the operational art. But the time is too short to do much more than to explain to one branch of the navy a bit about the others: to tell submariners a little about air and surface warfare, for example. That is not enough to give us naval officers who can think creatively in combat.

These problems cannot be solved by changing the content of the single-year course. The job cannot be done in one year. Instead, the first-year course should be used both to give a large number of naval officers the broadbrush look now provided and also to identify officers with aptitude for further schooling, especially in strategy and naval operations. Those officers should then attend a second-year course, modeled on the one at Fort Leavenworth. Selection for the second-year course should be looked on as a mark of highest distinction and be rewarded in career terms.

At the same time, junior courses should be extended as necessary to give more thorough treatment to naval tactics, with the emphasis on how to think tactically. Technical knowledge is very important, but it is the raw material of tactics, not a substitute for tactics. A navy that is technically excellent but unimaginative in its tactics will inevitably be pushed by its own rigidity and predictability into a war of attrition. The junior-level schools must teach tactics if our navy is to avoid this. Again, if that means more resources are needed for instructors, time for instructor preparation, course length, and so on—all of which eventually translate into money—they will be one of the best investments we can make.

The Air Force

The air force, like the navy, is highly technical, and most officer education follows suit. Despite the technical demands of air warfare, this is unfortunate. An officer may have to understand such matters, but he should never be a mere technician.[5] Officers who can lead, who can wrestle successfully with conceptual issues, who can think creatively about war and in war are as necessary in the air force as in the other services.

The air force currently has three schools that should educate air force officers toward these ends: the Squadron Officer School for first lieutenants and junior captains, the Air Command and Staff College for junior majors, and the Air War College for lieutenant colonels and colonels. All three are located together at Maxwell Air Force Base in Montgomery, Alabama. The Squadron Officer School offers an eight-and-one-half week course; the courses at the other two schools run for one academic year. Fifty-four percent of all air force officers attend Squadron Officer School, while only 14 percent of all officers attend Command and Staff, and only 12 percent the Air War College.

The Air War College and the Air Command and Staff College face a problem similar to that of the Naval War College. In the face of the almost exclusively technical background of most of those entering, a one-year course can do little beyond broadening the student's outlook. Neither air force school does this as well as Newport, although some changes have been made over the last several years that have brought some increased emphasis on the art of war. The air force's effort to focus more attention on warfare, called "Project Warrior," has helped in this.

At Air Command and Staff College, which on the whole seems somewhat more open-minded than the Air War College, the bulk of the curriculum hours are now devoted to studying war, and 10 percent of the curriculum is military history. However, just as at Newport, neither school produces educated tacticians or practitioners of the operational art. There simply isn't time. The air force, along with the navy, needs to establish a course parallel to the second-year course at Fort Leavenworth if it wants to have such people in key command and staff positions. It will not get them simply by "broadening" technicians.

Faculty problems at the Air War College and the Air Command and Staff College are similar to those elsewhere. Faculty members are chosen by the centralized personnel bureaucracy, with the schools having only a right of refusal; faculty preparation is minimal; and career rewards for serving as faculty are small or even negative. For a "fast tracker" in the air force, someone who is rising rapidly in rank, a three-year faculty tour is considered a setback, if not a terminal disadvantage.

Both air force colleges also seem somewhat weaker than their counterparts in the army and navy in identifying major issues for their students. Such questions as independent versus integrated bombing and which approach to fighter design is correct seem to be unknown to most faculty members and are generally allowed to pass unremarked in the classrooms. When a recent visitor asked the Air War College department heads what the major air-power issues were, the answers were uninspired: "limited resources," "the joint arena," "inadequate manpower for our force structure" (when precisely the opposite is the case), "becoming familiar with Air Force doctrine," and so on. It was evident the question of what the issues are was not often asked.

Identifying and wrestling with major air-power issues should be a principal function of both schools, and especially of the Air War College, since it is the air force's highest school. Both schools' faculties should be involved in doctrine development. And both faculties should be upgraded substantially, with deans of the colleges given the right to secure whomever they want as faculty. A year's faculty preparation would not be excessive, and career rewards for a successful tour as a faculty member should be high. Being selected as a faculty member should be one of the highest distinctions an air force officer can achieve.

In some ways, the third school at Maxwell, the Squadron Officer School, is the most interesting of the three. Though the course is short, just eight-and-one-half weeks, it is oriented toward leadership, military history, and teaching how to think, including how to think critically about air force policy and doctrine. The atmosphere is much freer than at the two higher schools, with faculty encouraging students to ask tough questions about air force bureaucracy and rigidity. In discussions with a visitor, students were highly positive about the way the school had got them thinking beyond technical issues. Many said the course had been their first brush with military history and that they planned to continue reading history after they left. Squadron Officer School also has an unusual degree of control over its faculty, since it systematically tries to identify students who show promise as future faculty members and bring them back later to teach.

For the air force's schools to be effective in spurring conceptual thought in the air force, one reform that goes beyond the schools themselves is vital. Air force officers must be given adequate freedom to publish controversial articles on military subjects. Today any article or paper written by an air force officer is subject to crippling censorship through the air force "policy review" process. Policy review is run by an office in the Pentagon. That office's approach is highly restrictive. Anything that disagrees with or criticizes air force policy is likely to be denied clearance. Even historical works are not infrequently denied publication. If an air force officer publishes without the policy review office's clearance, he takes serious career risks. In fact, the office sometimes makes explicit threats to officers' careers if they attempt to bypass or ignore it.

The effect is crippling. Most air force thinkers are aware of the policy review problem, and they respond the only way they can: they give up trying to write. The principal air force journal, *Air University Review,* finds it difficult to get air force officers to write for it. School faculties are greatly inhibited in doing what faculties must do if they are to be at the leading edge of thought in their field: write and publish.

This censorship must end. The Pentagon policy review office should be abolished. As long as an officer in the air force attaches a disclaimer stating that his views do not represent official policy, he should be allowed to publish freely on military subjects. This is the policy the other services generally follow, even though they are nominally under the same policy review process as the air force. As two air force captains recently wrote, "A free and open debate is the literary equivalent of capitalism—the concept that everybody can have his or her say (produce a product) and then the market place decides which idea is best (decision makers as consumers of ideas pick the solution they will apply). This type of discussion appears to be taking place in the other three services. Why are we in the U.S. Air Force so different that we cannot stand it?"[6]

The Marine Corps

If the army's new second-year course at Fort Leavenworth is the avant-garde in genuine military education, the Marine Corps' schools are the stragglers at the end of the column. That is both unfortunate and unnecessary. The Marine Corps' schools have a distinguished history, for it was through them that much of the highly innovative work on amphibious warfare was done in the interwar years, work that built the doctrine that carried Allied armies across every beachhead in World War II.

In addition, the marines have one school that reflects a concept the other services would do well to copy: The Basic School. Unlike the army, navy or air force, the marines send all their lieutenants through the same school as soon as they are commissioned. This is The Basic School. It is located in Quantico, Virginia, alongside the Amphibious Warfare School for captains, and the Command

and Staff School for majors and lieutenant colonels. The Basic School does two things. The first is the most important. It is "socializing" marine officers: leading them to accept certain values, standards, and images as defining what it means to be an officer of marines. The Marine Corps rightly puts great emphasis on this, much more than the other services. The traditional strength of the corps is its strong socialization, the strong acceptance by marines of the values and goals of the Marine Corps—combat effectiveness first among them—as their personal goals and values.

The Basic School does this socializing very effectively. Its effectiveness can be measured by the number of young marine officers who have joined the military reform movement in the corps, the movement for maneuver warfare, free-play training, and tactical experimentation. The fact that Marine Corps socialization today breaks down at the colonel/general level into bureaucratic behavior and clique politics is not the fault of The Basic School. No initial socialization can stand up indefinitely to the pressures generated by the officer surplus, the current promotion system, and an emphasis on personal, rather than institutional, loyalty.

Socialization is the very cornerstone of military effectiveness. It is sufficiently important that the army, navy, and air force should institute an equivalent of The Basic School. There are some dangers in this. It can happen that the wrong self-image is preached, one that reflects externals, not essentials. This has in fact happened to some degree at The Basic School, where the marine officer is currently defined too much in terms of how he looks in his uniform and his enthusiasm for jogging. But even with these deficiencies, the overall results of giving all lieutenants a common identity, a common definition of what it means to be a marine, are very positive.

The Basic School also has a second function: teaching lieutenants tactics. In this it is a miserable failure. Not only does it reduce tactics to techniques, to rote, formulistic, cookbook approaches, but the techniques it teaches are also dangerously obsolete. Defenses are still placed on forward slopes where the enemy can plaster them with artillery. Attacks are made in a line of men two deep, at a walk, just like the British at the Somme in 1916. It is as if the principal weapon in ground combat were still the smoothbore musket.

During one field exercise, a visitor to the Second Marine Division came across a defense set up by a recent Basic School graduate. He had dug an antitank ditch across the road and used the dirt from it to form a parapet with a firing step. His marines were lined up on the firing step. A senior noncommissioned officer who was with the visitor took one look and said, "My God, it's the siege of Vicksburg!" He was quite right. It was a tableau straight out of Mathew Brady's photographs.

Effective socialization can be combined with modern tactics and techniques as easily as with those rescued from museums. The Basic School tactics program needs complete revamping. Techniques should be those used on modern battlefields by light infantry. Tactics should not be confused with techniques and should be taught through free-play exercises, war-gaming, and historical case studies. Lieutenants must be taught tactics at the battalion level if they are to be able to employ their platoons wisely in maneuver warfare and with mission-type orders. None of this is difficult to achieve. All that is required are some senior leaders who want effectively trained and educated lieutenants, not a Basic School they can visit and say, "Isn't this great? It hasn't changed a bit since I went through thirty years ago."[7]

Amphibious Warfare School and Command and Staff School

Neither of these schools teaches how to think about and in combat. In both, the focus is on terminology, formats for orders, and staff procedures. The thought process that is tactics gets little attention. In 1983, the final examination in tactics at the Amphibious Warfare School was all true/false or multiple choice, with questions such as "The _____ stove is the primary heat source of the Ten Man Tent" and "The _____ is the basic ski technique utilized in a controlled movement downhill." In 1984, one student was flunked on a problem at the Command and Staff School because he went around a dug-in enemy beach defense instead of attacking it frontally.

Recently, there have been some praiseworthy attempts to improve the curriculum at the Amphibious Warfare School. Several lectures on maneuver warfare have been introduced.[8] Students are taken to a number of local Civil War battlefields to study the battles fought there. War-gaming critiques have begun to look at tactics, not just techniques. Unfortunately, while moving in the right direction, these changes still leave the bulk of the curriculum devoted to forms, formats, and terminology. And the incipient reforms at Amphibious Warfare School have not carried over to the Command and Staff College, where the curriculum remains dry, pedantic, and largely trivial.

While the faculty at both schools includes some highly competent individuals, the general quality is low, reflecting the low priority the schools have with the centralized personnel office. Faculty preparation is virtually nil. Several years ago, the noted Israeli military historian Martin van Creveld offered to spend six weeks at Quantico in the summer teaching the faculty. The offer was rejected, largely at the behest of the faculty, who had been told they would have to write a fifteen-page paper as part of the course work.

This dilettantism and the resulting poor quality of Marine Corps education is shameful and unnecessary. There is an abundance of younger marine officers well qualified to teach modern tactics and to teach them imaginatively. Effective reform of both the Amphibious Warfare School and the Command and Staff College requires revamping the curricula to emphasize tactics (and, at Command and Staff, the operational art) over procedures and formats, selecting school directors from among recognized Marine Corps thinkers, and allowing the directors to choose anyone they want from throughout the Marine Corps as faculty, regardless of career patterns. There should be a lengthy period of faculty preparation, probably a year, and faculty should be integrated into the doctrine development process to unify thinking and teaching. As should be the case at other service schools, successful service on the faculty should bring substantial rewards in career terms. And the Command and Staff College should have a second-year course modeled on that at Fort Leavenworth. With these changes, Quantico could again be the vibrant center of Marine Corps thinking it was in the 1920s and 1930s. And marine officers could receive what they now do not: a professional education.

The National War College
The National War College in Washington, D.C., is, in terms of its function (though not officially), the nation's highest military educational institution. It accepts officers from all four services, with the objective of preparing them for service in joint staff positions — on staffs, like that of the Joint Chiefs of Staff, that support commanders of multiservice groupings.

The National War College should be the place where we prepare joint- and combined-operations strategists and grand strategists, people who can advise our most senior commanders on these highest realms of the military art.[9] Over the last several years, there has been a sincere effort by the college to move in this direction. Some of the faculty are first-rate, people who understand military strategy and grand strategy and teach others how to think in the same terms.

Unfortunately, there is still a long way to go. The one-year course is neither focused on these subjects nor long enough to produce experts in either area. Further, the school is hurt by some of the "vacation" atmosphere that pervades the Army War College. One Capitol Hill staffer recently ran into a War College student he had known for some time. He asked him how the course was going. "We're winning," replied the student. "A war game?" asked the staffer. "No, we're winning what's important at the National War College—the volleyball tournament," answered the student.

The National War College needs to be reformed to focus intensively on the art of war at the joint and combined strategic and grand strategic levels. Volleyball is very nice, but it does not win wars. Only an intense, systematic approach to strategy and grand strategy will give us the kind of officers we need on top-level staffs.

Nor will a single-year course provide grand strategists. As at Fort Leavenworth, there should be a second-year course (or possibly an additional two years) for those who show the best aptitude for strategic thinking. We do not need a large number of thoroughly trained strategists and grand strategists, but we very definitely need some. We must make the needed investment in education to find and develop them.

Developing an officer corps that can think creatively about war and in war at every level—tactics, operations, strategy, and grand strategy—is vital for military effectiveness. It requires serious, extensive, and intensive military education in how to think, not what recipes and formulas to follow. That in turn means that at every school, faculty must be chosen carefully, as individuals, regardless of career patterns, not as sets of qualifications; be prepared thoroughly; and be rewarded very well for successful performance. Faculty members should have responsibility for developing concepts and doctrine as well as teaching them. Certain specified field units should be placed at the schools' disposal as experimental units where new ideas can be tested, creating a unity among developing, teaching, and testing doctrine. In many cases, more time must be devoted to military education. Educational establishments should have a top-priority claim on resources. And the curricula must focus on war, not management, formats for orders, English courses and the like, which currently consume a great deal of time at many of our military schools and colleges. Our goal, if we want a military that wins in combat, must be thinking warriors, not trained managers and technicians.

But reform of military education will not alone permit us to reach that goal. If we continue to have too many officers, most will still be compelled to spend the greater part of their career in jobs that have little or nothing to do with the art of war, jobs where their education will be largely irrelevant and where their knowledge will atrophy from disuse. They will continue to have only very short tours in real jobs as commanders or in important staff positions, because of the long line of fellow officers anxiously waiting to take their place. The bureaucracy and decision-by-committee generated by the officer surplus will continue to obstruct and often nullify even the best decisions by educated warriors. A reform of military education can only bring results if it is coupled with a drastic reduction in the size of the officer corps from the major/lieutenant commander level on up.

The Promotion System

There is yet a third component to reforming the officer corps: reforming the promotion system. The basic problem is that the current promotion system tends to promote the "organization man," the competent bureaucrat, the office politician, and the courtier, and weed out the warrior, the tactician, the leader, and the trainer. Educating warriors will not help if the promotion system later weeds them out.

Evidence of the predominance of the bureaucrat is presented by the personality testing done at the National War College. The students are given the Myers-Briggs Type Indicator, a personality test based on Jungian psychology. Most students are either ISTJs (Introverted, Sensing, Thinking, and Judging) or ESTJs (Extroverted, Sensing, Thinking, and Judging)—the typical managerial-bureaucratic personality. According to Otto Kroeger, a psychologist who explains the test's meaning to the War College students, if his students switched their uniforms for business suits, it would be next to impossible to distinguish them from the corporate executives he also tests. Kroeger stated, "The peacetime Army does not have the George Patton type. They've been weeded out. I know a number who have early-outed in the last ten years. The action types . . . the hardnosed risk-taking daredevils . . . said, 'I didn't come to push papers. I joined the action Army and there's no action.' " Dr. Richard Gabriel, the author of *Military Incompetence,* said in response to the test results: "I think the military school system is a more accurate reflection of the managerial ethos. The curriculum on balance stresses the acquisition of management skills versus leadership skills. . . . It's a rational response to an irrational system. If the brass rewards those skillful at bureaucratic battles, then skillful bureaucrats are what the system will turn out. They're going to spend the rest of their careers as bureaucrats, no question about that. The system rewards idiotic behavior. It has nothing to do with training soldiers."[10]

To be successful in combat, an officer needs two qualities above all others: strength of character and imagination. Strength of character is the single most important characteristic. To make the bold, often risky, decisions that bring great successes in war requires enormous strength of character. Many lives are at stake. The future of the nation may be at risk. The pressure to "play it safe," to do something that cannot bring great success and often cannot bring success at all but will "fail gracefully" is tremendous. Throughout history, most commanders have yielded to that pressure. That is why most wars have been bloody and indecisive. The bold stroke that wins quickly with little bloodshed, a stroke like the German attack through the Ardennes in 1940 or MacArthur's risky landing at Inchon, has been the exception. But the reformers' goal is to have the exception become the rule in our military. We want future Inchons, not future Antietams. And if that is our goal, our promotion process must above all identify and promote officers with strength of character.

But all boldness is not wisdom. The Charge of the Light Brigade was bold, but also stupid. Boldness coupled with a lack of imagination, or a lack of an ability to conceptualize a battle or a campaign—to see the enemy's weakness and think through how to strike at it—results in headlong charges into death. So strength of character must be coupled with what von Clausewitz called a "talent for judgment." Because in war few things are clear, because war is dominated by uncertainty and rapid change, by fog and by friction, this talent for judgment is composed in large part of imagination, of an ability to see with the mind more than can be seen by the eye.

The promotion system must seek out and promote such officers. Why doesn't it do so today? The fundamental reason is that our services have become bureaucracies, and bureaucracies are highly uncomfortable with people who have strong character and imagination. Anyone who has worked in a bureaucracy of any kind, military or civilian, government or private, has seen this. The person of strong character and imagination frequently upsets bureaucratic applecarts, what the military calls "rice bowls": parochial interests. His imagination leads him to question established ways of doing things, ways that many of his superiors have developed, find comfortable, and protect. His strong character leads him to make his dissatisfaction public, to challenge the entrenched bureaucratic interests and fiefdoms. He says things other people don't want to hear. He challenges his superiors' wisdom and, often, their legitimacy. He won't keep quiet when he is told to. Not infrequently, he may be somewhat abrasive personally, sometimes even eccentric. He does not "fit in" very well to the established routine. And he is penalized by not being promoted. The contradiction between the qualities we need in our officers to be successful in war and the qualities prized by our bureaucratic military institutions is fundamental.

Fortunately, there is something that can be done to curb the weeding out of officers with strong character and imagination. We can abandon "up or out."

Today an officer spends his career on a treadmill. By law, he must either be promoted at periodic intervals or resign or retire from the service. An officer generally comes before a promotion board three times in a given rank; if he is passed over three times, he must leave the service. When coupled with the officer surplus, the effect is to make everyone spend a great deal of time worrying about his career. Every officer knows that if he makes a career misstep, he is out. So he must be careful. He must not offend. He must not upset applecarts. He must be a "good organization man" to survive.

This environment is very unfriendly to the man with strong character and imagination—even more unfriendly than other bureaucracies where a person can be passed over for promotion but still stay in the organization. A person with strong character frequently cannot tolerate playing career games. Often he refuses to play them, which is why we lose many of our best officers early. They are weeded out or leave voluntarily in disgust.

Further, "up or out" institutionalizes the Peter Principle. The Peter Principle states that in any organization a person is promoted to the level at which he is incompetent. In the military, a certain type of person may, for example, be a very good company commander as a captain. But he may not have the ability to think broadly enough—to think at the division level—to serve as a battalion operations officer as a major. Under "up or out" he cannot be left a company commander. So up he goes, to a level where he will not be competent and where he usually will not find his job very fulfilling.

Ending "up or out" will not entirely solve the problem of promoting the bureaucrat instead of the warrior, but it will help. It will reduce the current fixation on promotion and the resultant careerism. It will allow an officer to trade off promotion for freedom to be himself, to let his strength of character be seen, to be imaginative even if he upsets some applecarts. His career may still suffer, but he will be less likely to be forced out. And eliminating "up or out" will reduce the Peter Principle's power. A competent company commander or fighter pilot will be allowed to stay just that for his whole career if he wants to.

The alternative promotion mechanism we should adopt is simple, and it is similar to one used in some foreign armies. If an officer wants a promotion, he must first ask for it. Then, he must be tested extensively, tested in his professional knowledge of the art of war at a level commensurate to the rank he seeks. His tests would be evaluated along with his previous performance record.[11]

These performance records and their evaluation process would also be changed. Fitness reports would not have "objective," fill-in-the-block sections as they do now. They would be based on questions to be answered by the officer's commander, such as "What are this officer's positive and negative qualities?" The process of evaluating these reports would also change. As one sociologist, wiser than most, once said, "You cannot study men, you can only get to know them." The current evaluation system, where boards of officers who do not personally know those being considered for promotion pass judgment on them on the basis of fill-in-the-block fitness reports, is counterproductive. It rewards not the warriors but the organization men, those who specialize in filling in blocks, making all the right moves, in what the military calls "ticket punching." Those deciding on an officer's promotion must be people who have worked directly with him, which means promotion authority must be decentralized to the regiment, the division, and the branch. Such a promotion system will undoubtedly, by some across-the-board numerical calculation, be "unfair." But fairness in identifying excellence and promoting it can only be local and subjective, so people can be judged as the individuals they are.

Without the weeding out process now established by "up or out," whereby a person is in effect fired if he is not promoted, another system for getting rid of unsatisfactory officers would be needed. Like the promotion system, it should be local. An officer's superior should simply have the right to fire him for cause. The right should be vested several levels above an officer's immediate superior, the cause should be explicit, and an officer should have a right of appealing to a still higher level of command. But the right to fire should not be so circumscribed that the military ends up like the civil service, where it is almost impossible to fire even the most egregiously incompetent. It should be closer to the system in a private corporation.

With the end of "up or out" must come some changes in the pay system. Every officer, regardless of rank, should be paid enough to provide his family with a middle-class standard of living. As his children grow in number and grow older, he will need more pay. Therefore, pay must give more weight to seniority than it does now. Currently, pay rises with rank and also with time in grade, but increases in pay are generally tied to promotion. That will be less the case with the end of "up or out." The longer an officer is in service, the higher his pay should be, with the goal of providing a middle-class standard of living to an officer who does not advance in rank. This would not eliminate financial reward for higher rank; a general with twenty years' service would still be paid more than a captain with twenty years' service. But the captain with twenty years' service would make enough to provide adequately for his family. Dr. Richard Gabriel has suggested another measure that would help dedicated officers and noncommissioned officers remain in the service without penalizing their families: allow the daughters and sons of any serving officer or NCO to attend tuition-free any state university for which they qualify. Dr. Gabriel states, "My discussions with majors and lieutenant colonels suggest that many leave because they cannot educate their kids on what they make." The suggestion is a good one and should be adopted as part of the reforms to the pay system.

Some may object that eliminating "up or out" and the automatic connection between higher rank and higher pay would discourage officers whose primary goal is upward mobility. If so, that would be to the good. Being a military officer should be a calling, a way of life, not a job or a career. Warfare is not just a business. The ethic of personal gain is not a healthy one in an officer corps. It is entirely appropriate that officers who seek more challenge in their work and can handle it should move up in rank, and they still would. For this type of person, the challenge is itself the reward. But those who want higher rank for reasons of prestige or higher pay should be discouraged. Careerism is not desirable in a military, and if these changes lead careerists to return to or remain in the civilian world, that is beneficial.

Finally, as part of the changes in the promotion system, we should make a major change in military retirement. Usually, the current military retirement system that permits an officer to retire after twenty years of service with 50 percent of his highest annual base pay is assailed for its cost. Currently, $18.4 billion is set aside from the defense budget for military retirement, and this is projected to rise to $45.8 billion by the year 2000. However, the cost is of less concern than three other disadvantages of the current system. The first is that, with 28 percent of all officers now retiring after twenty years of service, we lose a great deal of talent at its peak, when the individual is in his early forties. Second, we have too many officers who spend much of their time and effort during the last part of their career, the last three to five years (and sometimes more), preparing themselves for a second career as a civilian. Since the skills of the warrior are not very marketable in the civilian world, they are usually working hard at computer science, business management, or something similar. Our officers should concentrate on warfare, not acquiring civilian skills. Third, we get too many officers who are "retired on active duty." These are people who know they are unlikely to be promoted further, have consequently been assigned to what are looked on as dead-end jobs, and are simply waiting out their time, coasting until they have to retire. In terms of military effectiveness, they are liabilities, not assets.

We should replace the current retirement system with one that does not permit officers to collect retirement pay until thirty years after the date at which they entered the service, but that also vests them beginning in their tenth year of service. As in many civilian retirement systems, for each year of service beyond ten, an officer would be entitled to collect a certain additional percentage of his highest base pay as retirement. If he voluntarily left the service at, say, his eighteenth year, he would be entitled to collect retirement reflecting eighteen years of service once he had passed the date that would have marked thirty years of service. The same would be true if he were involuntarily separated under honorable circumstances; he would not lose his vesting. If officers were separated involuntarily because of a general officer surplus, such as one resulting from a reduction in the size of the service, they would be permitted to collect retirement from the date of separation regardless of whether they had reached the thirty-year mark or not. And officers currently in service who have served more than ten years would be "grandfathered"; they would continue to serve under the current retirement system.

Summary
Taken together, these reforms—reducing the size of the officer corps from the rank of major/lieutenant commander on up by at least 50 percent; refocusing military education on the art of war and how to think; and ending the "up or out" promotion system and the officer evaluation and pay and retirement systems that go with it—are at least as significant as the reforms needed in tactics, weapons, or training. In the long run, they are more significant, because they strike at some of the reasons for the current super-structure problems. If our officers are not adequately educated in war, deficiencies in tactics and doctrine are likely. So is misdefini-

tion of what constitutes quality in equipment, because the officers who write equipment specifications will not have a correct understanding of the battlefield. The officer surplus feeds the tendency to start new weapons programs we cannot afford and to continue programs for weapons that don't work, because those programs create jobs for surplus officers. The promotion system leads to deficiencies in almost every superstructure area, because it tends to promote bureaucrats, not warriors. Bureaucrats are not interested in things like training, doctrine, and tactics. They like to make decisions by committee consensus. They resist changes in force structure because they are comfortable with whatever is familiar. Their focus is inside the service, not on the outside, competitive world: the battlefield.

If we really want to solve our superstructure problems, we need to go after their roots. These reforms to the officer corps do just that. Their purpose is to give us a military that is run by educated warriors, not trained managers. As in the case of the reforms of the superstructure, they will be denounced and resisted by the milicrats, the bureaucrats in uniform. But they will be strongly supported by real soldiers, sailors, airmen, and marines. To them, these changes promise liberation from petty promotion politics, from the current system's repression of the officer with strong character and imagination, from education largely unrelated to the art of war, and from the institutional arteriosclerosis caused by the officer surplus. Most of our officers want to be warriors. We need a system that not only allows them to be, but also educates them and rewards them for being so. If we want to succeed in war, we need officers who are warriors above everything else.

6

The Weapons Development and Procurement Process

THE SERIOUS DEFICIENCIES in a number of the weapons we currently buy already have been documented. Deficient weapons are not just a waste of money. In combat, they result in our own troops being killed instead of the enemy's. One need only think of the American soldiers killed in World War II and in Korea trying to stop enemy tanks with the poorly designed bazooka, or the dead American infantrymen in Vietnam found clutching jammed M-16 rifles to realize the price paid for ineffective weapons. Weapons effectiveness is not just a political issue. It is a moral issue.

Usually, when we find deficient products, we also find a deficient process. Any system will make some mistakes, but the number of ineffective weapons in our inventory is substantially higher than can be explained by the irreducible minimum of human errors. We get ineffective weapons because of some basic defects in our understanding of what makes a weapon effective in combat; in our integration of weapons with soldiers, tactics, and training; and in the system by which we develop and procure our weapons. Until we change the system, we will not improve the quality or the affordability of our military equipment.

"Quality" in Weapons
What are the deficiencies in the current weapons development system? They begin with the way in which the current system defines quality in weapons. Very little research is done in the area

of weapons effectiveness—what makes a rifle, tank, or fighter aircraft in the hands of a soldier, sailor, airman, or marine effective in combat. As a result, the specifications the services set for new equipment often emphasize characteristics that are not important in combat, and they ignore those that are. Fighter aircraft provide a good example. Since the beginning of air combat, it has been evident to pilots that a fighter's ability to turn tightly is very important in a dogfight. But turning performance was not made part of U.S. fighter specifications until 1967.[1] Before that date, specifications emphasized only range, maximum speed, and altitude. In contrast, the Japanese had set a turning specification by 1935; any new fighter had to prove, in operational tests, that it turned at least as well as its predecessor or it would not be bought. Not surprisingly, the Japanese Zero turned much better than American fighters in 1941, giving the Japanese a major advantage.

Characteristics like range and maximum speed are used to define quality, even though—depending on the type of weapon—they may or may not actually mean much in combat, because they are easily quantifiable. In the current system, statistics are too often considered truth, and anything that cannot be quantified is disregarded as "subjective." This is an incorrect use of quantification. Quantification is useful only when qualities that are important in combat can be measured quantitatively. It is first necessary to determine what qualities are important. This can only be done historically, by carefully studying past combat. Then, it must be determined which qualities can be measured statistically and which cannot. Frequently, many of the most important qualities cannot be quantified.[2]

The overreliance on quantification has been made worse by the increasing use of computerized studies and analyses. In defense as in many other fields, many people believe a conclusion is valid if it is supported by a large quantity of computer paper. Computers are looked on as the modern equivalent to the oracle at Delphi. In a sense, perhaps they are, since Delphi was notoriously cryptic and subject to incorrect interpretation.

Part of the problem is the assumptions fed into the computers. These are too often based on the self-interested claims of weapons manufacturers or weapons program offices. A recent visitor observed a case of this in war-gaming at the Naval War College. The games were used to evaluate tactics, not weapons, but the problem is the same. In the games, weapons were assigned probabilities of kill that were extraordinarily high by historical standards. The Sparrow radar-guided air-to-air missile had an actual, demonstrated probability of kill of .08 to .10 during the Vietnam War. But in the games at Newport, it was given a probability several times that. Weapons that had no combat history, such as the Mark-48 torpedo, were given probabilities of kill that were high by comparison to virtually any weapon in actual combat. The navy did not want to believe that its weapons were not very effective, so the computers were told that they were effective. The results, in terms of skewing our tactics, are easy to imagine.

Most computer programmers will tell you that if assumptions fed into computers are wrong, the results will be misleading. Their saying is, "garbage in, garbage out." Too often in the military the motto is "garbage in, gospel out." Once data sheets come out of the computer, they are considered holy writ. Those results are then translated into requirements and specifications for new weapons designs. Not surprisingly, the designs often end up flawed.

Additionally, the mathematics in many of our combat models and simulations, in our operations research analyses, and in the associated studies are not sound. A typical technical report documenting a mathematical model will impress, if not awe, an intelligent layman with its profusion of symbols and the language of advanced mathematics—integrals, matrices, stochastic processes. The layman will not realize that there is much less there than meets the eye. Usually, the equations represent nothing that exists in combat, and the numbers they produce are misleading. Weapons systems simply do not behave in combat the way the equations imply.

Why? The answer is simple. Many practitioners of defense analysis view warfare as too complex and imprecise to represent exactly, so they simplify it. Naively plausible equations that lead to the "right" conclusions are sufficient. The equations are not intended to capture real physical phenomena, as are the equations of physics. They are a show used mainly to impress the viewer. And, because science is highly esteemed, using its trappings helps sell the product. Thus, the defense analysis industry couches its reports in the language and symbols of science. For the same reason, it ensures that those who write its reports are academically well qualified, often with advanced degrees in technical or scientific fields from excellent universities. But contrary to appearances, almost no one in defense analysis actually pursues the scientific method. Usually, they are paid to make "studies" or "analyses" with the best tools they have at hand, the trappings of science. The result is numerical quackery.

The shortcomings do not end with inappropriate mathematics. Our computer models are also glaringly incomplete. Fundamentals—vision, communication, and motion, for example—are so poorly treated that meaningful battlefield tactics geared to the characteristics of the weapons being modeled cannot be included. In particular, maneuver and surprise cannot be captured and consequently cannot play any role, despite their often decisive effects. Neglect of the fundamentals of combat so artificially simplifies the battle circumstances in which the weapons are employed that they appear to be much more effective in the models than they are in combat. That undoubtedly helps sell the product, but it certainly does not help us understand what constitutes quality in weapons nor does it help put effective weapons in our arsenal.

The combined overstatement arising from neglect of fundamentals as well as from inappropriate mathematics can be so great that many weapons systems are foredoomed to fall far short of their expected effectiveness in combat, even after all the usual design flaws and manufacturing problems are rectified. They never had the effectiveness our models attributed to them. Often new weapons prove inferior to the weapons systems they replaced.

The problems of ignoring nonquantitative factors, feeding ahistorical assumptions into the analysis and running the analysis on the basis of questionable mathematics and inadequate models are compounded with what might be called the "Fourteenth Street Factor." Fourteenth Street is Washington, D.C.'s red-light district. Service-oriented private entrepreneurs have been making substantial profits there for some time. But in recent years, their incomes have been made to look paltry in comparison with those of their counterparts in the defense business: consultants and analysts who specialize in telling their Defense Department clients whatever they want to hear regardless of the evidence.

The Washington beltway is crowded with defense consultants and defense analysis companies. Some of them—a minority—produce sound, competent, honest work. But they are not known collectively as the "Beltway Bandits" for nothing. Too many have found they can make a great deal of money through Defense Department contracts by the simple expedient of telling the client whatever he wants to hear. Does the client like large, complex fighter aircraft? Then a defense consultant knows he can make money by presenting him with a study showing large, complex fighters are more effective than small, simple fighters. Is the client in the airlift business? Then a study showing we need more airlift will find a ready buyer. Does the client like big aircraft carriers? Then he will buy a study that concludes big carriers will become less, not more, vulnerable as time goes on. And if a client is comforted by the conclusions of one study, he is likely to come back to the same consultant for more.

The Fourteenth Street Factor enables a military service, weapons manufacturer, or program officer to claim there is "independent" analysis confirming that what he wants to do, sell, or buy is correct. But the reason the consultant got the contract is that the client knew the analysis would not be independent at all. It would tell him what he wanted to hear and give him a new sales brochure for his product. Analysts and consultants who actually tell the client what they think the evidence shows don't tend to do very well in business. The way to wealth along the beltway is the way of prostitution.

How should we determine what constitutes quality in weapons? History is not only the best but also the only starting point. For each type of weapon—tanks, fighters, rifles—we need to do careful historical research into what has made past weapons of the same type effective or ineffective in combat. Only by adopting definitions of quality that reflect characteristics that have proved important in past and current combat—most important among them, those that relate to the people who use the weapons—can we hope to have a grip on what quality really means. Then, we need to add genuine scientific understanding. We need mathematical modeling that correctly and usefully analyzes those limited aspects of war and weapons that can be expressed in numbers. Quantification has a legitimate role to play, but only within boundaries established by historical study.

Design Competition

The second reform necessary to get effective military equipment is competition in weapons design. Today there is little genuine design competition. Most design competitions are strictly on paper; no competitive prototypes are built and tested in fly-offs and shoot-offs against each other nor against the weapon they are supposed to replace. Many weapons designs do not even face nominal competition. They are developed jointly by a single private contractor and the service bureaucracy.

In many cases there is nominal, but not real, competition. A good example is design work now going on for the navy's planned new attack submarine, the SSN-21 class. The navy says the design development is competitive. It has two different contractors, General Dynamics and Newport News shipyards, working on designs. But in reality, the competition is meaningless, because the navy has already set so many of the design characteristics itself that the competition is just over details. The navy has already set the size of the submarine, the design of the power plant, the hull form, and so on. There is no competition between, for example, a large submarine with a traditional design nuclear-propulsion plant and a much smaller submarine with an advanced-design nuclear plant, like some built by the Soviets and the French, much less even more advanced design ideas like modular submarines.

Further, in too many of the few cases where we have actually built prototypes of different designs and conducted competitions, we have bought the loser. We did that in the competition for the M-1 tank, the DIVAD antiaircraft gun, and the navy lightweight fighter, where the navy bought the F-17 (renumbered the F-18) that lost to the F-16 in the air force lightweight fighter competition.

Foreign weapons designs offer a major opportunity to increase design competition, but the services will generally go to great lengths to avoid buying a weapon designed overseas. When a competition was conducted between the M-1 tank and the West German Leopard, the Germans posted guards around their tanks at night to prevent what they suspected would be American sabotage attempts. They felt very strongly that the competition was rigged and that no matter how well their tank did, it would never be proclaimed the winner.

Another major opportunity for competition the services strongly resist is buying "off the shelf." Many items of militarily suitable equipment, ranging from boots and backpacks to communications equipment, are manufactured both in this country and abroad for civilian or military markets. In many cases, we could get better equipment more cheaply by simply buying a few of each and testing them competitively. Many soldiers will quickly tell you that you can get better boots, tents, backpacks, and other basic equipment on the civilian market than those issued by the military, and at lower cost. A number of navy chiefs (petty officers) told a visitor to a naval task group in the Indian Ocean that they could purchase ordinary electronic equipment from onshore Radio Shack stores ten times less expensively and several times faster than they could order through the naval supply system. But the military research and development bureaucracies strongly resist buying off the shelf, because it leaves them without a justification for their existence. It leaves them no role to play, which means no budgets, jobs, or prestige. So we continue to develop these products within the military, usually without any competition. Prices soar and quality plummets.

A key element inhibiting off-the-shelf buys, use of foreign weapons designs, and competition generally are "military specifications," usually called "milspecs." These specify in great detail certain technical characteristics for everything from mess kits through fighter engines and ship designs.[3] Most of them have little to do with what is actually important in combat. In fact, particularly in the area of electronics, advertisements for products aimed at the civilian market will often boast "not built to milspec," because many civilian consumers have come to realize that the milspecs just mean greater complexity and cost while doing nothing for performance.[4] The reason the Defense Department perpetuates milspecs is that they give the development bureaucracies control over competition. The bureaucrats can use the argument "these aren't built to milspec" to rule out many potential competitors and push in-house designs.

The usual way a weapon is designed today is that the relevant service bureaucracy works closely with a single contractor to produce a vast number of specifications the new system must meet. Most of these are not performance requirements, but exact places where parts must be placed, precise characteristics the weapon must have, and so forth. These specifications frequently are so lengthy they must be published in several volumes for a single weapon. Sometimes there is a competition to see who can best meet these specifications. But the specifications usually allow a designer little leeway. He is reduced to manipulating details. Further, the single contractor who has been involved with the service in designing the specifications has often managed to get them written in such a way that only he can meet them, so that he is assured of winning the "competition."

In the process of developing the specifications, each little subbureaucracy inside the larger service bureaucracy gets to add what it wants. It is "design by committee," and the usual result is that every "bell and whistle" gets added. It is much easier to build a committee consensus by saying "yes" to everyone than by telling someone "no" when he wants to add something. Each "fiefdom" has equal rights with the others, so there is often no one with the authority to say "no."

Furthermore, all these little bureaucratic interests had their say in the weapon the new one is intended to replace. So the new one usually reflects the same basic characteristics and embodies the same faulty understanding of weapon effectiveness. There is little room for innovation, because that would mean some military bureaucrat would have to say he previously had been wrong and we should go in a different direction. A missile community that has poured billions of dollars into radar-guided air-to-air missiles since 1948, and has yet to get one that really works, will never admit all that time and money were spent following a will-o'-the-wisp. Each community has its "rights" and its veto in writing the specifications for the new weapon, so we continue to plod down the same paths.

Nowhere in the current system is there any incentive to keep weapon costs down. The people who control the design and development process play no role in using the weapon in combat. Nor are numbers of weapons any concern to them—that falls into another bureaucratic bailiwick, that of the force planners. Every incentive actually works to drive costs up, by rewarding saying "yes" to new requirements and specifications with bureaucratic harmony. Nor is there any incentive to keep development time down. A major air force study, *Affordable Acquisition Approach,* showed how development times have increased dramatically over the past several decades. Comparing average development times of different systems of the 1950–1970 period with current times, the study found, for example, that development time for bombers had gone from 94 months to 169 and that for air-to-air missiles from 63 months to 104. It is now often twenty years or more between generations of major weapons. The Soviets gain a major advantage from the fact that their development time is much shorter. They have a shorter development cycle despite the fact that their society as a whole is much more bureaucratic and slow-moving than our own.

One major reason why our weapons development and procurement process takes so long and works so badly is that the bureaucracies in charge are so large. With so many involved, no one has much authority. No one is in a position to make an important decision. Everything is done by endless reviews, checks, and double checks, all of which take the form of committee meetings. With so many cooks playing in the stew, it is no wonder dinner comes late and badly seasoned.

What reforms are necessary? First, we need to reduce the size of these huge research and development and procurement bureaucracies. This doesn't just mean changing the names or moving the same committee meetings to another office. We have to cut them severely—discharge the people. Many of the employees are civil service civilians—get rid of them at the same time we retire our surplus higher ranking officers. Put the few functions that are really necessary into offices with few enough people so that individuals can make important decisions and we can see who made what decision. We must replace the committee consensus process with individual responsibility if anything is to be done right.

Second, we must select new weapons and other military equipment through real competition. In some cases, we can hold competitions among off-the-shelf equipment items already in production for civilian or foreign military markets. In cases where we are seeking a design that moves beyond anything now available, we should write a short list of performance requirements—what the system must accomplish in actual operational testing done comparatively against its predecessor—not a long list of specifications. The performance requirements themselves should reflect combat-based effectiveness analysis. It might be wise to have a rule that no requirement may be longer than ten double-spaced pages, with no annexes or appendixes allowed. No contractor who would later compete for the program should be allowed to participate in writing the requirements.

The small research and development offices that remain after the big bureaucracies are eliminated should evaluate the initial paper responses and identify the more promising. Generally, those chosen should represent a wide range of different approaches. Then, these should be built as prototypes. The prototypes should be tested for effectiveness in real shoot-offs and fly-offs, not in computer modeling.[5]

Competitions should reflect the reform discussed earlier: defining quality through historically based effectiveness analysis. Sound mathematical modeling, based on combat history, can also be useful, as long as the inherent limitations on quantitative analysis are respected. That analysis should give us the framework for the competition. Candidates should compete to see which do best in terms of the characteristics that matter most in combat.

Competition should largely, if not wholly, replace milspecs. Instead of saying, for example, "Milspecs require that you must have the dome light in the personnel carrier located at such-and-such a place, and it must put out so many lumens of light," we should see how the dome light actually works. Do troops hit their head on it? Can they read their maps by it? If so, it's effective.[6]

Foreigners should be welcome to compete in any design competition. The broader the competition, the more good new ideas we will get, and the better the chosen system will be. If a foreign design wins, we can build it here under license.

Finally, we should buy the winner. This seems obvious, but since we have in fact bought the loser in a number of competitions, we need to make it explicit. We need to be especially firm on this point where foreign designs are involved, since powerful interests inside and outside the government resist foreign-designed weapons.

Some may object that even this system could allow bureaucratic interests to pervert the process. That is true. If the "feather merchants" keep control of the new, smaller offices that oversee weapons research and development, we will still have problems. Administration or congressional politics could still result in pressure to buy a system that does poorly in a competition. How can we prevent the occasional turkey that may still slip through from going into production and endangering our soldiers?

Independent Operational Testing
We can preclude such a mistake through rigorous, independent operational testing of all new weapons and other military equipment. There are two different types of weapons testing: developmental testing and operational testing. The first takes place while a weapon is being developed, and it is of the "try it and if it breaks fix it" type. The object is to find and fix problems before the

weapon is considered ready for production—before it is a finished design. It is properly an iterative process.

Operational testing takes place after a design has been completed and after the manufacturer and the program manager say, "It's done, it's ready to go into service—and into combat." The purpose of operational testing is to see if that claim is valid. Good operational testing subjects the weapon to as many combat challenges as can be replicated in peacetime. It fills the weapon with fuel and ammunition and shoots at it with real enemy weapons. It puts it in the hands of ordinary soldiers to see if they can operate and maintain it easily, without contractor assistance. It is adversarial testing—trying to see if the weapon can be made to fail by applying combat stress to it. That is, after all, what an enemy will do to it in combat.

Strong, independent operational testing can be an effective check on any flawed weapons designs that slip through the reformed weapons development process. It could be a very effective check on the many ineffective weapons the current development process produces. Unfortunately, this makes it a threat to powerful interests inside and outside the Defense Department. In the recent past, operational testing has either not been truly independent or not had much clout or both. Operational testing designed to prove the system does work, to make the program manager and the contractor happy by keeping the money flowing, is all too common. In some other cases, the operational testing is honest and finds that something doesn't work, but the services just ignore the findings. The navy is notorious for this. Its operational testing squadrons for aircraft are proficient and honest. In their report on the F-18 they reportedly said, "As a replacement for the A-7, the F-18 unrefueled operational capabilities gained do not offset capabilities lost. . . . [The F-18] is not operationally suitable." The navy just ignored these findings and bought the F-18 anyway.

As noted earlier, in 1983 the Congress took some strong action on operational testing. Led by Senator David Pryor of Arkansas and the Congressional Military Reform Caucus, the Congress passed an amendment to the defense authorization bill that established a strong, independent Office of Operational Testing and

Evaluation in the Pentagon. The position of director was made a presidential appointment, with confirmation by the Senate. The director was given his own staff and the right to help design, monitor, and report on all operational tests. His reports were supposed to go directly to the secretary of defense and, unamended by the secretary, to the Congress.

The Defense Department bitterly resisted and resented this. It fought the amendment hard in the Senate but lost ninety-five to three. Then, the administration refused for eighteen months to appoint a director. A number of members of Congress urged the appointment of Colonel James Burton, the man who had blown the whistle on the rigging of the Bradley tests, but he was the last person the administration wanted. When it finally did appoint someone, in the spring of 1985, it chose an employee of one of the largest defense contractors, McDonnell Douglas, a person who, though he had worked extensively in developmental testing, had no experience in operational testing. Prior to his confirmation, the nominee met with the Congressional Military Reform Caucus. He was asked about a rigged test the navy had done with the F-18, a McDonnell Douglas product, when he was head of testing for the company. Although a McDonnell Douglas test pilot had flown the plane, he denied any knowledge of it. He was then asked, "If you had known, would you have blown the whistle—would you have let people on the Hill or in the press know what was going on?" He answered, "No."

Senator Pryor courageously led a fight on the Senate floor against this individual's confirmation, but only eighteen senators voted against him. The result is that the new Office of Operational Testing and Evaluation is neither strong nor independent. It is playing the same "go along to get along, keep everybody happy by keeping the money flowing" game that has too often undermined past operational testing and effective weapons.[7]

But under a strong director, the new office could play a major role in ensuring we do not buy worthless weapons. If program managers, contractors, and those in charge of weapons competitions knew they had to face rigorous, realistic, independent operational tests, it would put new discipline into their activities. If they knew problems could not be swept under the rug, they would have an incentive to find and fix them early or to acknowledge they have taken a wrong course from the start and cancel the program. Those weapons that complete development with major flaws in them would face a barrier they would find hard to cross. To ensure that, one rule would have to be absolute: no weapon would go beyond pilot production until it had passed its operational test. "No passing grade, no production" would have to be without exceptions. This rule, combined with a genuinely strong and independent operational testing office, could give us an effective guarantee that under the reformed development process, we would stop buying weapons that do not work in combat.

Procurement Reforms
The process of buying weapons involves more than getting good, effective weapons designs. We must also be able to keep costs down so we can buy the number of weapons we need. This need shows the relationship between efficiency and effectiveness. If our weapons production is so inefficient (or our designs so complex) that unit prices are very high, we will be unable to afford one of the most important qualities in weapons: numbers.

Today our weapons production is inefficient, unit costs are high, and we don't get the number of weapons we need. Some of this is due to the complexity of the weapons designs we have selected. But much is due to inefficiency among defense contractors and a defense procurement system that encourages that inefficiency.

Examples of the problems of high unit costs, decreasing numbers of weapons, and inefficiency among defense contractors are legion:

• In the early 1950s, we spent about the same amount of money we spend today, in real dollars (i.e., with inflation discounted) to buy fighters and tanks. But that money bought about five thousand fighters annually, and it buys only about three hundred per year today. It bought about six times as many tanks in the 1950s as it buys today.

• A frigate for the U.S. Navy costs about $400 million. A British Type 23 frigate costs $137.4 million.
• Overhead costs billed by defense contractors to the government are much higher than those that prevail in civilian markets, as are costs per hour and the number of hours needed to do a task. For example, the commercial electronics industry gets about $25 per standard work hour for the manufacture of such items as airline-quality radios, navigation equipment, and radars. One investigator found that the *lowest* cost per standard hour billed to the government for defense electronics work was $95. In general, the cost ran between $150 and $300 per standard hour. The highest that could be documented was $3,407, for work that was being done by people paid $3.93 per hour. The rest was overhead.
• Quality control in defense contracts is often poor. One specialist on defense procurement wrote, "We hire people to inspect (weapons made by private companies) and then rate them on having no Quality Deficiency Reports (QDRs). There are two ways to have no QDRs: (1) make it right the first time, or (2) ignore the defects. Unfortunately, we do mostly the latter, even on safety-of-flight items like jet engines." This translates directly into poor combat effectiveness, because if a weapon is poorly built, it is likely to malfunction in combat.

Why is military procurement so riddled with problems? Largely because, just as in weapons design, there is little competition. Americans argue, quite rightly, that competition in a free market is the best basis for an economy. But we do not apply that wisdom to defense procurement. Today only 6 percent of all defense procurement, measured in dollar value, is genuinely competitive in the classic, sealed-bid sense. In the other 94 percent one or more companies automatically get the contract. They know beforehand they will get it. They have no incentive to keep prices down —quite the contrary. Can you imagine what your local car dealer would charge you if he knew you had to buy a car and were definitely going to buy it from him, no matter what the cost? That is exactly how the Defense Department deals with the vast majority of its suppliers.

The effect of such widespread noncompetitive purchasing is that the defense industry is not really free enterprise. It is state capitalist. The corporations are nominally private, but they have such a close, symbiotic relationship with the Defense Department that they are really just an extension of it. They win contracts not by offering a better product (since there is little design competition) or a lower price (since there is little competition for production either). They win contracts by heavy lobbying of both the Defense Department and the Congress, by helping draft the specifications for a new weapon so only they can build it, by "building contacts" and "networking" with military officers and Defense Department civilians, by spreading prospective subcontracts into as many states and congressional districts as possible to build a constituency on Capitol Hill (the B-1 bomber is built in 37 states; the F-18 fighter in 21), and by using the "revolving door."

The term revolving door refers to the practice whereby a defense contractor hires the military officers or Defense Department civilians who oversaw his program as soon as they retire from the military or their Defense Department job. Savvy officers or Defense Department civilians know that if they "play the game" by keeping the dollars flowing to a contractor they are supposed to oversee, they are likely to be offered a well-paying sinecure by that contractor when they retire. As Tom Amlie, one of the inventors of the simple and highly successful Sidewinder missile, has said, "You know that if you play the game, when you retire some nice man will come around and offer you a well-paying job. If you make waves, if you raise uncomfortable questions about the program you are assigned to oversee, when you retire there will be no nice man."

What reforms can bring the efficiency we need to the defense business so that we can lower the prices of weapons and buy the number we require? First, competition must be the rule, not the exception. For almost all systems, once a weapon design is chosen, two separate contractors should be asked to produce it. Periodically, both must be required to rebid, with the contracts awarded on, for example, a 70-30 basis. The contractor with the higher bid should get just enough of the buy to keep him in business until the next round of competition, when he could offer a new, lower bid in hopes of getting the majority of the work.

This has been done in a few cases, with notable success. The best example is the 30-mm depleted uranium ammunition of the cannon on the A-10 close-support aircraft. The air force projected the cost, if it were produced on a sole source basis, as over fifty dollars per round. But when it was instead produced competitively, the price fell to just twelve dollars per round. The air force has recently moved to introduce competition for some jet engines on a similar basis, and the navy is also experimenting with this kind of competition.

Senator Charles Grassley of Iowa, who has been very active in the military reform movement, has introduced a bill to make competition the law. Called "creeping capitalism," it requires that the percentage of Defense Department contracts that are subject to competition must grow by 5 percent annually until it reaches 70 percent. "Creeping capitalism" would give the Defense Department and the defense industry time to adjust to the new world of capitalistic competition. Senator Grassley's bill should become law.

Second, defense contractors should have to provide warranties with their equipment. Today a contractor can make more money by supplying a defective system than a good one, because the Defense Department will pay him to fix the defects. Warranties would ensure that defective systems would have to be fixed at the contractor's cost, creating a strong incentive for good quality control and early identification of defects. Senator Mark Andrews of North Dakota authored an amendment to the FY 1984 defense appropriations bill that required warranties. Unfortunately, although the amendment was passed into law, it was subsequently weakened in ways that have allowed the Defense Department to avoid requiring warranties on many systems. The department argues that contractors will just raise their prices if we require warranties—which of course they will unless they face competition that gives them an incentive to keep prices down. But if coupled with competition in defense contracting, warranties can be an effective tool.

Third, we should close the revolving door. The Congressional Military Reform Caucus has led an effort to do this by passing a measure proposed by Representatives Charles Bennett of Florida and Barbara Boxer of California. Their proposal would provide heavy fines for any defense contractor who hired anyone from the Defense Department who had overseen that contractor's program within two years of the individual's retirement. It would also provide for fines and jail terms for anyone accepting a job in violation of the law. The Bennett-Boxer bill should become law.

Fourth, we should get soldiers, sailors, airmen, and marines out of the development and procurement business. These businesses are exactly that: businesses. They are inherently corrupting for any real soldier, not because money is passed under the table, but because they have nothing to do with the military art. They make a real soldier's education in and concern with warfare irrelevant and force him to become a manager and a businessman.

Real soldiers do need to be involved in two aspects of weapons design: setting the requirements and operational testing. Both of these relate directly to combat, and they should include soldiers from the field, people who will have to use the system once it is purchased.

But all the business management aspects of weapons design and procurement should be controlled by specialists in these fields. The French have an excellent system for doing this. French weapons development and procurement are largely controlled by a small specialist corps: the *Ingénieurs de l'Armament.* Only about 1,300 strong, they provide program managers for all major weapons programs for all three services, in addition to running other important functions in the research and development and procurement processes. They belong to no service: the *Ingénieurs* are in effect a separate service, with their own uniforms and ranks. This separateness, coupled with their specialization in development and procurement, gives them both greater expertise and greater objectivity than their American counterparts, who come from and remain part of one of the services and who do not specialize in program management through their entire career.

The French system is also strengthened by having a very strong, independent comptroller force. A French defense white paper states: "The financial Control Corps answers only to the Minister (of Defense). Inside the Corps itself, the watchword is independence; each comptroller is free to carry out the work assigned him in the way he pleases, and the conclusions he draws are personal." These comptrollers have the rank of four-star general, and many of them are young. It is not unusual for someone selected for this duty to be promoted directly from the rank of army captain to four-star general. They have the right and the duty to look into anything that seems in need of improvement. It is a very different approach from our rule-bound, regulation-strangled system. It relies on personal responsibility, not a vast collection of rules and directives. We should adopt a similar system.

The Secretary of the Navy, John Lehman, although opposed to any reform of naval force structure, is keen on improving efficiency, reducing weapons' cost, and cutting down the military bureaucracy. Recently, he attempted to take a step in this direction by ordering that 40 percent of all admirals be managerial specialists. In fact, such specialists should probably be civilians, not military personnel. But at least Secretary Lehman has acknowledged by his action that management skills and warfare skills are not interchangeable.

Summary
Competition in design and in procurement, coupled with performance requirements and independent testing that reflect historically based effectiveness analysis, can give us weapons that work at low enough prices so we can buy the number we need. It is time to put Adam Smith in the Defense Department. We have a military to defend free enterprise. We should apply that free enterprise to the military.

7

The Joint Chiefs of Staff and the
Office of the Secretary of Defense

ONE OF THE MOST BASIC PRINCIPLES of our government is civilian control of the military. The commander in chief of all American armed forces is the president—a civilian. The secretary of defense, the president's most important adviser on defense matters, makes many defense decisions on the president's behalf and is also a civilian. The Founding Fathers insisted that civilians sit in these important military positions to make certain the armed forces would be the nation's servant, not its master. In this, they were notably successful. We have never suffered a coup or even a serious coup attempt. We have never faced an internal military threat to our form of government. Even in the Civil War, the Confederates adopted a governmental structure largely identical to that of the Union they sought to leave—including a civilian president and civilian secretaries of war and the navy. There has never been an American Caesar or even an American Sulla.

One drawback of our system is that neither the president nor the secretary of defense is likely to be a military expert. A few have been; Lincoln had a better understanding of war than most of his generals. But we cannot assume we will have a civilian who understands war in either of these highly important positions. Usually, a president will be someone who has spent most of his life studying the art of getting elected, not the art of winning in combat. His background is most likely to be the profession of law; twenty-one of our presidents have been lawyers. In contrast, only five have been generals (only one in this century), and none have been admirals. The person chosen as secretary of defense will probably be a longtime associate of the president, a noted businessman or lawyer, or a fellow politician. Of our fourteen secretaries of defense since the office was established in 1947, only one, George C. Marshall, had followed a military career.

This means it is highly important for the safety of the nation that the president and the secretary of defense get the best possible advice on military matters. They must have advisers who are the military experts they themselves probably are not. The decisions and the final responsibility must rest with civilians. But there is a great difference in the quality of decisions we can expect from well-advised civilians and those who are presented only with poorly considered options, ill-prepared plans, and faulty recommendations.

The two agencies that provide most of the advice on defense policy to the president and the secretary of defense are the Joint Chiefs of Staff (JCS) and the Office of the Secretary of Defense. Both advise the secretary of defense directly. In addition, the president may meet with the Joint Chiefs personally whenever he chooses to do so. The Joint Chiefs are supposed to make recommendations on subjects such as military strategy, the size and structure of forces we need to implement our strategy, and what our chances of success would be if we undertook military action in a specific case.

The Joint Chiefs of Staff
How good is the quality of advice provided by the Joint Chiefs of Staff? It is notoriously poor. Examples abound:

• Since the current Joint Chiefs system was established in 1947, we have had exactly one significant, brilliant military victory, a victory that reflected out-thinking the enemy, not just bashing him with weight of metal. It was MacArthur's landing at Inchon in 1950. The Joint Chiefs finally approved the Inchon landing only one week before it was scheduled to take place, after expressing considerable misgivings for almost two months.
• In contrast, the plan for the Iran raid of 1979, which ended in tragedy and disaster in the desert, was approved by the Joint

Chiefs. That plan was so complex, failure was virtually certain.[1]
• At no time did the Joint Chiefs of Staff advise President Johnson
against undertaking a war in Vietnam, against continuing the war,
that we were losing—or that we were winning! No member of the
Joint Chiefs of Staff resigned in protest against the way the war
was being conducted. General William Westmoreland, the commander in Vietnam, said in his autobiography, "No commander
could ever hope for greater support than I received from . . .
General Wheeler and the other members of the Joint Chiefs."
• Each year the JCS presents a document describing the force
structure it says we need. Many hours of work go into devising
it. It is nearly useless to the secretary of defense, the president, and
everybody else, for the simple reason that the JCS ignores all
resource limitations in writing it. It assumes that funds are unlim-
ited, so it just calls for everything each service wants.
• One former chairman of the JCS, General David Jones of the air
force, has pressed for reform of the Joint Chiefs. He said of the
current JCS system, "The corporate advice provided by the Joint
Chiefs of Staff is not crisp, timely, very useful, or very influential.
And that advice is often watered down, and issues are papered
over in the interest of achieving unanimity . . . Individual service
interests too often dominate JCS recommendations and actions at
the expense of broader defense interests."

Last year, the Senate Armed Services Committee issued a 645-
page report that discussed in detail the problems in the JCS, among
other defense problem areas. In introducing the report to the Senate, the committee chairman, Senator Barry Goldwater of Ari-
zona, said:

A number of distinguished Americans who have served in key
positions, as well as a number of studies, have all concluded that
the JCS do not provide useful and timely military advice to their
civilian superiors. Former Secretary of Defense James Schles-
inger has said: "The central weakness of the existing system lies
in the structure of the Joint Chiefs of Staff . . . the recommendations and the plans of the Chiefs must pass through a screen
designed to protect the institutional interests of each of the separate Services . . . The unavoidable outcome is a structure in which
logrolling, back scratching, marriage agreements, and the like
flourish. It is important not to rock the boat. . . . The preferred

advice is generally irrelevant, normally unread, and almost always disregarded." Reports commissioned by the Executive branch in 1949, 1960, 1970, 1978, and 1982 reached these same conclusions. I regrettably have also reached the same conclusion: the Joint Chiefs do not provide useful and timely military advice. . . . You will hear over and over again the old maxim: "If it ain't broke, don't fix it." Well, I say to my colleagues: "It is broke, and we need to fix it."

Senator Sam Nunn of Georgia, the ranking Democrat on the committee, replied, "I agree with Chairman Goldwater: The system is broke, and it must be fixed."

Why do the Joint Chiefs of Staff provide such poor advice to the secretary of defense and the president? As elsewhere, the problem is systemic. It has little to do with the individuals who comprise the Joint Chiefs. The heart of the problem is that the Joint Chiefs of Staff are a committee, and they do business by seeking lowest common denominator, committee-consensus solutions to problems. The committee is made up, first, of the Joint Chiefs themselves and, second, of their staff. The Joint Chiefs are the heads of their respective services: the chiefs of staff of the army and the air force, the chief of naval operations, and the commandant of the Marine Corps. The chairman, the fifth member, is usually a former service chief. Each usually sees himself as the custodian of the institutional, bureaucratic interests of his service. The staff is constructed the same way. Officers come to the Joint Staff from their respective services and return to their services when their tour, usually of three years, is over. They are also expected to act as custodians for their services' bureaucratic interests. If they do not, they risk their careers.

The committee consensus process has been formally embodied in the JCS decision mechanism. When an issue arises, it is first written up by one of the staff officers in a draft called a "flimsy." This is then massaged through the system, with staff officers from each service either approving the draft or proposing changes. Once the flimsy has been thoroughly chewed on, it is rewritten as a "buff," a second draft that then goes through the same process.

That is in turn rewritten as a "green," a proposed final draft, and again, it is routed through all the different levels of the staff, where it must get numerous "chops" or approvals. One service can refuse to agree, or "purple," a JCS paper, which starts the whole "flimsy, buff, green" process over again. Only then does it go to the Joint Chiefs themselves to be put through the committee consensus process a fourth time.[2]

The committee-consensus nature of the "flimsy, buff, green" process is reinforced by the tendency of all the services to promote bureaucrats rather than combat-oriented leaders to the position of service chief. This, again, is not a comment on individuals but on the system. The military promotion process tends to advance the bureaucrat, the person skilled at keeping all the little subgroups and interests within a service happy, and weed out the combat-oriented officers. Naturally, the higher the rank, the more thorough this process has been, because of the greater number of promotion "wickets" an officer has had to pass through. The number of combat-oriented officers, people with strong character and imagination, who reach the top, the post of chief of staff, chief of naval operations or commandant, is necessarily small. A few make it, but not very many. When these senior products of bureaucracies gather in the "tank," the place where the JCS meet, they naturally seek the bureaucratic consensus that has been their lifelong object within their service.

What reforms are needed to enable the Joint Chiefs of Staff to give the secretary of defense and the president crisp, clear, competent military advice? A number of proposals for JCS reform have been put forward in the past several years.[3] Many of them focus on rearranging the relationships among the chiefs, the JCS chairman, and the secretary of defense. Several propose that the chairman be given more power.

Because the current promotion system generally chooses survivors of military bureaucracies as senior generals, service chiefs, and JCS chairmen, it is doubtful that rearranging the relationships among them will have much effect. The tendency of the Joint Chiefs to seek bureaucratic consensus, to sacrifice external effectiveness to internal harmony, cannot be eliminated until we change the type of people we promote to service leadership positions. That, in turn, cannot be done except through the overall reform of the promotion system already discussed.

However, one change in the positions of the service chiefs would be useful: they should not simultaneously be members of the Joint Chiefs and heads of their respective services. Anyone serving as a member of the Joint Chiefs should have that as a full-time job. Choosing senior military officers other than the service chiefs as JCS members would not achieve much in the way of reducing parochialism; the officers chosen would still have served for decades in a single service and would probably continue to regard themselves as spokesmen for that service's bureaucratic interests.

But it would give them time to perform their JCS duties. As the Senate Armed Services Committee report on defense organization states:

> The fact that the Service Chiefs do not have sufficient time to perform their two roles (service chief and JCS member) has been recognized for a long time. . . . The 1949 Eberstadt Report stated that: "A further source of the deficiencies of the Joint Chiefs lies in the fact that they are, as individuals, too busy with their service duties to give the Joint Chiefs of Staff matters the attention their great importance demands."

The committee report recommends that the JCS be replaced with a Joint Military Advisory Council "consisting of a Chairman and a 4-star military officer from each Service on his last tour of duty," i.e., senior officers not serving as service chiefs. The recommendation is good and should be adopted, to give the nation's most senior military advisers enough time to do their jobs.

Not much can be done to change the behavior of the JCS members themselves except as part of the overall reform of the officer corps. However, there is an area where reform can bring immediate benefit: the Joint Staff. Instead of the current Joint Staff, we need a National Defense Staff. It should have the following characteristics:

• Unlike the current Joint Staff, once an officer became a member of the National Defense Staff, he would be a member for his entire career. Promotion of National Defense Staff officers would be controlled by the staff itself. This would give its members a license to be objective. Today if a Joint Staff officer opposes what his service or branch wants, he ruins his chances for promotion, because his service and branch still control it. Because his promotion would be controlled by the National Defense Staff, a staff officer would be encouraged, not discouraged, to look beyond parochial service interests and perspectives.

• Officers would be chosen while young, probably at the rank of major/lieutenant commander. The intent would be to choose people before they developed a parochial service mind-set. Selection would put especially strong emphasis on strength of character; candidates would have to have shown such character in their previous service careers. Then, they would have to pass an extensive test. Passing would gain them entry into the National Defense Staff education system. This could either be a special school, probably of three years' duration, or a compendium of the curricula offered by the reformed command and staff colleges and war colleges, including the second-year courses in at least some of these. The candidates would have to demonstrate that they were the outstanding students in these courses in order finally to be selected as National Defense Staff officers.

• The National Defense Staff would have a strong internal ethic emphasizing frankness. The self-image of a staff officer would be that of someone who is as objective as possible in his work and who tells his superiors what he thinks whether or not he is asked for his views. If staff officers are courtiers, their intelligence and expertise will go for nothing.

• The National Defense Staff would be very small. The limit should be five hundred officers. From these five hundred, the staff that would replace the present Joint Staff[4] would be manned. Like all staffs, it would be much smaller than it is today. National Defense Staff officers would also be provided for key positions in some commands outside Washington, especially as operations officers on the staffs of theater commanders.

• As part of their continuing education and training, all National Defense Staff officers would periodically return to troop duties as unit commanders or staff officers. There should not be an "ivory tower" atmosphere in the National Staff. However, even when assigned to troop units, the National Staff officer's promotion would be controlled by the National Staff.[5]

217

• Finally, once the National Defense Staff was established, the individual service staffs would be forbidden to involve themselves in most war-fighting issues. This would further reduce parochialism and help accustom the Joint Chiefs to rely on the National Staff. The service staffs would still be necessary to guide each service's training and administration, but force employment should be guided by the expertise and objectivity of the National Staff, through their advice to the JCS, to the secretary of defense, and, through him, to the president.

All of this would be an advisory system, not a command system. The chairman of the Joint Chiefs, the chiefs themselves, and the National Defense Staff that would replace the Joint Staff would all be advisers, not commanders, just as they are today. All the command authority now resident in the secretary of defense and the president would remain exactly where it is now. The purpose of the reforms is not to diminish their authority, but to improve the quality of the military advice they get.

The Office of the Secretary of Defense
What of the other major source of advice to the secretary of defense and to the president—the Office of the Secretary of Defense (OSD)? While the JCS is supposed to be concerned with questions of military effectiveness, or "output," the Office of the Secretary of Defense is responsible for efficient management of resource "inputs": for the development, acquisition, and maintenance of equipment, facilities and supplies, which is to say, for a great deal of money.

OSD's activity, and indeed most of the activity in the Pentagon, is governed by a system known as the Planning, Programming, and Budgeting System (PPBS). This system was introduced by Secretary of Defense Robert S. McNamara in the early 1960s. In theory, it is a logical system, designed to insure that each year's budget is a coherent part of a long-range plan. PPBS first translates an overall national strategy into a detailed five-year defense plan. Then, the first year of this plan becomes the basis for the annual defense budget requests that are submitted to Congress. Everything fits together, and short-term budget decisions are made on the basis of a long-term plan.

The PPBS in Action

But in practice, it does not work. Instead of long-range goals shaping short-term program and budgeting decisions, the reverse happens. As discussed in Chapter 4, Chuck Spinney's book, *Defense Facts of Life: The Plans/Reality Mismatch,* describes how the pursuit of long-term objectives is undermined by the short-term pressures to start new procurement programs and to keep these programs going once they are started.

Spinney's description of how we pack the budget with too many procurement programs centers on five points. First, the Defense Department's five-year plans assume unrealistically high rates of growth in future defense budgets. Next, unrealistically low rates of growth in the operating budget are used to finance even higher rates of growth in weapons procurement. Third, notwithstanding a dismal track record of ever-increasing costs, the five-year plan optimistically assumes that most weapons will cost substantially less in the future than they cost today. To make matters worse, neither the Congress nor the Pentagon have the stomach to cancel large programs in order to relieve the increasing budget pressure. Finally, the pressure is magnified even further by the chronic tendency to start new, more complex programs, which often have unknown future costs. The result is a plan that is guaranteed to self-destruct. Moreover, since the plan always predicts things will get better in the future, it creates a perverse psychological incentive to avoid making hard decisions in the present.

Despite its seeming rationality in the real world, the PPBS results in decisions and plans that promote short-term individual procurement programs at the expense of long-term military effectiveness. Regardless of whether one believes the budget should increase or decrease, it is clear that if we continue to spend money this way, we will only make matters worse.

Why does PPBS do exactly the opposite of what it was intended to do? The system is based on two false premises. First, it wrongly assumes we know what our priorities are at the beginning of the planning process. Second, it presumes that we can predict the future with certainty.

It is well known that people with different backgrounds view the world differently. The Defense Department is made up of a large number of competing groups with very different backgrounds. Consequently, these groups hold differing sets of priorities. The army looks at the world differently from the navy or the air force. Research and development organizations have different priorities than logistics organizations. The strategic forces perceive different needs than the tactical forces.

The secretary of defense's planning problem is to synthesize these competing priorities into a coherent budget that best serves our nation's long-term defense interests and is fiscally realistic. He needs to understand the trade-offs among parochial needs in order to evolve his priorities. Given a set of meaningful priorities, the programming and budgeting tasks then become reasonably straightforward.

But the PPBS structure does not permit an investigation of competing priorities. The guidance produced by the front end of the PPBS is so vague that it does not filter competing needs. Without priorities, programming and budgeting are chaotic. The battles between the competing interests are never resolved.

In addition, the secretary of defense must try to plan in the face of great uncertainty. Although future threats and future budgets are unknown, he must make decisions today that often embody commitments twenty to thirty years into the future. However, the rigid procedures of the PPBS do not permit any exploration of how these long-term uncertainties could affect current decisions. For example, all the decisions shaping a five-year plan are based on a single projection of future budgets. The PPBS does not permit an investigation of how different future budgets might lead us to want to change these decisions.

Restoring Vitality to OSD Decision Making and Planning
John Boyd and Chuck Spinney have proposed some promising ways to reconcile the plans/reality mismatch. Their ideas are discussed at length in Spinney's book and in an unpublished briefing, entitled "Improving Defense Decisions: Revitalizing Policymaking and Budget Planning."[6]

Before summarizing their proposal, we should be clear on one point. Spinney and Boyd have proposed a concept for providing *better information* to decision makers. Neither their proposal, nor any other organizational solution, will work without the courage, character and commitment of real leadership—in Congress as well as in the Department of Defense.

Bearing this limitation in mind, the PPBS should be replaced by a macroplanning process. Macroplanning would provide a framework designed to permit rapid and easy syntheses of individual programs into rough estimates of alternative five-year programs known as macroplanning options; analysis of each planning option's strengths, weaknesses, and cost; and systematic examination of the possible long-term effects of current uncertainties surrounding future threats, budgets, and technological possibilities.

Macroplanning would consist of two steps. The first would be identifying alternative ways of coping with potential threats. The goal of the first step would be to understand our potential adversaries' weaknesses, strengths, constraints, and opportunities as well as our own. The alternatives would be the services' individual programs.

The second step would be combining alternatives into multiple macroplanning options. The strengths and weaknesses of each option would be analyzed and presented to senior decision makers who would select the "least painful." This "least painful" set of options would replace the vague guidance of the PPBS and would become the skeletal structure underpinning detailed programming and budgeting decisions. Thus, short-term individual decisions would be embedded in a coherent long-term overall perspective.

Macroplanning would provide OSD with a capability to shift its management focus easily from the "parts" to the "whole" and back again. Senior leadership would be able to convey its general intentions to those charged with managing individual programs. This would clarify where the individual programs fit in the "big picture" and permit real decentralization of authority and responsibility. Lower level management would be free to exercize initiative in the pursuit of generally understood objectives.

Macroplanning should not be interpreted as a scheme to increase centralization; on the contrary, it is a means to permit greater decentralization by providing better information to decision makers at all levels.

A Reorganization Proposal

Spinney also describes how OSD might be restructured to implement a macroplanning approach. The central idea behind his reorganization proposal is to institutionalize a set of checks and balances to stimulate and sharpen dialogue. His proposal would also result in a smaller, more efficient, less politicized OSD.

Currently, the OSD organization, with its panoply of two undersecretaries and twenty-two assistant secretaries, presents the secretary of defense with a span of control that is too complicated and too broad. Spinney argues that this could be replaced with a simpler organization consisting of four assistant secretaries as decision makers and an assistant to manage the macroplanning process.

The assistant for macroplanning, who would report directly to the secretary of defense, would head a small office consisting of no more than twenty people. He would be responsible for assembling the alternatives into planning options, presenting them to senior leadership, and ensuring that the detailed Department of Defense budget plan conformed to the priorities contained in the selected set of options. He should be a high-ranking career civil servant and would be appointed for a fixed term. In Spinney's words, he should have

> an impeccable reputation for moral integrity, personal strength, and drive. It is absolutely essential that he be perceived by the entire bureaucracy as an individual who is *not* pursuing a narrow agenda. It is for this reason that an apolitical career status is important. . . . his mission . . . is to lay out policy options and to ensure that the five-year program conforms to policy decisions. In this sense, he is *not* a policy maker; his mission is to make sure his boss, the Secretary of Defense, *is.*

This assistant should have a deputy from the National Defense Staff, since he will need to work closely with the staff in developing the planning options.

222

The first new assistant secretary in Spinney's proposal, the assistant secretary for force readiness and development, would have the mission of

> ensuring that our forces are maintained in a high state of operational readiness—defined broadly in terms of the development of military thought, the training of our people, and our material readiness. . . . (included) would be an important new organization responsible for the study of military history, the nature of conflict, and the development of a unifying body of knowledge to guide our nation's preparation for, and conduct of, war.

Relative to macroplanning, this secretary would be responsible for the identification and analysis of alternatives.

The function Spinney proposes is valid, but because the subjects are directly military, the position should be in the National Defense Staff, not OSD. A position of deputy chief of the national defense staff for force readiness and development should be created, with the duties described above. However, when engaged in macroplanning activities, the deputy chief would have direct access to the secretary of defense as well as the chairman of the JCS. This dual-hat position would permit the deputy chief to serve as the bridge between the resource management orientation of OSD and the military effectiveness orientation of the National Staff.

The second new secretary would be responsible for, in Spinney's words, "ensuring that the human and material resources are properly developed, procured, and supported." He would be the top resource manager in the Defense Department, concerned with all aspects of efficient management: of ensuring competition in hardware procurement, overseeing logistics and support or basing facilities, aligning recruiting with projected manpower needs, and so on. He would also oversee the research and development process. Relative to macroplanning, he would support the deputy chief for force readiness and development by providing resource-related information.

The third secretary, the assistant secretary of defense for policy, would absorb the functions currently performed by the under-secretary for policy. He would provide the threat analysis to the assistant for macroplanning.

Finally, the assistant secretary for budgeting and evaluation would be responsible for transforming the selected set of macroplanning options into a detailed five-year budget plan. In addition, he would conduct independent cost and effectiveness analyses of the alternatives developed by the deputy chief of the National Defense Staff and oversee the independent operational testing office discussed in Chapter 6. He would absorb the activities currently performed by the assistant secretary of defense comptroller and the directors of program analysis and evaluations and of operational testing and evaluation. The deputy assistant secretaries assigned to the operational testing and program analysis functions would be career civil servants appointed for a fixed time period. Their functions, which must include freedom to convey bad news, have become too politicized over the years. Accordingly, their independent evaluations would be submitted directly, and without interference, to the secretary of defense and the other assistant secretaries.

The macroplanning concept and the resulting reorganization are explicitly designed to attack the Pentagon's fundamental resource management problem, namely, the plans/reality mismatch. To attack this problem, we must make the long-term impact of today's decisions visible prior to making commitments. Macroplanning places current decisions in a long-term perspective. In contrast to the PPBS, which assumes priorities are known in advance, macroplanning acknowledges that different groups see the world differently and have different priorities. It provides a means for the secretary of defense to decide on an acceptable set of overall priorities. It is also designed to help individual program managers by providing information that permits them to shift from the "parts"—their programs—to the "whole"—the planning options —and back again.

The reorganization would reinforce the balance between the "whole" and the "parts" by incorporating checks and balances. For example, the power of the deputy chief of the National Defense Staff to advocate programs would increase the military voice in

OSD and provide a tighter link between budget plans and war plans. However, this increased power would be balanced by the improved overall perspective provided by the macroplan and the independent cost-effectiveness analysis provided by the assistant secretary for budgeting and evaluations. Responsibility for program advocacy would also be separate from the economic power derived from the resources needed for development and acquisition, and both of them would be separated from the evaluation of operational test results. The fixed-term assignment of career civil servants to positions that may require them to give bad news to senior officials and the streamlining of the whole OSD structure would reduce the politicization of OSD.

Summary

Adopting a National Defense Staff to replace the current Joint Staff and reorganizing the Office of the Secretary of Defense along the lines described are, once again, very major changes. They are sufficiently major to qualify as military reform. There will no doubt be intense resistance to them from the bureaucracies involved. But if we think we can solve our superstructure problems without reforming these two organizations, both of which have a great deal of effect on the superstructure, we are deluding ourselves. Our serious superstructure deficiencies mean that equally serious deficiencies exist in our defense processes, including the processes that provide advice to the secretary of defense and the president. Military reform means fundamental change in those processes. Nothing less will bring real improvement.

8

The Congress

WHEN ADVOCATES OF MILITARY REFORM talk to military audiences about the reform movement, officers in the audience frequently reply, "We agree with your description of the problems in the armed services. But what about the Congress? Doesn't it share responsibility for many of our defense deficiencies?" The answer is, "Of course." The Congress' approach to defense is today a large part of the reason we get decreasing defense at increasing cost.

The problems start in the formal process by which Congress tackles defense issues. Each year, both houses of Congress consider the defense budget three times through three separate processes and sets of committees. First, the Budget Committees of both houses of Congress recommend a defense budget figure as part of the total federal budget, and the Senate and House as a whole either accept or change that recommendation. Then, the Armed Services Committees of both houses go over the budget in great detail, attempting to look at most, if not all, of the approximately 4,840 "line items"—specific amounts of money for specific programs— in the defense budget. In FY 1985 the Senate Armed Services Committee produced 4,470 pages of committee hearings in eight volumes, changed 548 line items, and had to issue a report 527 pages long to explain to the Senate what it had done. When it completes its work, it sends an annual defense authorization bill to the whole Senate. Last year, 108 amendments to this bill were offered on the floor, and the Senate took nine days debating it. The

House goes through a similar process. Then, the whole thing is repeated! The Defense Subcommittees of the Appropriations Committees of both houses also consider the bill on a line-item basis and send forth a defense appropriations bill. How does it differ from the authorization bill? The only difference is that the appropriations bill is not supposed to provide more money to a program than the authorization bill did. The defense appropriations bill produces further chaos in the defense budget; in FY 1985, the two Defense Appropriations Subcommittees changed 1,848 line items.

Micromanagement

Because of the line-item focus and the large number of players involved, Congress tends to lose sight of the forest for the trees. It allows the Defense Department to make major policy errors while at the same time it drives the department to distraction with myriad minor changes to individual programs. Known as "micromanagement," this has been for some time a largely valid Defense Department complaint about Congress. Most congressional changes in line items are minor—a reduction or increase in funding of 10 percent or 20 percent. Very seldom does Congress actually cancel a program. In FY 1985, the Senate Armed Services Committee did not recommend canceling a single program, although the House Armed Services Committee did recommend canceling two.[1] But together, the authorization and appropriation bills changed 3,163 line items. Each change causes major perturbations in the Defense Department as contracts must be altered, programs slowed down or speeded up slightly, plans changed, and so on—all of which generate more meetings, paperwork, and committee compromises.

Micromanagement has been fueled by the tremendous growth in the number of congressional subcommittees dealing with defense and by the growth of congressional staffs. In 1964, the defense budget was considered by only four major committees, and the Armed Services Committees only authorized about 31 percent of the budget. Only six subcommittees were involved in the defense authorization and appropriation process. The Armed Services

Committees and the Defense Appropriations Subcommittees of the Senate and the House had a combined staff of just 47 people, and committee members relied almost exclusively on committee, not personal, staffs for their defense work. Today, eight major committees, with fourteen subcommittees, are involved fully in considering the defense budget; the Armed Services Committees and the Defense Appropriations Subcommittees alone have 132 staff members, to which the Defense Appropriations Subcommittees, the Budget Committees, and the Intelligence Committees add 222 more. In addition, most committee members have at least one personal staffer who works primarily or solely on defense issues. Just as in the Defense Department, the more people that are involved, the slower and more cumbersome the process becomes, and the more it becomes concerned with minutiae.

Sometimes the micromanagement is legitimate. The Congress will sometimes start a new line item or significantly modify one proposed by the Defense Department to reflect a disagreement over concepts or policy direction. For example, by significantly cutting or adding money for "Star Wars," Congress tells the administration it is less or more certain about the concept of strategic defense than is the president. But most line-item changes reflect minor management concerns or attempts to reduce defense spending by saving a nickel here and a dime there. The disarray they cause in the affected program frequently costs more than the cuts save.

Many committee members like micromanagement because it frees them from dealing with major issues. They shy away from taking on major issues because if they do, they may get in trouble politically if events prove them wrong. Not only does the line-item micromanagement devour all the time and effort of the Congress so little is left for major issues, but it also serves to generate an appearance that something is being done while, in reality, very little is. No member of Congress is likely to get in trouble over jiggling lots of small items, yet he or she can still project an image of doing a great deal to prevent defense waste. On the other hand, if a stand is taken on what strategy we should adopt, what kind of a navy we should build, or how to restructure the Joint Chiefs of Staff, events may prove the Congress member wrong in a way that will be hard to disguise.

Visitors to committee hearings will sometimes hear a committee member say to a witness, "Now general, can you assure me that what you are advocating is right?" The witness responds, "Yes, senator, you have my assurance." The senator's only reply is "Thank you very much." The senator sounds like a fool but is actually being clever politically. If something goes wrong, he can say, "Don't blame me. I just took the expert's word for it. I did not attempt to make a decision myself. Go blame him." The same thing can be seen when a committee withholds money until the secretary of defense "certifies" that something is correct. If it proves incorrect, he carries the blame, not the committee. Last year, the combined authorization and appropriations bills contained eight of these "certification" clauses.

Budget Myopia
Congress also avoids many of the most important defense issues by focusing almost exclusively on the defense budget. The defense budget is just one component of military effectiveness and not the most important. It is very rare in congressional hearings on defense to hear questions about style of warfare, officer education, what kind of people the promotion system is pushing forward, or training realism, because these do not show up as elements in the budget. Most questions focus on how much money we should spend for this or that. This reinforces the Pentagon's tendency to think much more about quantifiable matters such as equipment, which do show up in the budget, than issues relating to people or ideas. Many officers argue correctly that before the services can reduce budgeting and equipment to their proper priorities, the Congress must do so, because the Defense Department tends to focus on the areas that are of most concern to Congress.

Most congressmen justify their focus on the defense budget by saying they are trying to prevent waste. What they miss is that, if the armed forces are not effective in combat, *all* defense spending is waste. And the more issues like strategy, tactics, and the kind of officers we are promoting are neglected, the more likely it is that our forces will be ineffective in combat. If Congress really wants to prevent waste, it needs to reduce the time and attention given to the defense budget to its proper priority. By doing so, it can push the Defense Department to do the same.

Congrints

If the services have a partly legitimate complaint about congressional micromanagement, officers in the field have an equally valid one about "Congrints." A Congrint—short for Congressional Interest—is a request for information from a member of Congress, usually in a matter having to do with a constituent. If, for example, Private Johnny Jones is being hassled by his sergeant and complains to Mom, and Mom in turn writes her congressman, the congressman is likely to ask the service to look into it. That inquiry is a Congrint.

As soon as it is sent to the service involved, all hell breaks loose up and down the chain of command. Everyone drops what he is doing to round up every bit of information on Private Jones' tiff with his sergeant, in order to keep the congressman happy. This may seem like a trivial matter, until one realizes that in 1984, there were 123,130 Congrints.[2]

What can be done to alleviate the Congrint burden? There is no way to eliminate Congrints. They exist because constituents expect their congressmen and senators to perform a service for them, that of providing a "court of last resort" for people inside or outside the service who are having a problem with the military.

However, one step could be taken to alleviate the Congrint burden. The congressional liaison offices of the services, who first receive all Congrints, could assign them priorities. Today all Congrints get top priority in the field. But only a few of them are hot, burning issues for the member of Congress. Most are a routine service to a constituent. If most Congrints came to the field with a less than highest priority assigned to them, field officers would not feel compelled to let them interfere with whatever was going on at the moment. They could be dealt with as the routine matters most of them are.

The "Jobs" Factor

Another common congressional problem is the tendency of members of Congress to support a weapon built in their state or district whether the weapon is a good one or not. It is considered acceptable for a senator or congressman to set aside judgment on a weapon's effectiveness if it brings jobs and money to constituents. Unfortunately, bad weapons will get our own troops killed regardless of whose state or district they are built in.

Constituents generally understand this. Although some major defense contractors take the attitude, "As long as it makes a profit for our stockholders, we have fulfilled our moral responsibility; we have no responsibility to the soldiers," voters very seldom think this way. Most of them are willing to support congressmen or senators who tell them they are opposing a program that would bring them jobs because the weapon the program would produce is ineffective and, therefore, dangerous to our soldiers, and who explain why it is ineffective. One member of the Congressional Military Reform Caucus tells how a group of his constituents came to see him to get help obtaining an air force contract. The contract was for a weapon that not only does not work but also endangers the pilot who tries to use it in combat. At first, when the congressman explained why he could not support the weapon, his constituents replied, "We don't know anything about weapons. We just expect you, as our representative, to help get us these jobs. You know how high unemployment is back home." After explaining at length why the weapon was a bad one, the congressman finally said, "OK, what ratio of dead American pilots to jobs will you accept? One dead pilot for twenty jobs? One for ten? How about one for five? What should the cut off be?" They had not thought of it that way before—just as some members of Congress do not think of it that way. They forget that lives, not wasted dollars, are often the price for badly designed weapons. Once they saw it in those terms, the congressman's constituents said, in effect, "If that is the price for these jobs, we don't want them."

Incestuous Relationships

Another congressional failing is the "closed cycle." The closed cycle stems from the fact that although the Armed Services and Defense Appropriations Committees are supposed to be watchdogs over the armed services, a majority of their members consider the uniformed military and Defense Department officials the only real experts on defense. The only people the committees will believe are those they are supposed to be overseeing, which gives the Pentagon the happy situation that only it can testify effectively against itself. Seldom do these committees even hear outside witnesses. Last year the Senate Armed Services Committee heard only fifteen witnesses on the defense budget who were not from the Defense Department, and of those, seven were from other elements of the government or service lobbying groups, such as the Air Force Association. It is as if the Banking Committee heard few witnesses except spokesmen for the Federal Reserve, or the Committee on Environment and Public Works, few but spokesmen from the Environmental Protection Agency.

Why is this the case? Largely because the committees develop incestuous relationships with the armed services. This is not unique to these committees or to the Congress; the tendency of regulators to identify with the regulated is a long-standing problem with all oversight agencies. But it is a serious problem.

Some of this springs from politics. The Defense Department is adept at placing important defense contracts in the states of legislators who support them. A senator or congressman who has a "good relationship" with the department can help defense contractors get contracts, and the contractors in turn contribute to the member's campaign fund. Congressional staffers willing to "carry water" for the services can also look to rewards in the form of Defense Department or defense contractor jobs. The "revolving door" is not limited to Defense Department employees; those on Capitol Hill also get their reward. Recently, one member of the Armed Services Committee staff not only got a service job as principal deputy to an assistant secretary, he also continued to serve for some months as a committee staffer after he was told he was getting the job. His case is not an isolated one. Such conflict of interest is all too common on the Hill.

But most of the close relationship many members of the committees develop with the services is an emotional bond. They come to see the services generally, or one service in particular, as valiant battlers in the struggle for a strong defense, and they identify with them. The services not infrequently try to generate this kind of emotional tie. Nor can members of Congress really be condemned for this kind of bonding. Most military officers are trying to do a good job against heavy odds— odds made heavy by the weight of our own military bureaucracy. It is easy to identify with their struggles. Unfortunately, by identifying with a service or the Defense Department generally, members of Congress unwittingly help perpetuate our officers' problems by acting as defenders of "business as usual."

The "closed cycle" contributes to another major congressional failing: Congress' unwillingness to separate honest military advice, based on military thinking (sound or not), from bureaucratic preferences disguised as military advice. The people do not elect their representatives to be experts in the art of war, but they do elect them with the expectation they will be able to recognize baloney when it is being fed to them. It is not difficult, in many Armed Services Committee hearings, to see that the Defense Department witnesses are disguising bureaucratic preferences as military advice. It does not take a genius to see, for example, the navy's institutional identification with large aircraft carriers. Congress has a responsibility to separate that kind of bureaucratic preference from real military analysis. Today it almost totally neglects that responsibility. It pretends that it is getting military advice when it knows perfectly well it is actually being told what the bureaucracy finds comfortable.

The "closed cycle," defense committee identification with the services, and congressional unwillingness to separate military from self-interested bureaucratic advice all contribute to a very serious congressional failing: the failure to uphold the basic constitutional doctrine of separation of powers. Our Constitution deliberately creates separation of interests among the executive, legislative, and judicial branches of government, so that each will act as a check on the others. When a congressional committee becomes an extension of a department of the executive branch of government, it is uniting what the Founding Fathers wisely tried to keep separate. It is neglecting Congress' constitutional responsibility to cast a questioning eye on what the executive branch proposes. Instead of a system of checks and balances, we quickly find ourselves with an executive department bureaucracy that can do what it wants unchecked.

What Can Be Done?

There is one change in congressional procedures that would reduce the burden of congressional micromanagement and the time and attention the services must devote to Capitol Hill: eliminating either the defense appropriations or the defense authorization process. The original purposes of having a defense appropriations bill separate from the defense authorization bill were, first, to provide a more detailed defense budget at a time when the defense authorization bill only covered a limited portion of the budget and, second, to fit the defense budget into the overall federal budget. Today both of those functions are superfluous. Seventy-six percent of the defense budget is covered by the authorization bill, and the budget resolution, not the appropriations process, sets the overall defense budget total.[3] One of the two processes, authorization or appropriation, has become a fifth wheel, generating more micromanagement, more hearings, and more testimony, but not doing anything different from what has already been done by the budget resolution and by either the defense authorization or the appropriations bill. One is redundant. One should go.

What else can be done to change the way Congress looks at defense? Unfortunately, most of the problems have no mechanical solution, no solution based on changes in congressional procedures. Congress works the way it does because it wants to. Rules cannot prohibit a member of Congress from advocating what he knows are ineffective weapons because they would be built in his state or district. No rule can prevent members of the Armed Services or Defense Appropriations Committees from identifying emotionally with one or all services. No new procedure can compel committee members to separate honest military advice from bureaucratic preferences masquerading as military advice.

Nor is there any overall solution to Congress' microfocus and the micromanagement that results. If, for example, Congress were merely to authorize and appropriate funds in broad categories with little direction, the Pentagon would be delighted, because the few checks on its behavior the Congress now imposes would vanish. But that would not result in more attention to major defense issues, least of all on the part of the Pentagon. The relevant congressional committees do not focus on major issues because they do not want to. They could do so even under the current system, but they prefer the safety of microfocus. There is no way procedurally to compel a committee to look at issues it would rather ignore.

The only solutions are long-term, and they rest on education: education of the public and the press about defense issues so that they bring pressure on their elected representatives to address the real issues, not just budgetary trivia, and education of the representatives themselves about the potential cost to the nation of continued "business as usual" and about the alternatives to it. Neither will be easy. The military reformers discovered early in their work how hard it is to get press attention for nonbudgetary issues, such as style of warfare, officer education, and unit cohesion.

With the modern "science" of image-building, officeholders can present an image that is in fact contrary to what they are doing in Washington. Many of the legislators who most staunchly defend "business as usual" in defense, which is to say the perpetuation of our current military ineffectiveness, are those with the strongest "pro defense" images back home. Some nominal members of the Congressional Military Reform Caucus are equally staunch defenders of business as usual in arenas such as joint conference, where they are working behind closed doors.[4] Only if the press can be brought to look at the real defense issues and where members of Congress stand on them—in votes and actions, not just words —can the public hope to find out what its representatives are actually doing.

However, if the public can find out what is actually being done in Congress, it is likely to push its representatives in the right direction. The public has two basic perceptions about defense. The first is that we need a strong defense. The second is that the Pentagon is a bureaucratic Augean stable. Both perceptions are correct, and if the public can effectively persuade its representatives to reflect its views, Congress will at least have a valid starting point for its defense legislation.

The other way education can, over time, bring improvement is through education of members of Congress themselves. The fruits of this kind of education are evident in the continuing growth and increasing activity of the Congressional Military Reform Caucus. As a growing number of members of Congress are made aware of the fact that, with fundamental changes in policy direction, we *can* obtain an effective defense, they are joining the caucus and supporting reform. As the caucus grows in strength, it will compel the Armed Services and Defense Appropriations Committees to look at the broad policy issues they prefer to avoid. And it will be able to challenge those committees on the floor of the House and Senate if they seek to continue business as usual.

Ultimately, education of the press, the public, and the Congress about what really makes a military effective in combat, coupled with reform of the Defense Department itself, may lead to a new national consensus on defense. Then, congressional micromanagement and pork-barreling and the Pentagon counterpart of continual resistance to any congressionally mandated change will be ended. Because military reform addresses *both* of the public's basic perceptions about defense, the need for a strong defense and the need for reform of the Pentagon, it offers the potential basis for such a consensus. Consensus is, in fact, an explicit goal of the reform movement. The briefing of the Congressional Military Reform Caucus states at its outset, "We want military forces that can win when called upon . . . (and) we want the support of the nation for such forces, not for one or two years, but for the long haul—to 1990 and beyond."

Summary

If we can build a national defense consensus on the basis of military reform, many of the congressional problems discussed in this chapter will at least diminish. If the armed services, the public, the press, and the Congress are working in harmony, there will be far less need for micromanagement. Congressmen and senators will less often face pressure to support ineffective weapons built in their districts or states, because the Defense Department will no longer be requesting ineffective weapons. Members of Congress will be able to work for an effective defense by supporting what the Defense Department requests, while today, to support an effective military, it is often necessary to oppose the Pentagon.

If education is not as attractive a solution to Congress' problems in dealing with defense as some deus ex machina, it is nonetheless the only solution. Democratic institutions like Congress do not lend themselves to mechanistic solutions of major problems. They operate on the basis of consensus and beliefs, and only by building a new consensus can their behavior be changed.

PART

THREE

Changing The System

The problems discussed in Part
Two—those in the officer corps, the weapons development and
procurement process; the Joint Chiefs of Staff and the Office of the
Secretary of Defense; and the Congress— explain why we have so
many deficiencies in the defense superstructure. If the officer corps
is not well educated in the art of war, then concepts, doctrine, force
structure, and tactics are likely to be unsatisfactory. If the weapons
development and procurement process makes little use of competition, weapons are likely to be badly designed and overpriced. If the
Joint Chiefs of Staff and the Office of the Secretary of Defense make
their decisions by committee consensus, our strategy and grand

239

strategy are likely to be flawed, and our defense budget is likely to be incapable of moving us toward our long-term goals.

Why are the officer corps, the development and procurement process, the JCS, and OSD in such bad shape?[1] The majority of the people in each of these institutions is intelligent and well intentioned. Many of them are at least partially aware of the problems discussed in this book. Most share the frustration of the soldiers in the field with "the system." Why, then, does that system perpetuate itself?

The question can be answered with a single word: bureaucracy. Bureaucracy has what might be called the "reverse Midas touch." Everything it touches turns to garbage. It can take good people, intelligent, well-intentioned people, and turn them into office politicians, turf defenders, courtiers, moles burrowing blindly in narrow, parochial interests—in short, into bureaucrats—without their being more than dimly aware it is happening. Bureaucracy lies at the root of our military weakness, just as it lies at the root of much of the ineffectiveness of other government departments and the decreasing competitiveness of much of our private industry.

But if we are to solve our defense problems, we must do more than attach the label "bureaucracy" to them. We must understand what bureaucracy is, how its reverse Midas touch works, and what we can replace it with.

9

Bureaucracy

TODAY ALL FOUR ARMED SERVICES, the Joint Chiefs of Staff, the Office of the Secretary of Defense, the multitude of agencies that run the weapons development and procurement process, and all their various appendixes and extensions follow the bureaucratic organizational model. What exactly do we mean by "the bureaucratic organizational model"?

Bureaucracy is not just a pejorative term. It describes a particular way of organizing a company, department, or office. A bureaucracy takes the overall goals and purposes of the institution and breaks them down into ever smaller pieces until they constitute jobs—tasks that can done by a single individual. These jobs are usually very precisely defined, and people are usually placed into them not as individuals, but as a set of qualifications that matches the job description. The phrases "That's not your job" and, conversely, "That's not my job" are often heard in bureaucracies because bureaucracies define jobs quite rigidly.

Faced with these rigid job descriptions and the limits they impose, individuals within the organization cannot act on the basis of the organization's overall goal—what it is trying to do in the outside, competitive world. If they try to do so, they overstep their job descriptions and are told, "That's not your job." But the jobholders still need some system of values, if for nothing else than for prioritizing their time and effort. So they develop alternative values, unrelated to the organization's purpose. One is usually personal career success: getting promoted. Bureaucracies foster careerism and usually see it as something positive.

The other value most people who work in bureaucracies tend to develop is an unconscious one. They tend to see as most important those activities that take most of their time. These activities are seldom directly related to the external tasks or competitors—poverty if they work in the Department of Health and Human Services, Toyota if they work for Chevrolet, or the Soviets if they are in the military—but to other elements of their own institution: the competing office, program, or branch, the department immediately above or below them, or those for whom they produce a subproduct within their organization. The organizational decision process comes to be dominated not by considerations related to competing effectively in the outside world but by intra-institutional considerations.

This is the situation in which our intelligent, well-intentioned officers find themselves in the Defense Department. Intra-institutional preferences, habits, battles, and deals take up most of their time and set virtually their whole agendas. Anyone who attempts to subordinate them to the demands of the external world—the prospective battlefield—quickly finds himself the odd man out, a "loose cannon" who "doesn't understand" his real job, someone who does not know how to "be effective." If he persists in his unusual behavior, he usually pays with his career.

In the armed services, the power of intra-institutional considerations is reinforced by two factors not present in most civilian bureaucracies. The first is the "up or out" promotion system. The officer who is not promoted is in effect fired, so promotion takes on greatly added importance. The second is the fact that there is no lateral entry. Anyone who is a general or an admiral has spent a minimum of about twenty-five years in the same institution, looking at the world through the perspective of its many intra-institutional concerns. Large corporations often try to work around these blinders by bringing in a top executive from another company, even another field. That is never done in the armed services.[1]

The domination of the decision process by intra-institutional concerns is the hallmark of a bureaucracy, and it lies at the root of many of the problems discussed in this book. Why don't the services do a better job of educating officers in the art of war? The art of war has little relevance to the internal battles for resources, missions, programs, and prestige that occupy most of the time and attention of the senior military bureaucrats. Worse, officers who are better educated in the art of war are more likely to find deficiencies in "business as usual," leading them to call for institutionally unsettling changes. Why don't the services promote officers with strong character and imagination? Because both qualities lead such officers to put external effectiveness above internal harmony, again generating uncomfortable demands for change. Why do the Joint Chiefs of Staff have a system designed expressly to foster committee consensus, lowest common denominator decisions? Making decisions that way best protects parochial interests.

Why do the Joint Chiefs, the most senior personnel in the Office of the Secretary of Defense, the people who run the weapons development and procurement process, and most senior officers so adamantly defend "business as usual"? It is because *any* change is very painful to a bureaucracy.

The resistance of bureaucracies to change brings us to the bottom line of military reform. The dominant characteristics of combat are uncertainty and rapid change. Bureaucracies deal very poorly with both. Our armed services today are bureaucracies. Hence, the organizational model of our armed forces is *directly contradictory* to the nature of the environment in which they are supposed to operate.

This is the root reason why we cannot hope to achieve adequate military strength simply by spending more money, introducing more technology, or buying more weapons. Nor can it be achieved solely through the reforms discussed previously in this book: educating our officers better in the art of war, improving unit cohesion, redefining what constitutes quality in weapons, and so on. None of these changes will make a major, lasting difference so long as the organizational model of our defense establishment—and therefore its behavior—remains contradictory to the nature of war. Not only combat but also preparation for combat is inherently dialectical, because it involves an active and reactive hostile will. It cannot be

combined successfully with a type of institution that demands predictability and routine. The bottom line of military reform, therefore, is and must be *abandoning the bureaucratic organizational
model.*

But this most basic contradiction, the contradiction between
the nature of war and the organization of our armed services, is not
the only price the military pays for bureaucracy. The conservative
political activist Paul Weyrich discusses several other costs very
eloquently in a book chapter he wrote on bureaucracy:

> One is the price paid by people who are trapped inside a bureauc-
> racy. Today, more and more of us find ourselves in this situation.
> We go to work wanting to do a good job, to produce a good
> product, but the company or the union or the government de-
> partment won't let us. When we see a problem or a mistake, the
> bureaucracy says to us, "Shut up about it. It's not your job to
> worry about that. Besides, it will make the supervisor or the
> department head or the local union boss mad if you mention it.
> It will make him look bad." Or, maybe we have an idea about
> how the product or the way the office runs can be improved. We
> are told, "Don't rock the boat. That's the way *they* want it. Go
> along to get along."
>
> In government and private business, in big organizations and
> even in small firms, we hear this more and more often. Most of
> us don't like it. We want to do a good job. . . .
>
> And now we are told we can't do that. We are told we will
> ruin our chances for promotion, or even get fired if we try. We
> are told to "play the game," and sell our product and our country
> down the river in the process.
>
> So we come to hate our job. We can't get any satisfaction
> from it, because the bureaucracy won't let us do it right. Whether
> we are auto workers or businessmen or military officers, we feel
> we are caught up in a system that has something horribly wrong
> with it. But we can't see any way out. So we go through the
> motions, play the game to the degree we must to keep our jobs
> and try not to care.[2]

How many of our best officers will find this an all-too-accurate description of the situation they find themselves in, especially when assigned to a major headquarters, a development or procurement program, or, worst of all, the Pentagon! The "rules of the game" destroy all job satisfaction. "Committing truth" is a most serious sin. Anyone who balks at playing by the bureaucratic rules, which stipulate that the parochial interests of the program, the boss, the branch, or the service come first, is quickly counseled: "Don't you understand how the game is played? Don't you know you won't be effective unless you accept the rules?" Refusal to play the game is looked on as a fundamental breach of etiquette. And persistent, principled refusal brings swift retribution on the next fitness report, if not outright relief from the assignment.

Bureaucracy's destruction of the honest, well-intentioned employee or officer's job satisfaction is compounded by the fact that he often must sit back and watch the meteoric rise in the organization of his opposite: the courtier. The courtier has not changed much since he was described by Castiglione some centuries ago. He is the person who manipulates appearances and other people for his own personal benefit, flattering those who can help him rise, ignoring and despising those who cannot, projecting always an appearance of ability but seldom if ever producing a useful product. Usually deficient in real competence, he devotes his talents solely to his own career, trying to make up for his lack of substance with an ability to be pleasing to his superiors and a willingness to do anything in order to please.

The courtier's advent and proliferation in our bureaucratic armed forces is brilliantly described by a civilian professor at the air force's Squadron Officer School, Dr. Donald Chipman, in his article, "The Military Courtier and the Illusion of Competence":[3]

> A critic might point out there have always been courtiers. This, I do not dispute. Yet never have so many institutional forces encouraged the development of this character. The courtier develops not out of deviousness but out of the complexity in organizations that are process-oriented. Ultimately he arises out of the narcissistic culture in organizations that have allowed individu-

als to use their manipulative social skills for self-aggrandize-
ment.

The institutionalization of social skills has initiated new research on how to utilize this craft. Nationwide advice is available
on how to avoid work and yet succeed. Books and magazines
clearly present the message: Forget the job and concentrate on
refining your social skills. If you want a bigger salary and control
of others, then you must learn to grab for power. Since power is
the most important organizational ingredient, you must learn
how to get it and how to use it.

Although these books are for the corporate executive, many
of the suggestions have become a part of the military way. As the
military adopted corporate techniques, inevitably the courtier
followed.

Dr. Chipman's students at the air force's Squadron Officer
School, who are junior officers, receive his ideas very well. They
attempt to identify the courtiers among them. Very few of them
want to be courtiers and bureaucrats. The difficulty is that, as they
rise in rank, the current system gives them little option. They will
be compelled to adapt to bureaucracy or be pushed out of the
service by "up and out."

If the contradiction between the bureaucratic organizational
model and the kind of institutional behavior and people we need
for success in combat is evident, what is the solution? The answer
is another organizational model, known as the "corporative"
model.[4]

In the past few years, Americans have shown growing interest
in the way Japanese corporations are organized. We have discovered that the ability of the Japanese to produce very high quality
products is not due just to superior manufacturing technology. It
is because many Japanese workers approach their jobs differently
from many of their American counterparts. They do so because the
organizational model of most Japanese corporations encourages
them to. Those corporations follow the "corporative" model.

How does it work? The institution, whether it is a company, a
government department, or a military service, makes a great effort

to get its employees at every level to adopt the institution's *external* goals and purposes as their *personal* goals and values. These goals and purposes are constantly inculcated in everything the organization does, from starting the workday by singing the company song, through uniforms, the sharing of onerous tasks by management and workers alike, and the way the rewards and promotion systems work. The organization tries to get its members to reference everything they do on a day-to-day basis to its overall goals and purposes. People still have individual jobs, but they are expected to use their intelligence and initiative to work within and beyond those jobs to serve the organization's overall goals.

This creates a very marked contrast to the bureaucratic organization, because it reverses its rewards and punishment system. Whereas the bureaucracy punishes people who question what is done day-to-day because it fails to serve the institution's external purposes, the corporative institution rewards them for doing just that. Pressures still exist to put internal, parochial interests ahead of the external goals—that is human nature—but there is now a check on them. Throughout the organization, at every level, people who have been effectively inculcated with the institution's values, or "socialized," stand up and object. And when they do so, their superiors, instead of ruining their careers, listen to them and reward them.

A good illustration of the difference between the bureaucratic and the corporative institution was given by a professor from the University of Tokyo in a lecture at Stanford University. He told the story of an American bank that was not doing well and was bought out by a Japanese bank. The Japanese bank sent in new Japanese management. The American employees said, "Fine, we are willing to work for Japanese. Just tell us what to do differently." They expected detailed, specific instructions. The Japanese responded by explaining their values and goals.

The Americans did not know how to take this. They had gotten "pep talks" in the past, but they had always known they didn't mean anything. They were confused, and productivity continued to fall. But the Japanese were patient. They kept on explaining the company's goals and values and continued trying to get the employees to understand that they, not the management, were supposed to figure out how to accomplish those goals. Finally, the employees caught on. They began to take initiatives to serve the company's goals and values. Once they did so—once they became socialized—the bank's productivity took off, and it became highly successful. And the employees were much happier in their jobs.

The corporative institution is not just a Japanese phenomenon. Some American companies have long adhered to the corporative model—IBM is a good example. So have elements of our armed forces. Every service has pockets of corporativeness in it, most often in the field units. One service, the Marine Corps, still largely adheres to the corporative model at the more junior levels—lieutenant colonel and below—although it has become a bureaucracy at higher levels. As noted earlier, the main function of the Marine Corps' Basic School, through which all lieutenants pass, is to socialize, to inculcate a set of shared goals and values.

If military reform is to succeed, it must transform our bureaucratic services and equally bureaucratic civilian defense organizations, such as the Office of the Secretary of Defense, into corporative institutions. Only a corporative military can have the decentralization and initiative at every level needed for effectiveness in combat. Only a corporative military can focus sufficiently on the external world to overcome internal resistance to change.

How is this to be done? There is no single, mechanical change that can bring it about. Many of the reforms proposed in this book will assist in doing it. Mission-type orders that tell the subordinate what is to be accomplished but leave up to him how to do it will help. Reducing the size of the officer corps so that there is room for individual authority and responsibility will help. Creating long-range goals that permit everyone to understand the direction in which the institution is moving will help. Eliminating the "up-or-out" promotion system will help.

The task is an enormous one, because it means changing the way people think and behave. It will not be accomplished overnight, nor will it be accomplished without some mistakes. If we want the initiative that characterizes a corporative organization, we cannot have a "zero defects" atmosphere. Mistakes that result from taking the initiative must be accepted.

But it must be done. The bureaucratic model is inherently contradictory to the nature of war, and no military that is a bureaucracy can produce military excellence. If we just change the superstructure while perpetuating bureaucratic behavior, we will freeze in a new mold that will, in time, become as irrelevant as the present one. If we try to reform the officer corps, the weapons development and procurement system, the Joint Chiefs of Staff, and the Office of the Secretary of Defense, but leave them all bureaucracies, we will have changed only appearances, not substance. The final product, our combat units, will continue to be ineffective and uncompetitive in the outside world, the battlefield.

Can we do it? Yes, because so many of the people inside the services want to. They are the daily victims of bureaucracy, and they will be the first victims of its ineffectiveness in combat. As noted at the outset of this book, the most important element of the military reform movement is that inside the officer corps. Ultimately, our officers will decide whether military reform succeeds or fails, because military reform means changing the way their institutions think and behave.

10

Crosscuts

ONE OF THE MOST SURPRISING and rewarding aspects of the military reform movement is the way in which many people have seen its principles apply to broader aspects of their lives and work. As articles have been written and speeches given on military reform, a range of people have felt that the reformers have identified problems in the military that parallel problems they see in other fields.

Themes from the military reform movement do, in fact, cut across into many other areas. It may be worthwhile to explore briefly some of these "crosscuts."

The most obvious is the absolute requirement, in any field, to focus on the product. The military reform movement began with the realization that our military product—effectiveness in combat —was not what it should be. Despite the courage, dedication, and hard work of our soldiers, sailors, airmen, and marines, we were not doing very well in combat. And our defense establishment did not seem terribly concerned. The reason it was not very concerned is that it had lost sight of the product.

In this it was not alone. Many government departments seem content to produce a product of doubtful quality. So does much of private industry. In many companies, especially large ones, the quality of the product is no longer the top consideration. Railroads provide a good example. The product of a railroad is service to shippers, not trains. Yet for many decades, railroads have tended to say, "This is how we run our trains. Shippers will just have to

251

be satisfied with whatever level of service that gives them." They made the means, not the end, their highest priority. The resulting quality of service to shippers was such that many switched to trucks. A number of railroads are now realizing the shipper doesn't care how trains are run, he just wants to have his shipments arrive on time and in good condition. These railroads are beginning to offer guaranteed arrival times and other real services. But it took the harsh lesson of a fall in market share from 75 percent in 1929 to 36 percent in 1983 to teach them.[1]

The crosscut here seems to be: unless the product is the top priority at every level in the organization, product quality is not likely to be very high. When process rather than product becomes the top priority, the ability to compete declines.

Military reform has pointed out that we cannot get a stronger, more effective defense simply by spending more money. Similarly, adding more people may make an organization less, rather than more, effective. Our military effectiveness is reduced, not enhanced, by the large number of middle- and senior-grade officers we now have on roster.

We can see the same thing in many other government departments. Simply spending more money for education, health care, welfare, or foreign aid does not automatically give us better education, less illness or poverty, or more friends and allies in the world. It depends on *how* the money is spent—what the guiding concepts are. If the concepts are wrong, more money is likely to make the problems worse—as it has in areas like welfare, where some programs have inadvertently encouraged the breakdown of the family. This is not to say that the solution is simply to cut spending, as some urge for the military and others for human needs. As we have seen in the military, to improve effectiveness we need to spend less in some areas and more in others.

Similarly, making a government department or program larger by adding more people does not automatically make it more effective. Some of the largest government departments also seem to be some of the least effective, while some very small programs seem to produce good results. If what we have found in the military does

252

cut across to other government departments, we might help some of them by reducing the number of people in them, especially the number of people in supervisory or executive jobs.

Mergers provide a good example from the private sector of how spending large sums of money and increasing an organization's size can reduce rather than enhance performance (as many readers who have gone through mergers in the companies they work for can attest). Between 1973 and 1984, about $398 billion was spent by U.S. corporations on mergers and acquisitions. Some of these improved productivity. But a good number did not. Such major corporations as Mobil, Sohio, Exxon, Baldwin-United, and Pan Am invested billions of dollars in mergers that reduced, rather than raised, their earnings. According to one article, "in the past decade only one-third of all mergers have enriched the acquirer's stockholders, one-third have been a wash, and one-third have ended up costing investors money—sometimes lots of it."[2]

It seems there is another crosscut here: the effectiveness of an organization cannot be improved simply by throwing more resources at it—money or people. In fact, more resources may make the problems worse. Concepts and ideas, not more money or more people, must be the starting point. And fewer people, rather than more, may actually improve effectiveness.

A third crosscut seems fairly obvious: competition works. Competition, where the more successful competitors are rewarded with more money, improves the product. The few cases where real competition has been used to develop and procure military equipment have resulted in better products at lower costs.

Why then do we see so little competition in government departments? Obviously, some areas of government are not suitable for competition: we cannot have competing State Departments. But could we not benefit from competition in other areas, such as welfare? Could we not create competing approaches to reducing poverty in our cities, with each approach having its own office working in a different city to see which got the best results? The approach that worked the best could then be adopted generally.

What about private industry? Our economy is capitalist, but

there are some noticeable trends toward reducing competition. Many companies are seeking protection from foreign competition. Others look to government bailouts when they do not do well in the marketplace. To the degree that a corporation relates its profits more to cultivating relations with government than to how well its products compete in the marketplace, it ceases to be truly capitalist. And within the corporation, the concern with producing a quality product is likely to diminish.

Technology is very important in the military, as it is in the rest of our society. But one of the most important insights of the military reformers is that people and ideas are more important than equipment, including high-technology equipment. This seems to apply to civilian organizations as well. If the people in an organization are poorly led or poorly trained, if morale is low, if management is bad, if the organizational structure is faulty, if the product is poorly designed, if any of the many potential problems in the areas of people and ideas are occurring, adding high-technology equipment will not make the organization effective.

Too often, organizations attempt to improve their effectiveness by adding technology when the problem is not soluble with technology. They buy computers because they equate quantities of information with good information. The computers are used to make the process within the organization more complex, not less; to create rigidity, not flexibility; and to build new empires within the institution rather than a better product. They end up with more data that they do not use any better than the data they had before.

Many people found this out after they bought home computers. They tried using the computers to balance their checkbooks, store recipes, keep kitchen and workshop inventories, and so on. The computer would indeed do all these things. Unfortunately, it did them with much more work than the old, manual methods. Home computer sales have fallen as people have discovered their drawbacks and limitations.

Technology is no substitute for a sound institutional culture, for effective leadership, or for personal judgment. Computers are very useful for storing and retrieving data to help people make judgments. But too often we find the people being used to handle the data while they attempt to get the computers to make the judgments. Further, the more an environment is characterized by uncertainty and change, the more that human judgment is required. No machine is adaptable to change the way a person is. And our whole economy and society face a high and increasing rate of change.

Events in the corporate and civilian government worlds also confirm the military reform view that equipment quality should be measured by the equipment's usefulness, not the level of technology it embodies. Public enterprises, in particular, seem to become fascinated with technology for its own sake. Several years ago, there was an attempt to sell the city of Pittsburgh a high-technology transit system called Sky Bus. The plan was to use rubber-tired vehicles running on special "guideways," and the attempt to sell it was largely based on a "high-tech" appeal. Only after a long and bitter struggle did the city realize that it got exactly the same product from its existing trolley system, which it is now improving at a fraction of what Sky Bus would have cost.

All these cautions seem to add up to another crosscut: technology is not a deus ex machina. It is no replacement for correct policies toward people or for sound guiding concepts. Unless technology is considered for what it does rather than what it is, and what it does can be related directly to a problem, it is likely to do at least as much harm as good and cost a great deal of money in the process.

One of the military reformers' main concerns is the poor quality of military education. Instead of teaching how to think, it teaches what to do or what to think. Instead of anchoring the individual in the military culture—the basic ideas that frame the art of war, how they arose and why they are held valid, how successful commanders of the past have thought their situations through, what qualities a military needs for success, and so forth—it largely teaches mechanical skills, forms, formats, procedures, and terminology.

Civilian education seems to make many of the same mistakes.

It is no longer a liberal, classical education. It no longer anchors the student in his culture by acquainting him with its great ideas, thinkers, and books, with its history, literature, and philosophy. One recent article on the decline of education noted:

> Three years ago, when I was teaching at a major southeastern university, I asked freshmen honors students a set of twenty general knowledge questions. In what town was Christ born? Who painted *Guernica?* Name three of Shakespeare's plays. Who was the President immediately preceding Eisenhower? These were hardly "trivia" questions. High school graduates should be expected to have at least a passing familiarity with the landmarks of their culture. Still, more than half the students answered more than half the questions wrong. The heritage of this—or any—culture seemed to mean nothing to them. They were born yesterday and proud of it. They had learned next to nothing in high school.[3]

Just as officers who cannot think but can only follow recipes and formulas on the battlefield are soon reduced to helpless confusion by uncertainty and rapid change, so citizens who have not been educated are baffled and helpless in the face of social and economic change. They cannot understand what is happening or why, they cannot distinguish good changes from bad, they cannot adapt in a way that leaves them economically viable or personally secure.

Civilization depends on education. It is never more than one generation deep. It must be consciously transmitted from one generation to another, and the process of transmission is what rightly bears the name of education. It is not what most of our so-called educational institutions are doing now. Most are mere trade schools, teaching people machine-like skills in an age when machines can have those skills, but when we increasingly need people who can think through how to use machines.

That is crosscut number five: education is a requirement for effectiveness in anything. Education means civilizing, acculturating, teaching how to think, not what to do or what to think. We must reform our education system so that it once again provides true education.

Military reform makes a case for the power and importance of change. It notes that change, rapid change, is the essence of conflict. It argues that not only war but also preparation for war is inherently a dialectical process, because it is characterized by a multiplicity of active, contending wills. Any nation or armed service that freezes will find itself reduced to obsolescence and ineffectiveness as others change. The reformers propose major changes in many of the most basic aspects of our defense policy: weapons, ships, doctrine, personnel policies, promotion systems, even the basic organizational model of the armed services.

But military reform makes an equally powerful, if at first less obvious, case for constants. Most of the genuine novelties advocated by the reformers are in the area of military hardware. We live in a time when the society as a whole changes its hardware at a rapid rate, and it is not surprising that the need to do so carries over into defense. But even in the military, major changes driven by technology are rare. Despite all the talk about "technological revolutions in warfare" by the advocates of complex technology, such revolutions occur very seldom.[4]

Most of military reform consists of returning to the constants of the art of war, not moving in new and untried directions. Unit cohesion, maneuver warfare, officers with strong character and creativity, education based on military history and theory—these have all been important at least for hundreds, sometimes for thousands of years. The principal problem in our military is not that it has failed to try the new, but that it has forgotten the old and proven. It has neglected the basic verities of its profession.

What crosscuts do we see here into other areas? Civilian society, like the military, both faces and needs periodic changes in hardware. But are the major social and cultural changes taking place in our society really being driven by technology? Comparing the period from 1955 to 1985 with, as an example, the years from 1900 to 1930, it can be argued that socially significant technological change occurred more quickly during the latter. The first thirty years of this century saw the invention or significant proliferation of the automobile, the airplane, the telephone, and the radio, all of which have brought about basic changes in the way we live. In contrast, the last thirty years have seen only one such major change, the spread of television. Another may now be under way with the proliferation of computers, although it is not clear that will bring as much change as many expect.

However, truly massive change is being driven by nontechnological factors, such as the disintegration of the family, the replacement of education with mere training, the adoption of a morality based on fashion and status by many elements of the nation's elite, and, above all, by the collapse of the most basic concept of civilization, the concept of delayed gratification. Society, like our military, is forgetting or turning away from basic values.

Will we find that neglect of traditional values exacts a heavy penalty in terms of society's effectiveness? Will we discover through bitter experience that those traditional values are the underpinnings of our society's successes, its prosperity, its civil order, and its liberty? Will we learn the hard way that when they are abandoned, decay sets in, and with it national decline?

These are questions that should be high on our national agenda. They lead to crosscut number six: traditional values often have important, functional roles. They have not stood the test of time for no reason. If they are neglected, their neglect may exact a heavy penalty in the ability of an organization, small or large, to function effectively. Although change is itself a constant and an important one, it is not the only important constant.

The sixth crosscut relates to the costs of bureaucracy. One cost is obvious: the decline in the quality of the product and thus the ability to compete.

But bureaucracy exacts three other prices as well, all of them parallel to those identified in the military by the reform movement. The first is loss of job satisfaction. Those people who want to do a good job and who get satisfaction when they produce a good product suffer heavily in a bureaucracy. Often, the system simply won't let them do a good job; it throws up too many obstacles for anyone to overcome. In other cases, individuals in the profession or company can do a good job, but when they do they are penalized in terms of promotions, relations with colleagues, future business, or professional reputation. In either case, they come to hate their jobs. Since their jobs take up most of their time, the quality of their lives is not very high. They increasingly experience anomie and alienation.

A second price is the rise of the courtier. Courtiers are quite happy with bureaucracy; it is their milieu. But those who find the courtier's ways repulsive—ways that, to borrow a phrase from Samuel Johnson, combine "the morals of a whore, and the manners of a dancing master"—are distressed by having to work with, or worse, for courtiers. They are demoralized to see the courtier rise in the organization while honest, competent people are passed over, and they are distressed to see the courtier knowingly let the quality of the product decline while he manipulates other people and the organization for his own personal advantage. Again, job satisfaction is low.

A third price of bureaucracy, a price closely related to the rise of the courtier, is the growing assumption that everyone has a "hidden agenda." Not only does the person who is working to produce a quality product have to suffer from the presence and rise of the courtiers, but he also must struggle with the assumption on the part of many of his colleagues that he, too, has a "hidden agenda," a scheme for personal gain through manipulation of his job, his organization, and the people around him. Since it is "smart" and fashionable to have a hidden agenda, more and more people assume that everyone has one. The person who is honestly trying to do his work as well as it can be done finds increasing difficulty getting anyone to believe that is what he is doing. His colleagues and his superiors, unable to accept the fact that he is doing exactly what he appears to be doing—working to improve the product—keep asking, "Where is he coming from?" Directness and honesty are no longer accepted as genuine.

Each of these prices is a stiff one to pay for the bureaucratic organizational model. Together they add up to decreasing product quality, declining ability to compete (especially against imports), falling job satisfaction and quality of life, and the rise throughout the society of self-centered individuals at the expense of those who are trying to make some sort of contribution with their lives.

The last crosscut therefore is: it is time to move on a broad front to replace the bureaucratic with the corporative model. The benefits the corporative model can bring to the military and has brought to a number of corporations can be extended into almost every field, profession, and organization. This is not only an effectiveness issue; it is also a moral issue. If the structure of most of our institutions rewards cynical self-interest and penalizes honesty, the damage to the moral fabric of our society will be widespread and severe. Ultimately, it will be deadly to our society, our culture, and our nation.

The effectiveness of our institutions—their ability to produce a high-quality product—is not just a military issue. It applies equally to most other government departments and to many private corporations and institutions. The declining ability of our nation to compete is one of the most salient facts facing us in this latter quarter of the twentieth century.

The military reform movement might, therefore, offer a pattern of ideas for other reform movements. The same themes and principles might apply in many of our industries, in education, in labor-management relations, in Congress, in the media, in health care— across a wide range of activities in our national life. In each case, we should consider what the military reform movement has tried to address in the field of defense: the decline in the quality of the product and the specific changes that are needed to restore excellence, effectiveness, and the ability to compete and *win*. Our goal —the goal of all Americans—should be an American reform movement. Such a movement could enable us to pass on to our children the national greatness our forefathers so painfully built, and that we, the present generation, have as our highest responsibility to conserve, defend, and renew.

11

Conclusion

THOSE WHO TRULY CARE about the security of our nation must insist that the way we think about and discuss our defenses be fundamentally changed. Otherwise we risk obsolescence, irrelevance, or even catastrophic defeat.

This book urges basic reforms in our military institutions and thinking. Some reforms can be achieved with little disruption in day-to-day military activities. Others are sweeping and far-reaching. Almost all are controversial in one way or another. Those comfortable with things as they are will raise objections and give many reasons why changes cannot be made.

These objections are to be expected and, in fact, many already have been voiced in the short period of time since the military reform movement took shape. But if this book brings these quarrels to the surface and forces a wider and deeper public debate on the merits and demerits of specific reforms, then its principal purpose will have been served.

Concerned Americans must get over the notion that national defense should be left to the "experts." Thoughtful citizens seldom hesitate to form and render opinions on education, the economy, environmental issues, foreign policy, and a range of public concerns. But many of the same people seem reluctant to express similar opinions about their own security. Clearly, this has to do with feared ignorance of terminology or technology and respect for the expertise of those in military uniform. But with the current information explosion, sufficient knowledge is available to permit intelligent discussion of national security issues by those who care to do so.

Many of the so-called experts, those who have traditionally kept the defense debate among themselves, don't particularly welcome the thought of broad, informed public discussion about our military doctrines, training programs, types of weapons, shape of our naval shipbuilding program, and so forth. They don't relish accepting the burden of defining and defending basic premises that have become institutional dogma over the decades. It is much more comfortable for a small group of people to protect the status quo within its own small circle. But the military reform movement wants basic defense questions brought out into the open. It invites and encourages broad-based citizen participation in this debate. In fact, the only way traditional military institutions and attitudes will change is if aroused, informed, and concerned citizens demand it.

But the time is ripe for reform, because an increasing number of dedicated, patriotic Americans, including many in uniform, know there are serious flaws in our national defenses that dollars will not correct.

Reforming the military institutions of a major power in time of peace and relative security is one of the greatest tasks any society can undertake. But the very magnitude of this challenge itself offers hope. If we can undertake these reforms, we will demonstrate we can meet other equally daunting challenges—reforms in our education systems and tax laws, modernization of our industries and matching international competition, humanization of our corporate structures, and even the uniting of our nation behind crucial common goals.

The term military reform contains no special magic. The word *reform* merely means to change to a better state. Not all change is necessarily good, and the military reform movement does not advocate change for its own sake. Care must be taken that innovation and alteration is done with thoughtfulness and deliberation. The philosopher Santayana wisely said: "To reform means to shatter one form and to create another; but the two sides of this act are not always equally intended nor equally successful."

Many in the defense establishment are, by definition, threatened by reform. Those most comfortable with the present forms are going to resist shattering them most vociferously. The military reform movement hopes to put them to the demanding test of defending the status quo and the established ways of doing business —to force them to prove that all is well with the nation's defenses. If they can do so, they will win the debate and reforms will not succeed.

Those of us on the reform side, however, already are convinced all is not well, that in fact serious deficiencies lie just beneath the surface. Our burden is to create another form, one more effective and successful than the one that must be shattered.

There are debates currently underway to rearrange the military high commands, the Joint Chiefs of Staff, and the office of chairman of the Joint Chiefs. These discussions are worthwhile and all those concerned with defense should encourage them. But it would be a snare and a delusion to think that the serious institutional problems in our defense establishment can be solved by rearranging the organizational boxes at the top of the Pentagon. The problems are deeper and the solutions more profound. Reorganization is not reform. It can often be a façade to escape the harsh reality of reform. This must not happen. The issue is not who gives orders to whom or what powers the chairman of the Joint Chiefs has. The issue is the way we think about defense. That is what must change—and there is no easy way to bring that about.

Bureaucratic ways of thinking, institutional protectiveness, systems of promotion and reward, leadership qualities, definitions of threats, and government-contractor relationships, all must be scrutinized rigorously and revised. This is difficult, even painful. It is uncomfortable, often disruptive. But it must be done. There is no easy path to reform and a truly strong conventional national defense. And there will be few immediate rewards for those who take this narrower, untrodden path—except the knowledge that when the task is done the nation which we love will truly be more secure for future generations and that, above all else, America can win.

Notes

Preface

1. Mr. Polmar acted as Senator Taft's adviser with the support and encouragement of the secretary of the navy, J. William Middendorf.

Introduction

1. Harry G. Summers, Jr., *On Strategy: The Vietnam War in Context* (Carlisle Barracks, Pennsylvania: Strategic Studies Institute, U.S. Army War College, 1981), 2.

2. For a detailed discussion of our recent military failures, see Richard A. Gabriel, *Military Incompetence* (New York: Hill and Wang, 1985).

3. Denny Smith, Tom Tauke, Charles E. Grassley, and Nancy Landon Kassebaum, *The Need for a Defense Budget Freeze* (Jan. 31, 1985), 7.

4. Subsequently, as a major, John Boyd developed an energy maneuverability theory of air combat that quantified maneuver characteristics in a way that was useful to tacticians, aircraft designers, and fighter pilots alike. For a history of Boyd's work and the early origins of the reform movement, see Denny Smith, "The Roots and Future of Modern-Day Military Reform," *Air University Review* (September–October 1985), 33.

Chapter 1

1. China has an additional seventy-three Local Force divisions, which operate only within their home provinces. Soviet and Chinese figures are from *The Military Balance 1984–85* (London, England: International Institute for Strategic Studies).

2. Congressman Newt Gingrich, one of the most active members of the Military Reform Caucus, visited Verdun as a boy. He recalls:

> In 1958, my dad, a career infantryman in the U.S. Army, took us to Verdun, the greatest battlefield of World War I. We toured miles of concrete tunnels built through the mountains. We saw

Notes

huge cannons and examined tremendous old fortifications. In the town of Verdun itself, we saw houses that were still damaged after 42 years. Finally, we visited the Ossuary. This is the large building with a huge glassed-in basement that contains the bones of the 100,000 unidentified men whose bodies had been blown apart or decayed in the mud. The sights of that weekend trip convinced me that civilizations can die and that effective political and military leadership can mean the margin of survival for a nation.

3. For a detailed discussion of maneuver warfare, see William S. Lind, *Maneuver Warfare Handbook* (Boulder, Colorado: Westview Press, 1985).

4. For an excellent study of how an army must be structured to do maneuver warfare in combat, see Martin van Creveld, *Fighting Power* (Westport, Connecticut: Greenwood Press, 1982). For a further discussion of the changes needed in the U.S. Army today, see William S. Lind, "The Case for Maneuver Doctrine," in *The Defense Reform Debate,* Eds., Clark, Chiarelli, McKitrick and Reed (Baltimore, Maryland: The Johns Hopkins University Press, 1984).

5. Procurement of the Bradley should be halted immediately, and those already purchased should be junked. However, if procurement does continue, it is imperative that steps be taken to reduce its deficiencies. The army is considering such modifications as storing the TOW missile ammunition externally, adding armor designed to defeat RPGs, and enlarging the small top hatch. These modifications would not make the Bradley a good combat vehicle, but they would make it a better and safer one. They must be made to any Bradleys we retain.

6. While both the army and the marines have substantial quantities of what they call "light infantry," it is actually line infantry. Its tactics are largely linear and firepower-oriented, its mobility on foot is poor, and its logistics are cumbersome and road bound. The closest thing the U.S. currently has to true light infantry is the army ranger battalions, but even there, modern light infantry tactics are seldom practiced. At this time it is not clear whether the army's new Light Infantry Divisions will become genuine light infantry or just be more line infantry. The best works on true modern light infantry are several unpublished studies by Dr. Steven Canby and Franz Uhle-Wettler, *Gefechtsfeld Mitteleuropa: Gefahr der Übertechnisierung von Streitkräften* (Bernard und Graefe Verlag, 1980). The army has done an English translation under the title, *Battlefield Central Europe: The Danger of Overreliance on Technology in the Armed Forces.*

7. The relationship among fatigue, what the infantryman must carry, and courage was brilliantly observed by General S.L.A. Marshall, the great-

est combat historian of the twentieth century, in his famous book, *The Soldier's Load and the Mobility of a Nation* (Washington, D.C.: Combat Forces Press, 1950).

8. James M. Gavin, *On to Berlin* (New York: The Viking Press, 1978) 51–52.

9. This is not to say that some equipment, such as light, reliable, infantry radios, is not important. The army has yet to field a squad or platoon radio that matches a standard civilian CB radio for lightness or reliability.

10. Max Hastings, *Overlord: D-Day and the Battle for Normandy* (London: Michael Joseph Ltd., 1984), 166–167.

11. Edward N. Luttwak, *The Pentagon and the Art of War: The Question of Military Reform* (New York: Simon and Schuster, 1984).

12. However, it would not have addressed the main personnel constraints on rapid expansion, which are shortages of company grade officers, skilled technicians, and experienced noncommissioned officers.

13. These steps might also help lessen another problem in the NCO corps: overly rapid promotion. In order to improve retention, the services often promote NCOs into higher ranks, and thus higher pay, before their skills and maturity are adequate to deal with the greater responsibilities that come with the higher rank. By increasing pay and status at each NCO rank, adequate retention might be achieved without such rapid promotion.

14. Brigadier General E.S. Leland, Jr., *NTC Training Observations.* Unpublished army report, 18 November 1982.

15. The training at NTC uses lasers to simulate weapons, which permits kills to be counted. Called MILES, this system seems to be set up realistically at NTC, at least for tanks, in terms of the ratio of kills to shots. However, it can easily lead to unrealistic training. In many infantry training exercises, it is yielding a very high percentage of hits, which teaches false tactical lessons and results in overly cautious tactics. It also discounts the effect of artillery, further reinforcing the illusory benefits of cautious, slow-moving tactics. Unless MILES is carefully controlled and calibrated for realism, it can easily do more harm than good.

16. The Soviet division count includes Catagory II and Catagory III divisions, which require mobilized reservists to be brought up to full strength. However, several U.S. divisions also require National Guard units to be added to reach full strength, and the army as a whole would

add many mobilized reservists in wartime without raising the division count. The authors do not have the information required to calculate the comparative tooth-to-tail ratios after both the U.S. and Soviet armies are mobilized.

17. One of the most important changes the army's new doctrine must bring is much greater emphasis on reserves. The army tends to put most of its forces "on line," with only weak reserves. But in maneuver warfare, reserves are generally more important than the forces at the point of contact. And the weaker the army finds itself relative to an opponent, the higher the percentage of the force held in reserve should generally be.

18. The anticipated title is *Global Military Superiority.*

19. Reportedly, Napoleon's staff once presented him with a plan to defend France with a cordon similar to that on which NATO's defense is now based. He replied, "What is it for? To prevent smuggling?"

20. See David Greenwood's article in *Defence Minister and Chief of Staff,* no. 5 (1984).
RIM stands for Rechtstreekse Instooming In Mobilisabele Eenheden —Direct Intake Into Mobilization Units.

Chapter 2
1. Including exports to Canada and Mexico. Separate figures for overseas trade were not available.

2. A number of commentators have noted that the navy's "maritime strategy" may be more a budget strategy than an honest attempt to do anything militarily. It sounds good to many members of Congress and provides a salable justification for more ships.

3. On a worldwide scale; other navies may be serious opponents in their own home waters.

4. Equipped primarily with antisubmarine aircraft, carriers can be very useful for fighting submarines. But our carriers currently have only a small complement of antisubmarine aircraft for self defense (and not enough even for that).

5. The effects of the ban against thinking about force structure were evident to a recent visitor to the navy's premier intellectual establishment, the Naval War College at Newport, Rhode Island. On the grounds that "we need to think about how to fight with the fleet we now have," Newport is forbidden to think more than five years out into the future.

This effectively prohibits any thought about changes in force structure, since it is not possible to change the force structure much in five years. At the same time, Newport has been tasked with thinking about all levels of naval warfare—strategic, operational, and tactical. What happens? Few there are willing simply to throw up their hands and say, "It can't be done. It is not possible to think about naval strategy and naval campaigns intelligently or productively given the present force structure." Instead, they focus on developing new tactics—some of them quite imaginative and possibly effective. But they assume all these new tactics will be highly effective, and on the basis of that assumption, they become highly optimistic about the operational and strategic picture.

In real war, the enemy will have some tactical surprises of his own to offer, and he will also have counters to many of our tactics. Friction, the medium in which war is fought, makes most tactics far less effective than they appear to be in war games. Building optimistic operational and strategic plans on the assumption that all our tactical "neat ideas" work in combat is a good prescription for disaster.

Further this operational and strategic optimism is reinforced by a remarkably dangerous approach to intelligence. In many briefings on Capitol Hill and presentations elsewhere, the navy sings a tune of "the Soviets are virtually transparent to us, and we are opaque to them. We know how good (or bad) they are, and they know virtually nothing about us." Such optimism about intelligence is strewn about the site of many a defeat. It is particularly dangerous when facing Russians. Professor John Erickson once said, "What are the two great Russian specialties throughout history? Deception and ambush."

One can indeed say that, historically, the Russian navy has performed poorly, with exceptions in some areas, such as mine warfare. But for twenty-five or thirty years, the Soviets have worked diligently to improve their naval competence. And it has been forty years since the U.S. Navy engaged a serious naval opponent. In fact, neither we nor the Soviets can hope to be certain about the competence of the other. To a large degree, neither can be certain about his own competence.

The Soviet navy may prove incompetent. But to count on that would be very dangerous— especially to a nation whose national existence ultimately depends on control of the sea, as ours does. The Soviets can lose their entire navy and survive as a nation. We cannot.

6. Nelson also commanded maneuver-style, building the captains under him into his famous "band of brothers" so that each could act with independence and initiative because each knew how the others and the admiral thought. Nelson himself offered one of the best definitions of mission-type orders, which are central to maneuver warfare: "To serve my King and to destroy the French I consider as the great order of all, from which little ones spring, and if one of these little ones militates against it, I go back to obey the great order." At the Battle of Copenha-

gen, when his superior signaled him to withdraw even though he knew he was winning, he put his blind eye to the telescope and said, "I really do not see the signal."

7. They are, however, relatively small compared to super tankers.

8. At least those that hit the side of the ship. Those hitting the bottom may be another story.

9. During last year's hijacking crisis in the Mediterranean, the U.S. Navy reportedly lost the cruise ship *Achille Lauro* for twenty-four hours. It was finally located by Israeli radio interception.

10. Late nineteenth- and early twentieth-century monitors could also carry one or two such guns, but they were usable only in coastal waters and were seen primarily as shore bombardment ships.

11. Future antiship missiles will also be designed to select where they hit a ship, thereby increasing their lethality.

12. In fact, although our navy puts far more money and effort into shooting down enemy antiship missiles, fooling them seems to offer a much more effective defense. Most antiship missiles are radar guided, which makes them very vulnerable to being fooled by a radar reflector or radar transponder towed behind the ship. Because such devices give a stronger, cleaner return than the ship, many, perhaps virtually all radar-guided missiles can be "seduced" by them. Missiles that home on the heat released by a ship can also be fooled. Indeed, the only type of antiship missile not vulnerable to decoys would be one continuously controlled by a human operator, using infrared television guidance. So far, no navy is reported to have developed such a missile. But with our navy's relative disinterest in decoys and its extreme vulnerability to missiles that home on our own radars, which we operate virtually continuously under combat conditions, the antiship missile is a grave threat.

13. A hit that ignites the ammunition in the magazines will, of course, sink them.

14. Significantly, other navies, including the Royal Navy, now fly Vertical or Short Takeoff and Landing (VSTOL) aircraft—planes that can take off and land either with a runway like other airplanes or straight up and down, like a helicopter. VSTOL aircraft can still fly from a carrier after the flight deck has some holes in it, and they don't require vulnerable catapults for taking off. The United States Navy consistently understates the capability of VSTOL aircraft and refuses to use them.

Further, any damage to a carrier's vital sensors or communications facilities would take many months to repair, largely because of the lead time required to order new electronic equipment. We do not have much of an inventory of vital spare components. In addition, there are few U.S. Navy drydocks that can handle a damaged carrier. A modern war would probably be decided before a damaged carrier (or other major warship) could be returned to service.

15. Including cruise missile submarines.

16. In addition, the design of the SSN-21 has some serious defects. Norman Polmar has written:

> The Seawolf/SSN-21 is a torpedo/cruise missile attack submarine planned for construction in the 1990s, with the number "21" indicating a submarine for the 21st century. The submarine will be faster and deeper diving than the current Los Angeles (SSN-688) class, but will still be significantly inferior in performance to modern Soviet submarines, except for quieting and sonar performance. Also significant is the fact that the SSN-21 has not even met the list of desired characteristics developed by a committee of senior U.S. submarine officers—the so-called Group Tango.
>
> The SSN-21 is probably the best attack submarine that the United States can build at this time. That, however, is the problem. The U.S. Navy's submarine design community has been highly conservative in terms of submarine design, while holding to a single attack submarine class in series construction at any given time.
>
> As noted above, one area of U.S. submarine superiority has been sonar performance. The SUBACS sensor/fire control system intended for the SSN-21 has been touted as the system that will keep us ahead of the Soviet Union in the 21st century. Unfortunately, the SUBACS has become a model of Navy and industry (IBM) mismanagement and inadequate cost estimates. The entire SUBACS program has been reorganized and its goals reset, but even with these changes severe questions remain in the Navy and in industry about the future of the system and, in turn, about the relative effectiveness of the SSN-21.

17. According to an article in the *U.S. Naval Institute Proceedings,* the new German-built Argentine conventional submarine *Santa Cruz* cruised submerged for sixty-three hundred miles at an average speed of better than ten knots while snorkeling only about two hours per day. See Robert L. Scheina, "The *Santa Cruz*—A Record Setter," *U.S. Naval Institute Proceedings* (June 1985), 107–109.

18. The French navy is not building conventional submarines at present, although it has a substantial number in service. Most naval authorities

expect France to resume conventional submarine construction in the future.

19. For a good discussion of the possibility of such submarine dogfights, see Richard Pariseau, "How Silent the Silent Service?" *U.S. Naval Institute Proceedings* (July, 1983), 40.

20. We have one other type of torpedo, the Mark-46, which is virtually the only antisubmarine weapon now carried by our surface ships and aircraft. It is unreliable, easy to countermeasure, and has a very small warhead. It is a serious weak point in our entire antisubmarine effort. The navy is currently developing a replacement; whether it will be an improvement remains to be seen.

21. Or possibly fewer; four SSN-688s per year, although the current authorization rate, is unusually high in terms of the history of the SSN-688 program.

22. The navy is currently shifting its torpedo production to the Mark-48 ADCAP, a supposedly improved version of the Mark-48. It plans to increase torpedo production to fifty per month by 1990, a praiseworthy improvement over the current rate but still not sufficient; it would provide each U.S. attack submarine just one torpedo every two months in wartime. The real requirement is an open-ended capability to increase torpedo production rapidly in time of war. We simply cannot estimate in peacetime what our wartime consumption rate will be. That means it is also difficult to estimate what our peacetime torpedo stock and, therefore, production rate should be. But this is a case where prudence suggests too many are better than too few.

23. The DDG-51 has a helicopter landing pad but no hanger.

24. Most of the antiaircraft missile systems on our other surface combatants use the same basic principles as Aegis: search radars find the enemy, and other radars guide antiaircraft missiles to shoot him down. Some of weaknesses of this approach came to light in the Falklands War. The main antiaircraft missile system mounted on British warships—the Sea Dart—which is the British equivalent to Aegis in terms of its purpose (although it uses earlier technology), proved a failure. It shot down only five Argentine aircraft during the whole conflict, one of which was a helicopter and another a Lear jet, both easy targets. The British will not say how many Sea Darts they had to fire to get those five kills. But it is known they found their destroyers' missile magazines too small, which suggests they fired until those magazines ran out. Since the Falklands War, the Royal Navy has mounted antiaircraft guns on its ships to supplement the missiles.

Notes

Surface combatants have two other missions: fighting other surface ships and bombarding targets ashore. In terms of fighting the Soviet navy, the first is not particularly important. The Soviet navy is first a submarine navy, second a land-based air navy, and only thirdly a surface navy. Further, just as the easiest ways for the Soviets to sink our surface ships are with submarines and aircraft, so those are also the easiest ways for us to sink theirs. Surface engagements are not likely to play a large role in any naval war among major powers, except in coastal waters, where enemy missile boats may be present in large numbers.

In addition, our current cruisers, destroyers and frigates are not of much use for shore bombardment. They carry few guns and small ones: two five-inch guns are mounted on the CG-47 class cruisers, one five-inch on the DDG-51 class destroyers, and one three-inch on our most numerous class of frigates, the Perry class. Bringing a billion-dollar cruiser or destroyer close inshore, in range of hostile land artillery and missiles, to potter away with a couple of five-inch guns would generally not be very smart. We have recommissioned four World War II battleships for gunfire support, and these are powerful ships for that mission—although there are other ships that might be better for this purpose, such as the two Salem-class cruisers, which have smaller guns but a much higher rate of fire.

One final type of ship must be mentioned briefly: amphibious ships. These are ships designed to carry marines and their equipment. Today we have three marine divisions, but enough ships to carry only a bit more than one. The problem, as usual, is that the cost of each individual ship is too high to buy the number of ships we need. The navy has, however, taken one positive step with its newest amphibious ships, the LHD class. These ships are designed so that they can be converted to carriers for VSTOL aircraft and antisubmarine helicopters, if we find we need such carriers more than we need amphibious ships in time of war.

25. In 1979 and 1980, in response to congressional inquiries, the Congressional Research Service of the Library of Congress prepared or sponsored three significant studies on submarine design options: Alva M. Bowen, Jr., *Lower Cost Attack Submarines; Alternatives to the SSN 688 Attack Submarines: A Technological Survey,* prepared by the CADCOM company, a consultant; and *Non-Nuclear Powered Submarine Alternatives,* prepared by the Analytic Advisory Group, Inc. These studies make it clear that there are far more submarine design options than the very few the navy is willing to consider.

26. Including one cruise missile class, the "Oscar."

27. The merchant ship *Atlantic Conveyor* was sunk by a single Exocet in the Falklands War. However, it proved no more vulnerable than HMS *Sheffield.*

28. The U.S. Navy has had a similar system for modular weapons and sensors in development for some time, called SEAMOD (recently renamed Ship Systems Engineering Standards, which includes more than the modules program). But it has been very much on the back burner, kept alive only by congressional interest. In 1979, the Senate Armed Services Committee, in its report on the annual defense authorization bill, suggested that the new DDG-51 class of destroyers be built with modular weapons and sensors. However, the navy ignored the committee's suggestion, and the DDG-51 is not modular except in some minor details.

29. The smallest practical size is probably about eight thousand tons, the minimum size of a small aircraft carrier. It might prove most economical to build several standard sizes, each alike as to hull and propulsion plant. Because hulls built to merchant standards are relatively inexpensive, it may be desirable to build HASCs significantly larger than the planned load of aircraft, weapons, or sensors requires, and fill the remaining space with a fireproof material that floats. Larger hulls also have the advantage that, in a heavy sea, a large ship can maintain high speed more easily than a small one.

30. Guns for gunfire support, at least up to five inch, can also be modularized. And while a destroyer normally carries only one or two such guns, a medium-sized HASC configured for gunfire support should be able to carry four to six, depending on how the module receptacles were arranged. Bombardment rockets could also easily be containerized and mounted on a HASC.

HASCs would also provide the additional amphibious ships we need. With their flat top deck for helicopters and a RO-RO bow or stern, they would be well configured for this role. Troop living spaces would be containerized and carried on the second deck or the top deck on ships not operating aircraft. Landing craft would be built on the SEABEE system now used by some merchant ships, wherein barges are carried on and launched from the ship.

31. The navy argues such expansion in the number of aircraft carriers is unaffordable, because each carrier requires four to six escorting cruisers or destroyers. As noted, these escorts are largely ineffective, and the "requirement" for them stems from the bureaucratic imperative to give the "surface union" its share of the pie. HASCs would in many cases be grouped, but the functions currently assigned to escorts, antiair and antisubmarine warfare, would largely be performed by aircraft from the HASCs. If antiaircraft missiles prove themselves in rigorous, realistic, honest tests, some HASCs in a group would probably be configured to carry them, but the ratio of missile ships to aircraft carriers would be nowhere near the current ratio of surface escorts to carriers.

32. The number of jobs for American merchant seamen has shrunk from 48,273 in 1965 to 13,530 in 1984. Such a reduction in the number of trained seamen should be of serious concern to a nation which is by geography a maritime state.

33. Beyond HASCs, only a few special purpose surface warships should be built. The U.S. Navy does need to improve its shallow water capabilities, lest it end up like the Spanish Armada, unable to reach the Duke of Parma's army in the Netherlands to carry it to England because the hostile Dutch controlled the shallow coastal waters. The worldwide proliferation of fast missile boats and small conventional submarines means any attempt to land marines or use air power to influence a battle ashore could mean a fight for the waters along the littoral. At present, the whole U.S. Navy has just six fast missile boats. More should be built, perhaps as many as one hundred. They would be highly useful for challenging the Soviet navy in waters it tends to regard as its own, such as the Baltic. They could serve as precursors of our main fleet in the Persian Gulf, the eastern Mediterranean, and the waters around Japan. Some could be equipped with a dipping sonar to locate submarines. They would be supported by HASCs modularly equipped to serve as mother ships.

Our mine warfare capabilities, offensive and defensive, should be substantially increased. Every year, the navy agrees in congressional hearings that mine warfare is its neglected stepchild. It points out that the Soviets have the largest stock of naval mines in the world. It concurs that one of the few strong traditions in the Soviet navy, dating to the time of the Imperial Russian Navy, is the tradition of effective mine warfare. But it does little to procure new minesweepers. We now have just twenty-one minesweepers, all of which date back to the mid-1950s. We have just begun to build some new ones, but plan no more than thirty-one. To keep open Boston, New York, Newport News, Charleston, Kings Bay, Georgia, Pensacola, New Orleans, San Diego, San Francisco, Seattle, Pearl Harbor—just to mention the ports of most direct importance to the Navy—we will have just thirty-one minesweepers, plus a few helicopters equipped for minesweeping.

Modern mines are easy to lay and hard to sweep. We should build a force of at least one hundred modern minesweepers. Further, we should develop new mines for offensive mine warfare, procure them in quantity, and adopt the German system of minelaying "belts" that strap around the outside of a submarine to allow all our subs to serve as minelayers.

Finally, we should move quickly to permit the navy to convert existing merchant marine containerships to antisubmarine aircraft carriers in wartime. The navy had a program to do this, called ARAPAHO. The idea was simple: containerize the support services for antisubmarine helicopters, put the containers on a containership on top of the regular cargo, and lay a simple army engineering bridge over the containers to serve as a flight deck. The antisubmarine helicopters would come from the Naval

275

Reserve. But the active-duty admirals saw ARAPAHO as a possible alternative to their beloved frigates and destroyers, so just after it completed a series of successful tests, they canceled the program. The Royal Navy, which learned the importance of basing aircraft on merchant ships in the Falklands War, quickly snapped ARAPAHO up and put it to sea. The ship that evacuated British army troops from Beirut in 1984 was an ARAPAHO ship. We should revive ARAPAHO and buy enough sets of equipment to convert at least thirty containerships to small carriers in time of war.

34. Elmo R. Zumwalt, Jr., *On Watch* (New York: Quadrangle/The New York Times Book Co., 1976), 63–64.

35. The Royal Navy's approach is similar to what is recommended here.

Chapter 3

1. Or six, if the Coast Guard and the Civil Air Patrol are counted. Both have military functions in time of war.

2. This somewhat startling fact is often overlooked because helicopters are not thought of as "real" aircraft. But in terms of cost, they are. The army's AH-64 Apache attack helicopter costs $10.5 million, a million dollars more than the air force's F-16A fighter.

3. A good example came to light several years ago in a Senate hearing. The air force was at that time producing a close-support aircraft, the A-10, while the army was developing its close-support aircraft, the Apache attack helicopter. An Armed Services Committee staff member asked the army representative, "Are the missions for the advanced attack helicopter compatible with what a fixed-wing aircraft can do?" The army spokesman, Brigadier General Charles E. Canedy, replied, "We have had great dialogue with the [air force] air staff at the chief level to include the chairman, which suggests that they are complementary in nature. Both services have said both are required, and we see no problem." Trials that pitted the A-10 against the AH-64 to see which performed the mission best were never held.

4. However, in neither case was the common purchase voluntary. They were both forced on the services by Secretary of Defense Robert S. McNamara.

5. A "bounce" is a pilot's term that generally means a single-pass attack.

6. For the F-16A. The F-16A was the first model of F-16 procured by the air force. It is now procuring the F-16C, which costs $13.3 million. Despite this higher cost and the "improvements" it reflects, the F-16C is substantially inferior as a fighter to the A model. Maneuverability and

agility are both notably less. The F-16A price is given here because, of
the two models, it is the one we should be procuring.

7. The air force claims better results today in training exercises with the
latest model Sparrow. The question is whether today's exercises simulate
combat more realistically than did those of the early 1960s that led the
air force to expect so much from earlier models of the Sparrow.

8. However, major uncertainties remain. Radar-guided missiles may
work poorly even against large, unmaneuverable bombers because of
electronic countermeasures, formation effects, and even sluggish maneuvers.

9. The next generation of radar-guided missiles, the AMRAAM, is supposed to avoid this by putting the radar in the missile. However, AM-
RAAM has encountered severe development problems. It is highly questionable whether so small a radar will be effective when the much larger,
more powerful radars carried by fighters generally have not been.

10. For a good account of German independent bombing in World War
I and its postwar effects on German air doctrine, see Raymond H.
Fredette, *The Sky on Fire,* (New York: Harcourt Brace Jovanovich,
1976).

11. This also reflected technical and industrial limitations, but German
analysis of World War I independent bombing was a major factor.

12. Massive deep interdiction campaigns against German military logistics in specific combat theaters were also undertaken as part of the
independent bombing campaign. "Operation Strangle," directed against
the Germans in Italy, was the largest, involving about fifty thousand
sorties and around twenty-six thousand tons of bombs dropped. Like
other similar campaigns, "Strangle" was a failure; the German armies
in Italy got the minimum quantities of supplies they needed to keep
fighting.

13. Nor did the bombing of German and Japanese cities cripple those
countries' war production. German war production, production of aircraft and tanks in particular, reached its peak in the fall of 1944. The
Japanese economy, including war production, was largely brought to a
halt by the end of the war, but the primary cause was the destruction
of the Japanese merchant marine and heavy mining of Japanese home
waters, not bombing of Japanese cities.

14. We tried yet another "Operation Strangle" in Korea. Despite the
bombing, the Chinese armies fighting along the 38th parallel got the
supplies they needed to sustain pressure in a stalemated conflict. In fact,

there was a dramatic increase in Chinese artillery shellings in the last year of the war, and the Chinese were able to launch a vigorous, if limited, offensive just before the cease-fire. Despite massive independent bombing in the Vietnam War—we dropped more bombs on Laos alone than we dropped on Germany in World War II—the North Vietnamese still won the war.

15. Pierre Sprey has developed an excellent briefing on the changes needed.

16. According to a pro-helicopter source, 5,604 helicopters were shot down in Vietnam, of which 3,571 were recovered and repaired. Another 2,610 were lost to other causes. Information from Harry W.O. Kinnard, "Army Helicopters: Why?" *Armed Forces Journal* (May 1982), 58. Other sources put Vietnam losses as high as ten thousand helicopters. Grenada losses may have been as high as eighteen, or about 20 percent of the force. See Gabriel, *Military Incompetence,* 180.

17. For navy and air force HARM antiradar missiles, which are designed to home in on the radars of enemy antiaircraft systems.

18. Figures include assets held at army level.

19. Pierre Sprey has a briefing that describes this aircraft in detail.

20. This was again confirmed by analysis of air support during the Grenada operation. The navy's air after-action report states, "The biggest factor in deterring enemy forces was the M-61 gun (on the A-7E attack aircraft)." From "Lessons Learned: Urgent Fury." Unpublished navy report, November 17, 1983.

21. The navy plans to reengine the F-14, which should improve energy maneuverability, but the large size will remain a serious problem.

22. Reports about how the F-18 compares with the F-16 as a fighter remain inconclusive. The F-18's engines reportedly have an unusual degree of responsiveness, which is a major asset. However, its larger size works against it.

23. The navy is currently considering the acquisition of blimps to serve as early-warning aircraft.

24. Marine air procedures are also a problem. In exercise after exercise, the air is provided to the ground commander when it is convenient for the aviators to do so, not when the ground commander needs it. The result is periodic "whooshes" over the battlefield and air controllers calling over the radio, "Does anybody need an airplane?" not an air focus

of effort. In its procedures and attitudes as well as its aircraft, marine air has become more of an independent air force than the part of the "Air/Ground Team" the Marine Corps likes to talk about. Today that team exists largely in rhetoric.

25. The famous German Stuka dive-bomber was inspired by Marine Corps experiments with dive-bombing.

26. They are also drawn off by the debilitating practice of contract maintenance, in which hired civilians maintain much of the services' equipment. Skilled NCOs can leave the service and return to do the same job as a contractor's employee at three times the pay. If war comes, the contractors leave, and who will then do the maintenance? The practice of contractor maintenance must be stopped.

27. Reportedly, the increasing emphasis on procurement in the Israeli defense budget has resulted in recent cuts in flying time and sorties. If the reports are correct, the effects on Israel's long-standing air superiority could be severe.

28. The Israelis regularly train by pitting one whole squadron against another.

29. Luttwak, *Pentagon and Art of War,* 166 –167.

Chapter 4
1. From *A3: Affordable Acquisition Approach.* Unpublished air force study, February 1983.

2. The study has recently been published as a book: Franklin C. Spinney, *Defense Facts of Life: The Plans/Reality Mismatch* (Boulder, Colorado: Westview Press, 1985).

Chapter 5
1. Benjamin F. Schemmer, "Internal Army Surveys Suggest Serious Concerns About Army's Senior Leaders," *Armed Forces Journal* (May 1985), 18–20.

2. There are some shortages of officers in these ranks in special skill areas, but overall there is a large surplus.

3. While the purpose of reducing the size of the officers corps is to improve effectiveness, not save money, the reduction would save between $1.5 and $2.5 billion annually, assuming retirement pay were calculated on the basis of two-and-a-half times years of service times terminal basic pay, which is the current formula.

4. One former instructor at the Air Force Academy wrote:

> Cadets "study for the exam." They have to take that approach because the curriculum is so crowded that they cannot learn for the pleasure of learning. They also rarely question what is told them. They don't want interpretations nor do they want to devise their own interpretation. . . . they want the correct answer. Education at the Air Force [Academy] is analogous to taking a shower under a fire hose. From my experience, education should entail a vigorous swim in a relatively calm pool.

5. During a dinner several years ago, John Boyd said to the famous German general Hermann Balck, "You know, general, with your extraordinarily quick reactions (still very evident despite Balck's eighty-plus years), you would have made a great fighter pilot." Balck's instantaneous response was, "Ich bin kein Techniker"—I am not a technician.

6. See Tom Lytle and Alex Gimarc, "More Simplistic Solutions," *Air University Review* (July-August 1985), 103.

7. Infantry officers get further schooling in tactics in the Infantry Officers' Course after graduation from The Basic School. IOC is much better than TBS in the way it teaches tactics, and marine lieutenants speak highly of it. However, it still does not teach modern tactics—tactics in maneuver warfare.

8. Under the name "common sense tactics"; a better "buzzword" for maneuver warfare might be "genius operations."

9. "Joint" operations include more than one service; "combined" operations include allied forces.

10. *The Washington Post Magazine,* November 4, 1984, 50.

11. Tests are necessary to encourage officers to read the literature of their profession. Unless they know they will be tested on it, most will not take the time to read it. However, tests can have some negative side effects. Most worrisome is the danger that they would screen out some officers who do not "test well," but who would be gifted combat commanders. The best protection against this would be the decentralization of promotion authority called for below. If a potentially highly competent combat leader did poorly in a test, it would be fully appropriate to set the test results aside in considering his promotion.

Notes

Chapter 6

1. And then only because of John Boyd's involvement.

2. For instance, having a fighter that is hard to see is a tremendous advantage in combat, but no single engineering number can quantify that vital quality.

3. To illustrate how pervasive milspecs are, there is even one for taco shells. It is eighteen pages long! See Jeffrey Denny, "Are Milspecs the Culprit?" in *Military Logistics Forum* (June 1985), 29.

4. In a recent interview, Ben R. Rich, president of a division of the Lockheed Corporation, said, "Have you ever sat and listened to a radio in a fighter airplane? It squawks, it creaks—you can't understand it. But my kids can buy a 'Walk Man' that has tremendous fidelity. The manufacturer doesn't have to meet any military specs." Quoted in *Defense Science 2003+* (June-July 1985), 72.

5. Both the F-16 versus F-17 and the A-9 versus A-10 competitions followed exactly this format, with great success.

6. Without such troop tests, no milspecs can ensure that the dome light or anything else actually works.

7. The office received widespread acclaim for submitting a tough report on DIVAD to the secretary of defense just before he canceled the program. However, that credit may not have been deserved. Reportedly, the director of the operational testing office had prepared a very weak report that could have been used to justify a decision for or against DIVAD. But two days before the secretary was to make his decision, a separate Pentagon office, defense research and engineering, released within the Pentagon its own very negative report on DIVAD. The operational testing director demanded the report be recalled, which was done, but more copies were returned than had been released, indicating the Xerox machines had been at work and the cat was out of the bag. The operational testing director then frantically rewrote his own report, borrowing heavily from the other report, so as not to appear too weak.

Chapter 7

1. Gabriel, in *Military Incompetence,* states, "The planners, in a number of instances, subordinated operational requirements to other considerations, such as interservice rivalry and the need to sustain the bureaucratic consensus underpinning the plan. . . . the plan rested heavily on a previously established consensus—a consensus that removed responsibility for failure. . . . To many, the failure of the Iran raid was simply bad luck. The truth is that it was almost predestined to fail."

2. These terms were recently dropped by the JCS in an effort to disguise how the process works, but the substance of that process remains unchanged. There is a compressed version of the process for urgent issues, but the full system is used for most issues.

3. The most recent are contained in the Senate report noted earlier: *Defense Reorganization: The Need for Change,* (Staff Report to the Committee on Armed Services, United States Senate, October 16, 1985).

4. Including the Office of the Joint Chiefs of Staff (OJCS).

5. They would probably, though not necessarily, return to the service whence they came. But their fitness report during their tour of field duty would be written by the National Defense Staff, not the service.

6. These ideas expand on an air force proposal Boyd and Spinney coauthored in 1974 with Colonel James Burton and Lieutenant Colonel Raymond Leopold.

Chapter 8
1. In FY 1986, the House and Senate Armed Services Committees individually canceled thirty programs. But when they got together in the joint conference, they restored every one of them.

2. The Defense Department estimates that response time might average five hours per letter. In addition to the 123,130 written Congrints, the Defense Department also responded to 599,000 telephone calls from Congress in 1984.

3. The largest category in the remaining 24 percent is military personnel, which are also authorized indirectly by authorizing personnel levels rather than actual dollar amounts.

4. One procedural change that would help is opening the meetings of the joint conference whenever classified material is not being discussed—which is most of the time. Many of the worst "insider" deals are cut behind the closed doors of the conference meetings.

Introduction to Part Three
1. The following discussion, which is of models for hierarchical institutions, does not apply to Congress because it is a different type of institution: a confederation. That is not to say that its problems are less, only different.

Chapter 9
1. One industry that very seldom permits lateral entry even at relatively low levels and between companies in the same industry is the automobile

industry. In the opinion of a number of management specialists, this has contributed substantially to the parochialism that made the industry so vulnerable to foreign competition.

2. *Future 21: Directions for America in the 21st Century,* eds. Paul M. Weyrich and Connaught Marshner (Greenwich, Connecticut: Devin-Adair, 1984), 185–196.

3. Donald Chipman, "The Military Courtier and the Illusion of Competence," *Air University Review* (March-April, 1981), 53–62.

4. Also known as the "socialized" model. In this context, the term "socialized" has nothing to do with socialism. "Corporative" refers to the medieval, not the modern corporation.

Chapter 10
1. John Kneiling, a transportation consultant, has been attempting for years to get railroads to realize this basic point.

2. "The Decade's Worst Mergers," *Fortune* (April 30, 1984), 263–270.

3. John Agresto, "The Humanities and the Condition of American Education," *The Journal of Family and Culture* (Spring 1985), 10–11.

4. The nineteenth century saw just two technology-driven revolutions in land warfare: the introduction of the rifled musket in the 1850s put an end to the Napoleonic tactical offensive, and the proliferation of railways later in the century gave a decisive advantage in operational mobility to the defender. The trench warfare of World War I was not a revolution brought about by barbed wire, the machine gun, and quick-firing artillery; as Mathew Brady's photographs of the siege of Petersburg in 1865 show, the rifled musket had already driven men into the trenches. The primary revolution in World War I, the restoration of the tactical offensive in 1918 by the Germans, was based primarily on new ideas, not technological breakthroughs, although the light machine gun and new techniques in artillery control were important. The revolution predicted by the air-power enthusiasts of the 1930s still has not materialized, unless nuclear weapons are employed. The only partially technological revolution in ground warfare in World War II was the Blitzkrieg, which married tanks and other mechanized vehicles with the German infantry tactics of 1918.

Index

Aircraft *(continued)*
  F-16 vs. F-17 competition, 28ın
  F-17, 116, 197
  F-18, 116, 120, 135, 137, 138,
    206, 278n
    cost: 120; estimated vs.
      actual, 152; projected
      decrease vs. actual
      change, 154
    operational testing, 202,
      203
    purchases, projected vs.
      actual, 154
  F-86, 5, 151
  F-100, cost, 147
  F-104, cost, 147
  Harrier VSTOL, 116
  jinking, 47–48
  P-3, 137
  procurement
    costs, 4
    FY 1953–FY 1956,
      compared to FY
      1982–FY 1985, 148
  S-3, 136
  Short Takeoff and Landing
    (STOL), 137
  Soviet MiG-15, 5–6
  Soviet MiG-21, size, 120
  Vertical or Short Takeoff and
    Landing (VSTOL), 104, 137,
    138, 139, 270n
    implications for pilot
      training, 142
Aircraft carriers, 22, 83–89. *See
  also* Surface ships
  aircraft on, 89, 135
  antisubmarine aircraft on, 136,
    268n
  battle group, costs, 88
  costs, 88
  damage repair time, 88, 271n
  escorts, requirement for, 274n
  light, 101. *See also* High
    Adaptability Surface
    Combatant (HASC)
  missile damage, 87
  Nimitz class, 83

number of, 88
numbers needed, 105
relevance of, 136
specific vulnerabilities, 87
U.S. Navy's emphasis on, 83
vs. submarines, 80
vulnerability of, 83–89, 135
Air defenses, 131–133
  effectiveness of, 131–132
  Soviet, 131
  of Soviet divisions, 133
  suppression weapons, cost, 131
Air Force Academy, 166–168
  education at, 28ın
Air forces. *See also specific air
  force*
  concepts, 117–131
  noncommissioned officers,
    141–142
  officer surplus, 140–141
  organization, 143–145
  personnel, 140–142
  ratio of aircraft to people, 144
  training in, 142–143
  unit cohesion in, 140
Air Force Systems Command,
  144
Air National Guard, 141, 145–146
  reform efforts within, 73
Air Reserve, 141, 145–146
Air University Review, 176
Air War College, 173–175
Amlie, Tom, 206
Ammunition
  supplies, 22
  for training, 63
Amphibious ships, 273n, 274n
  LHD class, 273n
Amphibious Warfare School, 176,
  178–180
AMRAAM, 277n
Andrews, Mark, 207
Antiaircraft gun. *See also*
  DIVAD
  radar-controlled, 47–48
  Soviet ZSU-23, 133
  visually controlled, 47–48
  Vulcan, 133

Index

Index

ABOUT THE MAKING OF THIS BOOK

The text of *America Can Win* was set in Times Roman by ComCom, a division of The Haddon Craftsmen, of Allentown, Pennsylvania. The book was printed and bound by Fairfield Graphics of Fairfield, Pennsylvania. The typography and binding were designed by Tom Suzuki of Falls Church, Virginia.